Evidence-Based
Public Health Practice

This book is dedicated to the ones I love: John C. Beck and Ingvard.

Evidence-Based Public Health Practice

Arlene Fink

University of California, Los Angeles
The Langley Research Institute

Los Angeles | London | New Delhi
Singapore | Washington DC

Los Angeles | London | New Delhi
Singapore | Washington DC

FOR INFORMATION:

SAGE Publications, Inc.
2455 Teller Road
Thousand Oaks, California 91320
E-mail: order@sagepub.com

SAGE Publications Ltd.
1 Oliver's Yard
55 City Road
London EC1Y 1SP
United Kingdom

SAGE Publications India Pvt. Ltd.
B 1/I 1 Mohan Cooperative Industrial Area
Mathura Road, New Delhi 110 044
India

SAGE Publications Asia-Pacific Pte. Ltd.
33 Pekin Street #02-01
Far East Square
Singapore 048763

Acquisitions Editor: Vicki Knight
Associate Editor: Lauren Habib
Editorial Assistant: Kalie Koscielak
Production Editor: Brittany Bauhaus
Copy Editor: Sarah J. Duffy
Typesetter: C&M Digitals (P) Ltd.
Proofreader: Wendy Jo Dymond
Indexer: Maria Sosnowski
Cover Designer: Michael Dubowe
Marketing Manager: Helen Salmon
Permissions Editor: Adele Hutchinson

Copyright © 2013 by SAGE Publications, Inc.

Printed in the United States of America

Library of Congress Cataloging-in-Publication Data

Fink, Arlene.

Evidence-based public health practice / Arlene Fink.

p. cm.
Includes bibliographical references and index.

ISBN 978-1-4129-9744-7 (pbk.)

1. Public health. 2. Evidence-based medicine. I. Title.

RA440.85.F56 2013
362.1—dc23   2011039063

This book is printed on acid-free paper.

11 12 13 14 15 10 9 8 7 6 5 4 3 2 1

BRIEF CONTENTS

DETAILED CONTENTS

ABOUT THE AUTHOR

Arlene Fink (PhD) is professor of medicine and public health at the University of California, Los Angeles, and president of the Langley Research Institute. Her main interests include evaluation and survey research and the conduct of research literature reviews as well as the evaluation of their quality. Dr. Fink has conducted scores of evaluation studies in public health, medicine, and education. She is on the faculty of UCLA's Robert Wood Johnson Clinical Scholars Program and is a scientific and evaluation advisor to UCLA's Gambling Studies and IMPACT (Improving Access, Counseling & Treatment for Californians with Prostate Cancer) programs. She consults nationally and internationally for agencies such as L'institut de Promotion del la Prévention Secondaire en Addictologie (IPPSA), in Paris, France, and Peninsula Health, in Victoria, Australia. Dr. Fink has taught and lectured extensively all over the world and is the author of more than 110 peer-reviewed articles and 15 textbooks.

ACKNOWLEDGMENTS

Writing a textbook in digital times is challenging. I have been helped in this task by the hundreds of students and colleagues throughout the years who taught me the value of clear explanation and the importance of robust research. There are simply too many to list, but you know who you are, and I am grateful to you. I am also most appreciative of my small family who was there for me every day as I labored away.

If you think the book taught you something or advanced the field, please ascribe some of its best features to the reviewers. They were extremely helpful, and I tried to incorporate as many of their suggestions into the text as I could and still meet my deadlines. Specifically, I am grateful to W. Douglas Evans (The George Washington University), Linda Agustin Simunek (Nova Southeastern University), Rojann R. Alpers (Arizona State University), Deric R. Kenne (Kent State University), Laura C. McKieran (The University of Texas), Alexandra Evans (The University of Texas), Lyn Paleo (University of California, Berkeley), Richard Culbertson (Tulane University), and Carl Hacker (The University of Texas). I hope I can meet you all one day and thank you in person.

A book, no matter how excellent in purpose and content, needs a team to produce it. My team at Sage is the greatest. Vicki Knight is simply the very best editor I could have asked for. I hope that we have morphed from editor and author to friends. I would also like to acknowledge the essential contributions of Lauren Habib, Kalie Koscielak, Brittany Bauhaus, Helen Salmon, Adele Hutchinson, and Michael Dubowe.

Presentation of Useful Forms and Questionnaires. The book provides detailed examples of the forms used to record data as the reviewer does an abstraction. In addition, examples from the literature are presented to show how systematic literature reviews should be reported.

Emphasis on the Importance of Ethical Research. The book discusses the ethics of research with human subjects, research misconduct, and concerns associated specifically with evidence-based practice.

❖ WHAT ARE THE CONTENTS OF THE BOOK?

Chapter 1. Public Health Practice and the Best Available Evidence

This chapter discusses evidence-based public health's defining characteristics, including how to evaluate community health and health service needs and cultural values and how to use the best available evidence to meet the needs. It also explains the differences between evidence-based medicine and evidence-based public health. The distinction is important. Evidence-based public health practice is concerned with reducing risks and promoting health regardless of disease and focuses on communities and populations, whereas evidence-based medicine is primarily interested in preventing disease and curing illness in individuals. Chapter 1 is also concerned with explaining where evidence originates, with a particular emphasis on evidence collected from evaluation and effectiveness research. Other types of research used in evidence-based public health practice are also discussed, including epidemiology and health services research.

Because current evidence-based practices are often found on the web, Chapter 1 provides an extensive list of websites to go for information and differing perspectives on evidence-based public health

Chapter 2. Community Health and Health Service Needs and Evidence-Based Programs

This chapter explains the differences among seven categories of health needs or risks: social, behavioral, administrative, environmental, communal, physical, and educational. It describes the characteristics of commonly used methods for identifying and assessing needs and priorities, including analysis of large statistical databases, key informant techniques, community forums, focus groups, the nominal group process, the Delphi technique, the RAND/ UCLA Appropriateness Method, surveys, asset mapping, and consensus development conferences.

Once community health and health services needs are identified, the search for relevant programs begins. Chapter 2 describes how to identify and evaluate online evidence-based program databases, such as those maintained by the U.S. Agency for Healthcare Research and Quality and the Centers for Disease Control, and explains how to evaluate the quality of online health information websites.

Chapter 3. Finding the Best Available Evidence: Questions, Practical Concerns, and Ethics

This chapter focuses on finding the best available evidence. It teaches the steps in conducting a research literature review, and it explains how to choose an online bibliographic database that is likely to result in articles on evaluated public health programs and practices, use the PICO method to formulate questions to focus a literature review search, create search terms from the research questions to guide the literature review, and use Boolean operators (e.g., *and, or, not*) when searching the research literature. Chapter 3 also discusses how to identify the components of two practical literature review screens, such as language; research design; the characteristics of the experimental and comparison programs; data collection dates and duration; and study sponsorship, outcomes, participants, and settings.

The best available evidence comes from ethical research, and Chapter 3 discusses ethical issues that accompany research with human subjects, describes the characteristics of research misconduct, and explains the ethical concerns associated with evidence-based public health practice.

Chapter 4. Research Design, Validity, and Best Available Evidence

The goal of this chapter is to teach readers how to review research design and threats to the validity of the results because of the design. It therefore tells readers what to look for rather than how to do it.

Chapter 4 explains the characteristics of commonly used research designs in studies to define and meet public health program needs and describes the methods that statisticians, epidemiologists, and other health researchers use to ensure that experimental and control groups are equivalent

CHAPTER 1

PUBLIC HEALTH PRACTICE AND THE BEST AVAILABLE EVIDENCE

Evidence-based public health practice uses the best available evidence to make informed decisions about programs, campaigns, initiatives, and policies to improve the health and well-being of countries, communities, and families. Effective public health practice systematically identifies gaps in health and health care and tracks down evidence-based programs to close those gaps. The evidence comes from a systematic study of completed and publicly available research on program effectiveness.

This chapter gives an overview of evidence-based public health practice and discusses the characteristics of high-quality research to evaluate program effectiveness. Subsequent chapters describe and explain how to practice evidence-based public health by (a) identifying community and population values and needs for health services through public contact and analysis of data, (b) tracking down available evidence-based programs to meet the needs, (c) analyzing the quality and strength of the evidence, and (d) evaluating and reporting on the results.

communal lifestyles and beliefs that affect well-being (views on what really constitutes a healthy diet), while physical needs refer to external social factors (access to fresh fruit and vegetables). Other needs may be environmental (for safer schools or better transportation to health clinics) and genetic (the identification of genes that cause or regulate susceptibility to diseases such as cancer).

Data for evaluating needs come from epidemiological databases and from reviews of existing databases such as those maintained by the Centers for Disease Control and Prevention (CDC) and other public health agencies. Additional sources of information about community needs come directly from interviewing and observing the affected population.

2. **Tracking down the best available evidence on programs and practices that potentially meet the needs.** This means identifying and reviewing online bibliographic databases such as PubMed to locate appropriate articles and studies. PubMed is a service of the National Library of Medicine. Some agencies, such as the Agency for Healthcare Research and Quality, maintain databases of evaluated programs. Evidence-based public health practice requires learning where to search for programs that are useful for the community.

3. **Collecting the best available information on appropriate programs and practices.** The best available information is accessible, valid, and useful. Information is accessible when it is recorded and reachable by the public. Determining validity requires skill in assessing the quality of a study's research design, measurement choices, statistical methodology, and findings. Appropriate programs are those for which the benefits in terms of improving public health outweigh the risks and hassles of implementation. Useful programs are those that solve community problems and meet their needs by reducing community members' health risks and improving their health and well-being. Evidence is imperfect, and practitioners should seek the best evidence available, not the best evidence possible (Brownson et al., 2009).

4. **Selecting programs that fit together with community and population needs and values.** A *community* is any population of people who are bound together by their risks, resources, and beliefs. People with the same chronic disease, pathological gamblers, and people who share an occupation may be said to belong to the same community. In some cases, a community is identified by its geographic location.

Community values are the community's or population's beliefs, preferences, concerns, and expectations. Evidence-based public health practice uses various methods to learn about values. These include living in the community; surveying and meeting regularly with community members to find out about their values, beliefs, and preferences; and enlisting the community to participate directly in the research.

5. **Evaluating the impact on health and well-being of putting the selected programs into practice.** There at least two purposes for doing the evaluation. The first is to find out whether the new or improved evidence-based program satisfies the community's needs. Did it improve the health-related behavior of providers, patients, and systems? Was care appropriate, with benefits outweighing risks? Without overuse of services? Without underuse of services? Were public health goals achieved? Public health goals include measures of general health status (such as healthy life expectancy, chronic disease prevalence), health-related quality of life and well-being, and health disparities. Public health goals can be found on the websites of the U.S. Department of Health and Human Services Healthy People series (http://www.healthypeople.gov/2010 etc www.healthypeople.gov/2020/about/tracking.aspx) and the World Health Organization (http://www.who.int/entity/en).

A second purpose for doing the evaluation is to find out whether, and in what places, the program needs improvement. Did all segments of the community benefit equally? If not, do we need a special campaign to reach those who were left out? Did the program's effects continue after the experimental or transitional phase? If not, do we need to do a better job in training the staff to take over?

EVIDENCE-BASED MEDICINE AND EVIDENCE-BASED PUBLIC HEALTH ❖

Evidence-based public health practice relies on evaluation researchers to test and report on the effectiveness of new programs and initiatives. The historical basis for public health practice's dependence on evidence, and ultimately on evaluation research, is found in evidence-based medicine.

Evidence-based medicine came into health care consciousness back in the mid-1990s. Its most traditional definition is the "conscientious, explicit, and judicious use of current best evidence in making decisions about the care of individual patients" (Sackett, Straus, Richardson, Rosenberg, & Haynes, 2000, p. 1). Over time, the definition has been expanded and sometimes includes the use of current best evidence in making decisions about the health of communities.

Evaluating medical interventions for safety and effectiveness in an experimental way has probably existed for many hundreds of years. Among the first recorded evaluations is one that dates back to biblical times. Daniel of Judah compared the health effects of a vegetarian diet (the intervention) with those of the Royal Babylonian diet (control group) over a 10-day period. The Book of Daniel (1:15–16) records the findings:

> At the end of the ten days their appearance was better and their bodies healthier than all the young men who had been eating the royal delicacies. So the warden removed their delicacies and the wine from their diet and gave them a diet of vegetables instead.

According to Sackett et al. (2000), five of the originators of evidence-based medicine and the authors of an extremely influential textbook about it, its roots lie in Chinese medicine. In the reign of the Emperor Qianlong (1711–1799), a method known as *kaozheng* (practicing evidential research) was apparently used in relation to Confucian medical texts. Sackett et al. also identify the ideas of evidence-based medicine with postrevolutionary Paris clinicians, at least one of whom rejected the pronouncements of authorities that vivisection was good for cholera.

It was only in the 20th century that evidence-based medicine really evolved to affect almost all fields of health care and policy. Professor Archie Cochrane (1972/1999), a Scottish epidemiologist, through his book *Effectiveness and Efficiency: Random Reflections on Health Services* and subsequent advocacy, was responsible for the increasing acceptance of the concepts behind evidence-based practice. The explicit methodologies used to determine "best evidence," however, were largely established by the McMaster University research group led by David Sackett and Gordon Guyatt. The term *evidence-based medicine* first appeared in the medical literature in 1992 in a paper by the Evidence-Based Medicine Working Group.

So are evidence-based medicine and evidence-based public health practice the same? Not exactly. In evidence-based medicine, each physician's clinical expertise is used as the basis of judgments for applying research findings to the care of *individual* patients. This means that when physicians (also nurses, social workers, psychologists, occupational therapists, and so on) are presented with research findings or data on groups of people (such as diabetic patients, substance abusers, or people injured at work), they must use their clinical expertise to translate the research into care for each individual patient with diabetes, substance abuse, or injury, respectively.

Evidence-based public health practice works outside of the direct clinical encounter. It focuses instead on analyzing research findings or data to make decisions for communities or populations of people.

There are important differences between the disciplines of public health and medicine, which are helpful in understanding the application of evidence-based approaches to practice, as illustrated in Table 1.1.

Table 1.1 General Differences Between Public Health and Medicine

	Public Health	**Medicine**
Primary Focus	Populations and communities	Individuals
Emphasis	Prevention	Diagnosis and treatment
	Health promotion	Treatment
	Whole community	Whole patient
Paradigm	Interventions aimed at environment, human behavior and lifestyle, and medical care	Medical care, lifestyle
Organizational Lines of Specialization	Analytical (epidemiology)	Organ (cardiology, gastroenterology)
	Setting and population (occupational health, school health)	Patient group (pediatrics, geriatrics)
	Substantive health problems (nutrition, epidemics such as HIV)	Etiology, pathophysiology (oncology, infectious disease)
	Skills in assessment, policy development, and assurance	Technical skill (radiology)

SOURCE: Adapted from Fineberg, 2003; Reprinted with permission from the National Academies Press, Copyright 2003, National Academy of Sciences.

Another way of contrasting medicine and public health is to ask, Why do people die in the United States? Medically minded individuals usually respond by listing the major causes of death in terms of disease: heart disease; cancer; stroke (cerebrovascular disease); chronic lower respiratory diseases; accidents; Alzheimer's disease; diabetes; influenza and pneumonia; nephritis, nephrotic syndrome, and nephrosis; septicemia (see CDC, 2011b). Public health people respond differently, listing risk factors. For example, they may point out that 19% of Americans die of tobacco-related illness, 14% from poor diet and lack of exercise, 5% from alcohol-related disease, and 2.5% from gun injuries (McGinnis & Foege, 1993). Public health is in the business of identifying risks, regardless of disease, and devising strategies to enable people and populations to avoid these risks. This role is often described as health promotion, that is, changing exposure to risks in the environment or modifying unhealthy behaviors (Bloom, n.d.).

How do the differences between medicine and public health affect evidence-based public health practice? The short answer is, not as much as you might think. Both are dependent upon identifying the highest quality—best—available evidence-based programs. Perhaps most important, evidence-based public health and evidence-based medicine both accept the fundamental idea that evidence replaces anecdote in making health care and health policy decisions. Here are two definitions of evidence-based public health:

1. Evidence-based public health is the conscientious, explicit and judicious use of current best evidence in making decisions about the care of communities and populations in the domain of health protection, disease prevention, health maintenance and improvement (Jenicek, 1997).

2. Evidence-based public health is the development, implementation, and evaluation of effective programs and policies and public health through application of principles of scientific reasoning including systematic uses of data and information systems and appropriate use of program planning models (Brownson, Gurney, & Land, 1999).

The first definition sounds very much like the definition of evidence-based medicine, with an emphasis on making decisions about communities and populations (rather than individual patients) based on current best evidence. The second definition calls for use of scientific reasoning and systematic use of data and information systems, key components of the methods for obtaining best evidence.

Kohatsu, Robinson, and Torner (2004) draw appropriate parallels between evidence-based public health and medicine because both are concerned with asking questions, collecting relevant evidence to answer those questions, and evaluating the effectiveness of the process and its outcomes. Evidence-based public health focuses on understanding and preventing disease and promoting health in communities. Evidence-based medicine tends to focus on diagnosis and treatment (although primary care or generalist medicine is also concerned with prevention) in individuals.

According to the American Public Health Association, evidence-based practice and policy explores the processes of systematically finding, appraising, and using scientific research as the basis for developing sound practices. The knowledge gleaned from this research is used to develop policies and practices that improve health outcomes and performance as well as allow for more efficient use of resources. Policy makers are also provided with a better understanding of the science, ensuring that policy decisions are based on the best information available.

Table 1.2 provides a list of websites that you can go to for more information about evidence-based public health.

Table 1.2 Websites for More Information on Evidence-Based Public Health

Agency for Healthcare Research and Quality: www.ahrq.gov

American Public Health Association: www.apha.org

Centers for Disease Control's Guide to Community Preventive Services: www.thecommunityguide.org

Centre for Evidence-Based Medicine (Toronto): http://ktclearinghouse.ca/cebm

The Cochrane Collaboration: www.cochrane.org

The Evidence Network (United Kingdom): www.kcl.ac.uk/schools/sspp/interdisciplinary/evidence

HealthLinks: Evidence-Based Practice (University of Washington): http://healthlinks.washington.edu/ebp

Healthy People 2010 and 2020: www.healthypeople.gov/2020

The Lamar Soutter Library, Evidence-Based Practice for Public Health (University of Massachusetts): http://library.umassmed.edu/ebpph/

National Cancer Institute: www.cancer.gov

World Health Organization, Regional Office for Europe: Data and Evidence: www.euro.who.int/InformationSources/Evidence/20010827_1

CURRENT BEST AVAILABLE EVIDENCE FOR ❖ PUBLIC HEALTH PROGRAMS AND THE ROLE OF EVALUATION RESEARCH

Evidence-based public health practice uses the best available evidence to make informed decisions about programs, campaigns, initiatives, and policies to improve the health and well-being of countries, communities, and families. A primary source of the evidence is evaluation research (also called program evaluation).

Evaluation research uses the scientific method to provide evidence of a program's effectiveness. As part of evidence gathering, evaluations collect data on the extent to which program participation influences outcomes, impact, and costs. Evaluations can also be used to study current program effectiveness and how to improve effectiveness in the future.

Example 1.1 provides two evaluation research summaries or abstracts.

Example 1.1   Abstracts of Two Evaluation Studies

1. Munch and Move: Evaluation of a Preschool Healthy Eating and Movement Skill Program (Hardy, King, Kelly, Farrell, & Howlett, 2010)

Background. Early childhood services have been identified as a key setting for promoting healthy eating and physical activity as a means of preventing overweight and obesity. However, there is limited evidence on effective nutrition and physical activity programs in this setting. The purpose of this study was to evaluate *Munch and Move*, a low-intensity, state-wide, professional development program designed to support early childhood professionals to promote healthy eating and physical activity among children in their care.

Methods. The evaluation involved 15 intervention and 14 control preschools ($N = 430$ [students]; mean age 4.4 years) in Sydney, New South Wales, Australia and was based on a randomised-control design with pre and post evaluation of children's lunchbox contents, fundamental movement skills (FMS), preschool policies and practices and staff attitudes, knowledge and confidence related to physical activity, healthy eating and recreational screen time.

Results. At follow up, FMS scores for locomotor, object control and total FMS score significantly improved by 3.4, 2.1 and 5.5 points more (respectively) in the intervention group compared with the control group ($P < 0.001$) and the number of FMS sessions per week increased by 1.5 ($P = 0.05$). The lunchbox audit showed that children in the intervention group significantly reduced sweetened drinks by 0.13 serves (i.e., 46 ml) ($P = 0.05$).

Conclusion. The findings suggest that a low intensity preschool healthy weight intervention program can improve certain weight related behaviors. The findings also suggest that change to food policies are difficult to initiate mid-year and potentially a longer implementation period may be required to determine the efficacy of food policies to influence the contents of preschoolers lunchboxes.

2. Evaluation of REAL MEN (Freudenberg et al., 2010)

Purpose. This study assesses the impact of REAL MEN (Returning Educated African-American and Latino Men to Enriched Neighborhoods), an intervention designed to reduce drug use, risky sexual behavior and criminal activity among 16–18-year-old males leaving New York City jails.

Methods. Participants ($N = 552$) were recruited in city jails and randomly assigned to receive an intensive 30-hour jail/community-based intervention or a single jail-based discharge planning session. All participants were also referred to optional services at a community-based organization (CBO). One year after release from jail, 397 (72%) participants completed a follow-up interview. Logistic and ordinary least squares regression was used to evaluate the impact of the intervention on drug use, risky sexual behavior, criminal justice involvement, and school/work involvement post release.

Results. Assignment to REAL MEN and, independently, use of CBO services significantly reduced the odds of substance dependence (odds ratio [OR] = .52, $p \leq .05$; OR = .41, $p \leq .05$, respectively) 1 year after release. Those assigned to the intervention spent 29 fewer days in jail compared with the comparison group ($p \leq .05$). Compared to non-CBO visitors, those who visited the CBO were more likely to have attended school or found work in the year after release (OR = 2.02, $p \leq .01$).

Conclusions. Jail and community services reduced drug dependence 1 year after release and the number of days spent in jail after the index arrest. While these findings suggest that multifaceted interventions can improve outcomes for young men leaving jail, rates of drug use, risky sexual behavior, and recidivism remained high for all participants after release from jail, suggesting the need for additional policy and programmatic interventions.

The evaluation abstracts in Example 1.1 are typical evaluation reports. But are the studies valid? The only way to find out is to systematically analyze each study's quality. Looking at the abstracts, you can see that *doing* an evaluation requires skills in research design, statistics, data collection, and interpretation. Doing evidence-based public health requires skills in *reviewing* the evaluator's work, including the quality of the research design, statistical methods, data collection, and interpretation.

EVALUATION AND EFFECTIVENESS ❖ RESEARCH: DEFINITIONS AND METHODOLOGICAL CONSIDERATIONS

Evaluation is an essential part of public health; without evaluation's close ties to program implementation, we are left with the unsatisfactory circumstance of either wasting resources on ineffective programs or, perhaps worse, continuing public health practices that do more harm than good (Vaughan, 2004). Because of evidence-based public health's close ties to evaluation research, learning how to identify and only use the highest quality evaluation studies is essential.

The **program** or intervention is the focus of evaluation research. The term is a generic name for interventions, treatments, campaigns, and initiatives. A program consists of activities and resources that have been specifically selected to achieve beneficial outcomes. An example of a program is the 10-session school-based cognitive-behavioral intervention to reduce children's symptoms of PTSD resulting from exposure to violence. Other examples include an education campaign to promote a community's acceptance of the need for polio vaccinations or the 1-year intensive lifestyle intervention consisting of diet and physical activity.

According to the CDC (2011a), the term *program* is used to describe the object of evaluation, and it applies to any organized public health action. The CDC uses a broad definition so that the framework can be applied to almost any public health activity, including the following:

- direct service interventions
- community mobilization efforts
- research initiatives
- surveillance systems
- policy development activities
- outbreak investigations

major methods used in analyzing the comparative outcomes and costs of programs (Drummond, Richardson, O'Brien, Levine, & Heyland, 1997).

Program funders have been increasing their demands for economic evaluations of public health programs. Their justification is based on the realization that resources for programs are scarce, the resources have alternative uses, people have different needs, and there are never enough resources to satisfy everyone's needs.

The application of cost-effectiveness measures to meet one group's needs over another's has ethical implications. For instance, the elderly, the mentally ill, the homeless, children with special needs, and others may be excluded from access to certain programs because they are not expected to benefit a great deal from them, a particular problem when the programs are expensive. Moreover, people with special needs have traditionally been excluded from research because they are not "interesting" enough, do not yield reliable data (because they have multiple complex problems), or are not able to participate in research. As a result, the available data may be insufficient to measure the effectiveness, let alone the cost-effectiveness, of any given program for these groups. Critics of the use of economic evaluation also point out that what is "effective" sometimes differs between clinicians and researchers. If so, then what is "cost-effective" will also differ.

❖ EVALUATION RESEARCHERS AND OTHER EVALUATORS AND RESEARCHERS

Evaluation research is usually included as a subdivision of the much larger field of evaluation, which has been described by the American Evaluation Association (www.eval.org) as a profession composed of persons with varying interests, potentially encompassing but not limited to the evaluation of programs, products, personnel, policy, performance, proposals, technology, research, theory, and even evaluation itself. Evaluation research shares some of the purposes that are delineated by the American Evaluation Association in connection with other forms of program evaluation. These include contributing to informed decision making and more enlightened change, precipitating needed change, and empowering all stakeholders by collecting data from them and engaging them in the evaluation process.

The similarity between evaluation researchers and other program evaluators usually ends with the choice of method they use to achieve their aims. Some evaluators based their methods on disciplines as diverse as organizational theory, political action, or social networking, and these usually do not apply to effectiveness research. Evaluation researchers do scientific studies to determine the effectiveness of programs. Their methods are often indistinguishable from and shared with other health and social scientists.

When evaluators do **research**, they are participating in systematic processes of inquiry aimed at discovering, interpreting, and revising information about programs (Fink, 2005). Evaluation research uses the **scientific method**, which is a set of techniques for investigating phenomena and acquiring new knowledge of the natural and social worlds, based on observable, measurable evidence.

The scientific method is also characterized by the belief that a study's activities must be objective so that the scientist cannot bias the interpretation of the results or change the results outright. Another basic expectation is that the researcher will make available complete documentation of the data and the methodology for careful scrutiny by other scientists and researchers, thereby allowing them the opportunity to duplicate and verify the results. Enabling this replication of results is a scientific and ethical imperative.

In fact, the field of **ethics**, also called moral philosophy, is directly associated with scientific research. Ethics involves systematizing, defending, and recommending concepts of right and wrong behavior. Because evaluations always include human participants, the evaluator must demonstrate that the study design attends to ethical principles and respects participants' privacy, ensures that the benefits of participation are maximized, and provides all participants with equal access to the benefits. The criteria for including and excluding participant must be justified, and there must be a sufficient number of participants so that a program has a chance to prove itself. Also, the data collection and analysis must be appropriate and valid. Research that is not sound is unethical in itself because it results in misleading or false conclusions that, when applied, may result in harm.

Reading and reviewing evaluation research requires expertise in research design and statistics. Evidence-based public health practice is characterized by teams of people who work together because their skills and expertise complement one another's.

Evaluation researchers rely on the scientific method, a characteristic they share with all social researchers who strive for the "truth." The main difference is that evaluation researchers specifically study the effects of programs, interventions, campaigns, initiatives, interventions, and policies on participants.

Other scientists, such as epidemiologists, study patterns of health and illness in the population. Health services researchers examine how people get access to health care, how much care costs, and what happens to patients as a result of this care. The main goals of health services research are to identify the most effective ways to organize, manage, finance, and deliver high-quality care; reduce medical errors; and improve patient safety.

Evaluation, epidemiology, and health services research sometimes shares purposes or methods. If a program or intervention is involved, then the study is an evaluation. Example 1.4 contrasts evaluations and other types of research.

Example 1.4 Evaluation Research: Yes? No?

A. Research Objective: To investigate the effectiveness of acupuncture compared with sham acupuncture and with no acupuncture in patients with migraine.

Is this objective likely to be consistent with evaluation research purposes?
Answer: Yes. The researchers compare three interventions: acupuncture, sham acupuncture, and no acupuncture. (No acupuncture is considered an intervention in this case because the absence of acupuncture does not mean the absence of anything at all. The no acupuncture group may be on medication or other forms of therapy.)

B. Research Objective: To determine the effectiveness of an abuse-prevention curriculum designed to empower women with mental retardation to become effective decision makers.

Is this objective likely to be consistent with evaluation research purposes?
Answer: Yes. The intervention in this study is an abuse-prevention curriculum.

C. Research Objective: To estimate 1-year prevalence and correlates of alcohol abuse, dependence, and subthreshold dependence (diagnostic orphans) among middle-aged and elderly persons in the United States.

Is this objective likely to be consistent with evaluation research purposes?
Answer: No. The researchers are not planning to analyze the implementation, outcomes, impact, or costs of a program or intervention. This is an epidemiological study of alcohol misuse among older U.S. adults.

D. Research Objective: To clarify the concepts of coping with pain and quality of life (QoL) and to present a literature review of the strategies that children with recurrent headaches use to cope with their pain, the impact of recurrent headaches on children's QoL, and the influence of personal characteristics (such as age, family support) on headache, coping, and QoL in children.

Is this objective likely to be consistent with evaluation research purposes?
Answer: No. The researchers are not planning to analyze the process, outcomes, impact, or costs of a program or intervention.

The difference between evaluations and other studies covering relevant public health topics is presented in Example 1.5.

Example 1.5   Two Studies, One of Which (Study 1) Is an Evaluation

1. What Are D.A.R.E.'S Effects on Alcohol, Tobacco, and Marijuana Use? (Vincus, Ringwalt, Harris, & Shamblen, 2010)

    We present the short-term results of a quasi-experimental evaluation of the revised D.A.R.E. (Drug Abuse Resistance Education) curriculum. Study outcomes examined were D.A.R.E.'s effects on three substances, namely students' lifetime and 30-day use of tobacco, alcohol, and marijuana, as well as their school attendance and academic performance. The study comprised students in 17 urban schools, each of which served as its own control; 5th graders in the 2006–2007 school year constituted the comparison group ($n = 1,490$), and those enrolled as 5th graders in the 2007–2008 school year constituted the intervention group ($n= 1,450$). We found no intervention effect on students' substance use for any of the substance use outcomes assessed. We did find that students were more likely to attend school on days they received D.A.R.E. lessons and that students in the intervention group were more likely to have been suspended. Study findings provide little support for the implementation and dissemination of the revised D.A.R.E. curriculum.

2. Does Community Violence Exposure Predict Trauma Symptoms in a Sample of Maltreated Youth in Foster Care? (Garrido, Culhane, Raviv, & Taussig, 2010)

    Previous studies find that childhood exposure to family and community violence is associated with trauma symptoms. Few studies, however, have explored whether community violence exposure (CVE) predicts trauma symptoms after controlling for the effects associated with family violence exposure (FVE). In the current study, CVE and FVE were examined in a sample of 179 youth with a recent history of maltreatment. CVE was associated with trauma symptoms after controlling for FVE, but FVE was not associated with trauma symptoms after controlling for CVE. In addition, negative coping strategies (e.g., self-harm, interpersonal aggression) partially mediated the association between CVE and trauma symptoms. These findings are discussed in terms of their implications for interventions aimed at addressing the needs of children exposed to violence.

Study 1 in Example 1.5 is an evaluation of the D.A.R.E. program's effectiveness in reducing exposure to alcohol, tobacco, and marijuana. Study 2 is concerned with finding out whether exposure to community violence predicts trauma symptoms in youth in foster care. No program is included in this study, and so it is not an evaluation.

Table 1.4 shows the relationship among evaluation research and evidence-based public health practice.

Many programs go unevaluated or are poorly done. The need for scientific evaluations is worldwide and encompasses programs from local initiatives to global health programs. In 2010, *The Lancet*, a world-renowned journal, published a UNICEF-commissioned evaluation of its Accelerated Child Survival and Development Program ("Evaluation: The Top Priority for Global Health," 2010). The results of the evaluation did not

Table 1.4 Evaluation Research and Evidence-Based Public Health: Compare and Contrast

	Evaluation Research	**Evidence-Based Public Health Practice**
Objective	Produces valid evidence about the effectiveness of programs and practices Effective programs promote well-being and access to high-quality health care among communities and defined populations	Identifies, reviews, evaluates, and summarizes existing evidence regarding needs and effective programs and practices
Methods	Uses scientific method to design studies, collect information, and analyze and interpret data about the process, outcomes, impact, and costs of programs	Uses prespecified and transparent systems for grading the quality of the research and rating the strength of the evidence Uses the best evidence available to select programs and policies within the context of community needs and values
Ethical Concerns	Respects participants' rights to privacy and ensures they have an understanding of the risks and benefits of participation	Uses only research data that come from ethical research (e.g., evidence of an ethics board review)

match with the extravagant claims UNICEF had made about the program in 2005. The editorial stated,

> Evaluation must now become the top priority in global health. Currently, it is only an afterthought. A massive scale-up in global health investments during the past decade has not been matched by an equal commitment to evaluation. This complacency is damaging the entire global health movement. Without proper monitoring and accountability, countries and donors—and taxpayers—have no idea whether or how their investments are working. A lack of knowledge about whether aid works undermines everybody's confidence in global health initiatives. . . . Research will not only sustain interest in global health. It will improve quality of decision making, enhance efficiency, and build capacity for understanding why some programmes work, while others do not. . . . Evaluation matters. Evaluation is science. And evaluation costs money. (p. 526)

Table 1.5 contains a list of evaluation reports and articles that will give you an introduction to the contents, methods, and format of typical evaluation studies.

Table 1.5   Sample Evaluation Reports and Articles

Belansky, E. S., Cutforth, N., Delong, E., Litt, J., Gilbert, L., Scarbro, S., et al. (2010). Early effects of the federally mandated local wellness policy on school nutrition environments appear modest in Colorado's rural, low-income elementary schools. *Journal of the American Dietetic Association*, *110*, 1712–1717.

Belsky, J., Melhuish, E., Barnes, J., Leyland, A. H., & Romaniuk, H. (2006). Effects of Sure Start local programmes on children and families: Early findings from a quasi-experimental, cross-sectional study. *British Medical Journal*, *332*, 1476–1478.

Chien, A. T., Li, Z., & Rosenthal, M. B. (2010). Improving Timely childhood immunizations through pay for performance in Medicaid-managed care. *Health Services Research*, *45*(6p2), 1934–1947.

Ciaranello, A. L., Molitor, F., Leamon, M., Kuenneth, C., Tancredi, D., Diamant, A. L., et al. (2006). Providing health care services to the formerly homeless: A quasi-experimental evaluation. *Journal of Health Care for the Poor and Underserved*, *17*, 441–461.

Diamant, A. L., Brook, R. H., Fink, A., & Gelberg, L. (2001). Assessing use of primary health care services by very low-income adults in a managed care program. *Archives of Internal Medicine*, *161*, 1222–1227.

Fink, A., Elliott, M. N., Tsai, M., & Beck, J. C. (2005). An evaluation of an intervention to assist primary care physicians in screening and educating older patients who use alcohol. *Journal of the American Geriatrics Society*, *53*, 1937–1943.

Fishbein, M., Hall-Jamieson, K., Zimmer, E., von Haeften, I., & Nabi, R. (2002). Avoiding the boomerang: Testing the relative effectiveness of antidrug public service announcements before a national campaign. *American Journal of Public Health*, *92*, 238–245.

Fox, P. G., Rossetti, J., Burns, K. R., & Popovich, J. (2005). Southeast Asian refugee children: A school-based mental health intervention. *International Journal of Psychiatric Nursing Research*, *11*, 1227–1236.

Freudenberg, N., Ramaswamy, M., Daniels, J., Crum, M., Ompad, D. C., & Vlahov, D. (2010). Reducing drug use, Human Immunodeficiency Virus Risk, and recidivism among young men leaving jail: Evaluation of the REAL MEN re-entry program. *Journal of Adolescent Health*, *47*, 448–455.

Goodpaster, B. H., DeLany, J. P., Otto, A. D., Kuller, L., Vockley, J., South-Paul, J. E., et al. (2010). Effects of diet and physical activity interventions on weight loss and cardiometabolic risk factors in severely obese adults. *JAMA: The Journal of the American Medical Association*, *304*(16), 1795–1802.

Hardy, L., King, L., Kelly, B., Farrell, L., & Howlett, S. (2010). Munch and Move: Evaluation of a preschool healthy eating and movement skill program. *International Journal of Behavioral Nutrition and Physical Activity*, *7*(1), 80.

Hay, J., LaBree, L., Luo, R., Clark, F., Carlson, M., Mandel, D., et al. (2002). Cost-effectiveness of preventive occupational therapy for independent-living older adults. *Journal of the American Geriatric Society*, *50*, 1381–1388.

(Continued)

Table 1.5 (Continued)

Hedman, E., Andersson, G., Andersson, E., Ljotsson, B., Ruck, C., Asmundson, G. J. G., et al. (2011). Internet-based cognitive-behavioural therapy for severe health anxiety: Randomised controlled trial. *British Journal of Psychiatry*, *198*, 230–236.

Klesges, R. C., Obarzanek, E., Kumanyika, S., Murray, D. M., Klesges, L. M., Relyea, G. E., et al. (2010). The Memphis Girls' health Enrichment Multi-site Studies (GEMS): An evaluation of the efficacy of a 2-year obesity prevention program in African American girls. *Archives of Pediatrics and Adolescent Medicine*, *164*, 1007–1014.

Lobera, I. J., Lozano, P. L., Ríos, P. B., Candau, J. R., Del Villar y Lebreros, G. S., Milan, M. T. M., et al. (2010). Traditional and new strategies in the primary prevention of eating disorders: A comparative study in Spanish adolescents. *International Journal of General Medicine*, *3*, 263–272.

Lovera, D., Sanderson, M., Bogle, M. L., & Vela Acosta, M. S. (2010). Evaluation of a breastfeeding peer support program for fathers of Hispanic participants in a Texas special supplemental nutrition program for women, infants, and children. *Journal of the American Dietetic Association*, *110*, 1696–1702.

Petry, N. M., Weinstock, J., Morasco, B. J., & Ledgerwood, D. M. (2009). Brief motivational interventions for college student problem gamblers. *Addiction*, *104*, 1569–1578.

Polaschek, D. L. L., Wilson, N. J., Townsend, M. R., & Daly, L. R. (2005). Cognitive-behavioral rehabilitation for high-risk violent offenders: An outcome evaluation of the violence prevention unit. *Journal of Interpersonal Violence*, *20*, 1611–1627.

Runyan, C. W., Gunther-Mohr, C., Orton, S., Umble, K., Martin, S. L., & Coyne-Beasley, T. (2005). Prevent: A program of the National Training Initiative on Injury and Violence Prevention. *American Journal of Preventative Medicine*, *29*(5S2), 252–258.

Rydholm, L., & Kirkhorn, S. R. (2005). A study of the impact and efficacy of health fairs for farmers. *Journal of Agricultural Safety and Health*, *11*, 441–448.

Sheeran, P., & Silverman, M. (2003). Evaluation of three interventions to promote workplace health and safety: Evidence for the utility of implementation intentions. *Social Science and Medicine*, *56*, 2153–2163.

Stein, B. A., Jacox, L. H., Kataoka, S. H., Wong, M., Tu, W., Elliott, M. N., et al. (2003). Mental health intervention for school children exposed to violence: A randomized controlled trial. *Journal of the American Medical Association*, *290*, 603–611.

Wells, K. B., Sherbourne, C., Schoenbaum, M., Duan, N., Meredith, L., Unutzer, J., et al. (2000). Impact of disseminating quality improvement programs for depression in managed primary care: A randomized controlled trial. *Journal of the American Medical Association*, *268*, 212–220.

Wheeler, M. T., Heidenreich, P. A., Froelicher, V. F., Hlatky, M. A., & Ashley, E. A. (2010). Cost-effectiveness of preparticipation screening for prevention of sudden cardiac death in young athletes. *Annals of Internal Medicine*, *152*, 276–286.

In addition to evaluation research, evidence-based public health practice uses research from many fields, including epidemiology and health services research, for data on needs, methods, and best practices (Brownson et al., 2009). For example, suppose a health district was interested in improving childhood immunizations. A study in the journal *Health Services Research* reveals the impact of a "piece-rate" pay-for-performance program (Example 1.6).

Example 1.6   Improving Timely Childhood Immunizations Through Pay for Performance in Medicaid-Managed Care (Chien, Li, & Rosenthal, 2010)

Objective. To evaluate the impact of a "piece-rate" pay-for-performance (P4P) program aimed at rewarding up-to-date immunization delivery to 2-year-olds according to the recommended series.

Data Sources/Study Setting. Plan-level data from New York State's Quality Assurance Reporting Requirement and claims data from Hudson Health Plan for 2003–2007. In 2003 Hudson Health Plan, a not-for-profit Medicaid-focused managed care plan, introduced a U.S.$200 bonus payment for each fully immunized 2-year-old and provided administrative supports for identifying children who may need immunization. This represented a potential bonus of 15–25 percent above base reimbursement for eligible 2-year-olds.

Study Design. Case-comparison and interrupted times series.

Principal Findings. Immunization rates within Hudson Health Plan rose at a significantly, albeit modestly, higher rate than the robust secular trend noted among comparison health plans. Supplementary analyses suggest that there was no significant change in preexisting disparities during the study period, and that children with chronic conditions have significantly greater odds of being fully immunized during the entire study period.

Conclusions. This study suggests that a piece-rate P4P program with appropriate administrative supports can be effective at improving childhood immunization rates.

Summary of Chapter 1: Public Health Practice and the Best Available Evidence

Words to Remember

abstracts, best available evidence, clinical trials, community-based participatory research, cost-benefit, cost-effective, cost minimization, cost utility, effectiveness, efficacy, ethics, evaluation research, evidence-based public health practice, experimental group, experimental studies, health services research, Healthy People, impact, implementation evaluation, needs, observational research, outcomes, participatory evaluation, process, program, public health, qualitative, quantitative, research, research ethics, scientific method, study quality

Evidence-based public health practice is characterized by it use of the best available evidence to make informed public health practice decisions. It is a means of identifying community needs, tracking down information from evaluation research to find potentially effective programs, assessing the quality of the research or evidence supporting the programs, and evaluating the impact of introducing the programs into practice. Evaluation research is a systematic method of assessing the process, outcomes, impact, and costs of a program or intervention. Scientific evaluations aim to produce valid research evidence about the effectiveness of programs and practices.

Evidence-based public health uses evidence from evaluation research to guide decision making about programs. Evaluators do the research. Evidence-based public health practitioners review the research requiring them to have skills in evaluating study quality. In addition to evaluation research, practitioners use data and methods from health services research and epidemiology.

THE NEXT CHAPTER

Chapter 2 discusses how to analyze community needs and preferences for services and identify high-quality programs and services to meet them.

EXERCISES

1. List five defining characteristics of evidence-based public health.

   Answer:
   - Evaluating needs for new or improved programs or practices
   - Tracking down the best available evidence on programs and practices that potentially meet the needs
   - Collecting the best available information on appropriate programs and practices
   - Selecting programs and practices that fit together with community and population needs and values
   - Evaluating the impact on health and well-being of putting the selected programs into practice

2. Define evidence-based public health practice.

   Answer:
   Evidence-based public health practice uses the best available evidence to promote the health and well-being of communities and populations.

3. Explain the similarities and differences between evidence-based public health practice and evidence-based medicine.

   Answer:

   Evidence-based public health and evidence-based medicine are both concerned with asking answerable questions, collecting relevant evidence to answer the questions, and evaluating the effectiveness of the process. Evidence-based public health practice focuses on understanding and preventing disease and promoting health in communities. Evidence-based medicine tends to focus on diagnosis and treatment in individuals. Both require skills in identifying and evaluating existing knowledge from research.

4. Describe methods for obtaining best available evidence.

   Answer:

   Systematic review of the literature, especially evaluation research findings or comparative effectiveness studies.

5. Explain and justify the use of evidence-based public health practice.

   Answer:

   Evidence-based public health practice replaces anecdote with the findings of the best research that is publicly available. It provides reasonable confirmation that a program or practice will improve public health.

6. How does evidence-based public health practice use evaluation research or program evaluation findings?

   Answer:

   Evidence-based public health practice uses evaluation findings in guiding decisions regarding which programs to support.

7. Explain whether each of these is an evaluation study or not.
   a. **Research Objective:** To evaluate a randomized culturally tailored intervention to prevent high-HIV-risk sexual behaviors for Latina women residing in urban areas.
   b. **Research Objective:** To determine the efficacy of a spit tobacco (ST) intervention designed to promote ST cessation and discourage ST initiation among male high school baseball athletes.
   c. **Research Objective:** To study drivers' exposure to distractions, unobtrusive video camera units were installed in the vehicles of 70 volunteer drivers over 1-week time periods.

   Answer:
      a. Yes. This is an evaluation study. The program is an intervention to prevent high-HIV-risk sexual behaviors for Latina women in urban areas.
      b. Yes. This is an evaluation study. The intervention is a spit tobacco intervention.
      c. No. This is not an evaluation study. The researchers are not analyzing the process, outcomes, impact, or costs of a program or intervention.

8. Define the major characteristics of evaluation research.

Answer:

- Produces valid evidence about effectiveness of programs and interventions by studying their process, outcomes, impact, and costs
- Uses scientific method to design studies, collect information, and analyze and interpret data
- May add a participatory dimension to ensure that evidence obtained is evidence that matters (meets needs, values, and expectations of stakeholders)
- Respects participants' rights to privacy and ensures that they have an understanding of the risks and benefits of participation

9. Read the following five statements and tell whether you agree or disagree with each or do not have sufficient information to agree or disagree.

Statement	Agree	Disagree	Cannot Tell (Not Enough Information)
1. If a report provides detailed descriptive statistical information about a program (e.g., number of people who participated in the program, how many of them benefited, duration of the program), that is proof that the program is effective.			
2. To qualify as an effective program, you need at least one of these: data on how program participants' outcomes compare to nonparticipants'; comparable outcome data from established databases; long-term data on outcomes for one or more groups of people.			
3. Once you find an effective program, it doesn't matter if you change parts of it to meet your needs as long as you stay true to the program developer's intentions.			
4. Effective programs are usually less costly than ones that are of unproven effectiveness.			

Statement	Agree	Disagree	Cannot Tell (Not Enough Information)
5. Evaluation reports do not need to include information on program activities such as staff training and monitoring of quality and adherence to the study's implementation because such information is not needed to arrive at a conclusion about a program's effectiveness.			

10. Compare these four definitions of evaluation.

- Evaluation research is a systematic method of assessing the process, outcomes, impact, and costs of a program or intervention. Scientific evaluations produce the best research evidence about the effectiveness of programs and new knowledge about social behavior. For research evidence to matter, it must be accurate and helpful to the evaluation's users.

- The key to a successful program or project is evaluation. Evaluation provides formative feedback that helps guide a program as it is being implemented. It also provides summative data that clearly demonstrate that the program is accomplishing its stated goals and objectives. Without effective evaluation, the program staff may fail to document important impacts the program has on its participants. It may also fail to recognize how different components in the program are affecting the participants or participating institutions. In an era of limited resources for educational programs, those programs that can document their success in having an impact on their participants and in using resources efficiently will be at an advantage for ongoing funding.

- The purpose of evaluation is to produce information about the performance of a program in achieving its objectives. In general, most evaluations are conducted to answer two fundamental questions: Is the program working as intended, and why is this the case? Research methods are applied to answer these questions and to increase the accuracy and objectivity of judgments about the program's success in reaching its objectives.

- The generic goal of most evaluations is to provide "useful feedback" to a variety of audiences, including sponsors, donors, client-groups, administrators, staff, and other relevant constituencies. Most often, feedback is perceived as "useful" if it aids in decision making. But the relationship between an evaluation and its impact is not a simple one—studies that seem critical sometimes fail to influence short-term decisions, and studies that initially seem to have no influence can have a delayed impact when more congenial conditions arise. Despite this, there is broad consensus that the major goal of evaluation should be to influence decision making or policy formulation through the provision of empirically driven feedback.

- Describe how to identify and evaluate online evidence-based program databases such as those maintained by the Agency for Healthcare Research and Quality and the Centers for Disease Control and Prevention (CDC)
- Distinguish between primary and secondary data
- Describe the advantages and disadvantages of using secondary data
- Explain how to evaluate the quality of health information websites

❖ IDENTIFYING HEALTH AND HEALTH CARE RISKS OR NEEDS, PREFERENCES, AND VALUES

Evidence-based public health practice begins with identifying gaps in available programs and policies to prevent disease and promote well-being (see Table 2.1). The gaps are the **risks** or needs. A systematic effort to identify community needs is called a **needs assessment**. Needs are intertwined with values and preferences, which together affect priorities for programs and services. For example, a community may need more social services for the elderly but may prefer to spend most of its resources on preventing violence in teens.

Needs can be arranged into seven categories: social, communal or epidemiological, behavioral, environmental, educational, administrative, and genetic.

Social needs usually refer to the community's perceptions of its problems. For example, one community may see gang warfare or teen violence as its major problem, while another may regard the unemployment of its youth as the most pressing need.

Epidemiological needs refer to problems that can be documented to affect a large number of people in the community. For example, school records may reveal inadequacies in meeting the health needs of special education students in a school district, and a review of the state's statistics on low-weight births may reveal higher than state averages for three counties. Data on communal or epidemiological needs usually come from very large national and state databases such as those maintained by the CDC (www.cdc.gov), the U.K. Department of Health, Public Health Statistics (www.dh.gov.uk/health/category/publications/statistics), and the Australian Institute of Health and Welfare (www.aihw.gov.au).

Behavioral needs refer to individual and communal lifestyles and beliefs that affect a community's well-being. Abundant evidence exists, for example, that some communities rely on diets that are high in fat and that this contributes to high rates of obesity and to concomitant illnesses in those

Table 2.1   Exploring Seven Categories of Needs

Need	Explanation	Question/Comment
Social	People's perception of their own needs	What are the community's needs and preferences? Does the community have the resources to solve its health risks? How readily can the community implement programs?
Communal/epidemiological	Assessment of problems that characterize specific groups in a community	Information comes from analyses of large databases and vital statistics.
Behavioral	Determination of individual and community lifestyles or behaviors that contribute to existing needs	For instance, these may include dietary preferences that lead to obesity and diabetes or customs regarding receipt of prenatal care.
Environmental	External social and physical factors that contribute to risks	For instance, how healthy are the foods served to children in school cafeterias? How accessible is prenatal care? Fresh fruits and vegetables?
Educational	Individual and community knowledge, attitudes, skills, and self-efficacy beliefs	A major question is how these factors interact to assure the implementation of new programs and practices.
Administrative	Policies and resources prevailing in the organizational context that might facilitate or hinder program implementation	What are the barriers to implementation (e.g., staff commitment, lack of space)?
Genetic	Inherent or built-in genetic risks and predispositions	How can we integrate our intrinsic genetic risks and predispositions, environmental risks and exposures to provide insight into how disease outcomes are determined?

communities. Another example is that prenatal care may be viewed by some in Community A as a necessity, while in Community B it may be seen as an attempt to make a medical problem out of a natural process.

Environmental needs refer to social or physical factors that are external to an individual or a community. For example, if access to nutritious food is limited in a community, then it will be difficult to implement a program to instill good eating practices.

The CDC also provides public health data through its Morbidity and Mortality Weekly Report (MMWR). The data in weekly MMWRs (Figure 2.2) are provisional, based on weekly reports to the CDC by state health departments.

The MMWR provides public health information AND evidence-based recommendations for solving public health problems. For instance, in 2010 (MMWR: 2010:59: 1541-1545), the MMWR reported on adverse childhood experiences that were reported in 2009 by adults in five states. Such experiences include verbal, physical, or sexual abuse as well as family dysfunction such as domestic violence or substance abuse. The report concluded that such events are common and associated with multiple mental and physical health problems, and it recommended evidence-based prevention programs such as home visitations and parenting programs.

The U.S. Census and the CDC also provide user-friendly ways to get population data. Suppose you were considering a public health campaign to improve the proportion of older people in the population who receive flu shots in California. To find out about the proportion who are already receiving the shot (Figure 2.3), you can use data from the CDC's Behavioral Risk

Figure 2.2   Morbidity and Mortality Weekly Report (MMWR) From the CDC

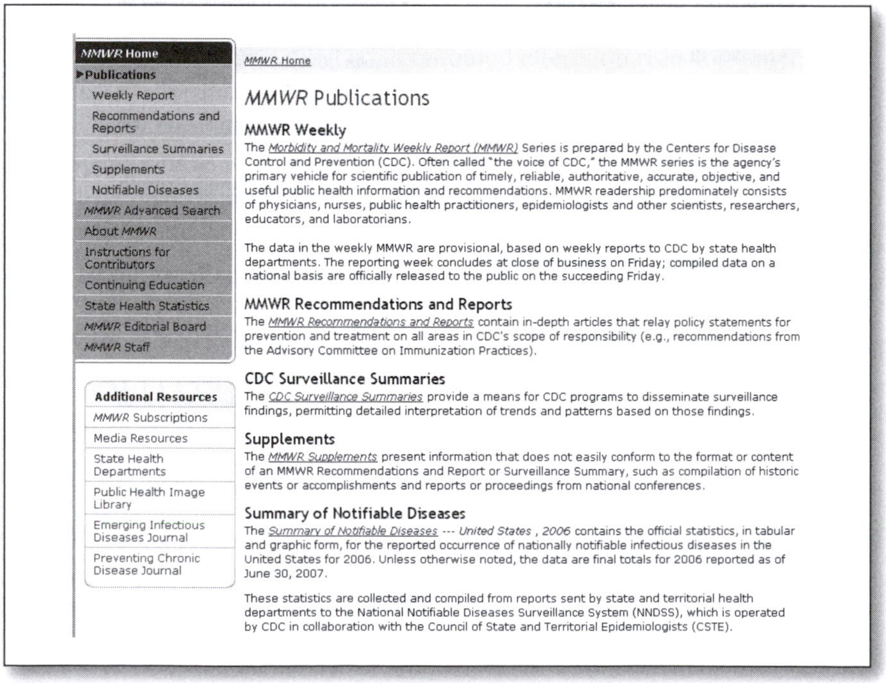

Figure 2.3   Percentage of People 65 Years of Age and Older Who Had Influenza Vaccinations in the Past Year (2001–2009)

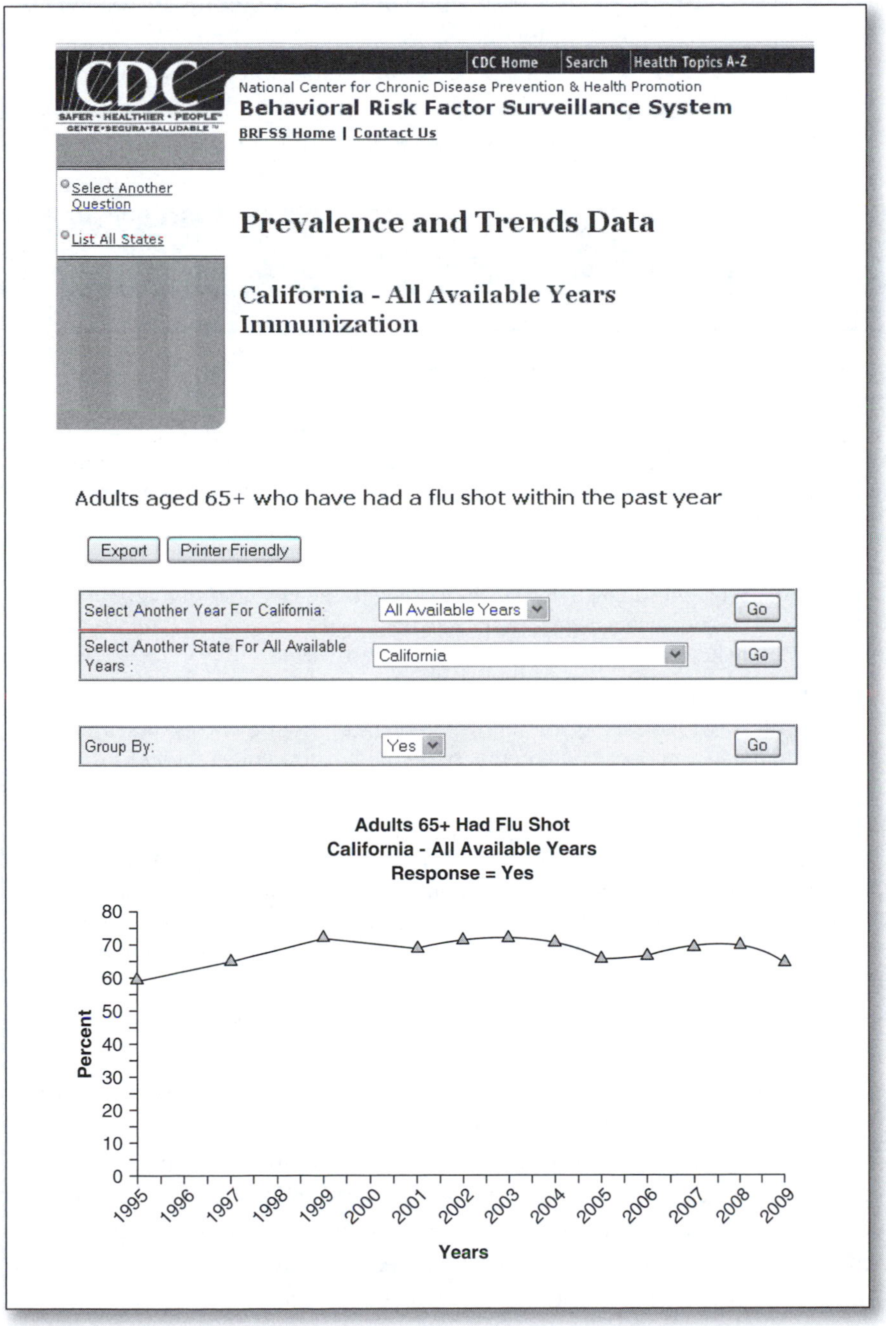

Factor Surveillance System (BRFSS) website (www.cdc.gov/brfss). BRFSS is an ongoing telephone health survey system that has been tracking health conditions and risk behaviors in the United States yearly since 1984.

The data can be refined by gender, and you can compare California's performance with that of other states.

An illustration of the use of secondary data analysis is presented in Example 2.1. In the example, the authors use data from the California Health Interview Survey to study the health of rural adolescents.

Example 2.1 Large Database in Use: Adolescent Rural Health (Curtis, Waters, & Brindis, 2011)

Context: Adolescence is a pivotal developmental period for the establishment of positive health and health practices. However, developmentally propelled risk behaviors coinciding with barriers to health services may increase the propensity for untoward health outcomes in adolescence. In addition, the sociocultural context of the rural environment can present challenges to the health of adolescents. Limited data on rural adolescent health, particularly among population subgroups, hinder the ability to adequately advocate for adolescent health prevention services.

Methods: A secondary analysis of the 2005 California Health Interview Survey Adolescent questionnaire was conducted. Selected survey items corresponding to the Healthy Youth 2010 objectives were analyzed for 663 adolescents aged 12–17 residing in rural regions of California. Adolescent subgroup analysis included race/ethnicity, age, and poverty level.

Findings: Adolescent health issues of particular concern in this study include sexual health, substance abuse, mental health, and risk factors for obesity. Predictably, risk behaviors increase with the age of the adolescent. Minority and poor youth demonstrate the greatest vulnerability to untoward health outcomes.

Conclusion: Significant risk behaviors and health concerns exist among the rural adolescent population, particularly among poor and minority youth, arguing for the creation and preservation of prevention services for youth in the rural community. Future research using alternative sampling methodologies may be necessary to adequately represent the higher-risk adolescent in the rural community. More data are needed on vulnerable adolescent populations in the rural community in order to adequately advocate for prevention services.

Researchers can create subsets of data from existing databases that meet their specific study needs. For instance, suppose an alcohol researcher wanted to study the prevalence of women's use of alcohol in the United States. The researcher might use one of the databases maintained by the National Institute on Alcohol Abuse and Alcoholism to create a data set that only contained information on women. If the researcher planned to study women 65 years of age and older, the data set would include that subpopulation.

The analysis of data from existing databases is called **secondary data analysis**. Tutorials for using specific U.S. databases are available online at the appropriate websites. The National Center for Health Statistics (www.cdc .gov/nchs), for instance, offers a tutorial for accessing and using the National Health and Nutrition Examination Survey. This database contains information on the health and nutritional status of adults and children.

Secondary data are used by researchers and program planners because it is comparatively economical to do so. Many databases are free or relatively low in cost. Although professional skill is needed in doing the data analysis, the costs in time and money are invariably less than the resources needed to do primary data collection. Primary data are collected by researchers to meet the specific needs of their study.

Why Evidence-Based Public Health Practice Uses Secondary Data

- Sometimes primary data collection simply is not necessary because the available data solve the problem or answer the question.
- Secondary data sources are less expensive and time-consuming than are primary sources.
- Secondary sources of information can yield more accurate data for some variables than can primary sources. For instance, data collected by governments or international agencies in surveys of health behaviors and health problems are accurate. The data collection methods and processes are often perfected over time with large numbers of people.
- Secondary data are especially useful in the exploratory phase of large studies or program-planning efforts. They can be used to determine the prevalence of a problem and to study whether certain members of a given population are more susceptible to the problem than others.

What Evidence-Based Public Health Practice Should Watch For

- The definitions of key variables that the original researchers use may be different from yours. Definitions of terms such as *quality of life* or *severity of illness* may vary considerably from time to time and country to country.
- The information in the database may not be presented exactly as you need it. The original researchers collected information on people's

been presented to session participants and they have had an opportunity to ask questions or briefly discuss the scope of the topic, they are asked to take a few minutes to think about and write down their responses. The session moderator then asks each participant to read, and elaborate on, one of his or her responses. These are noted on a flipchart. Once everyone has given a response, participants are asked for a second or third response, until all of their answers have been noted on flipchart sheets posted around the room.

Once duplications are eliminated, each response is assigned a letter or number. Session participants are then asked to choose up to 10 responses that they feel are the most important and rank them according to their relative importance. These rankings are collected from all participants and aggregated. Here is an example:

Response	Participant 1	Participant 2	Participant 3	Columns Inserted Here for Participants 4–12	Relative Importance of Each Response
A	ranked 1st	ranked 2nd	ranked 2nd		5 participants ranked A 1st
B	ranked 3rd	ranked 1st	ranked 3rd		7 participants ranked B 3rd
C	ranked 2nd	ranked 3rd	ranked 1st		6 participants ranked C 2nd
D	ranked 4th	ranked 4th	ranked 4th		12 participants ranked D 4th

Sometimes the results are given back to the participants in order to stimulate further discussion, and perhaps a readjustment in the overall rankings is assigned to the various responses. This is done only when group consensus regarding priorities is important.

The nominal group process can be used in a wide variety of settings. For example, it was used to collate information for the development of a mental health program for victims of drought in rural Australia (Sartore, Hoolahan, Tonna, Kelly, & Stain, 2005). Twenty-three participants were recruited in consultation with rural mental health organizations. They were asked questions about the best mental health service strategies for minimizing and responding to the mental health impact of drought. Three general strategies emerged: community building and education about the physical, financial, and mental health effects of drought; cooperation between and coordination among agencies in delivering mental health and other drought support; and continuity and planning of improved mental health services.

Delphi Technique

The **Delphi technique** is a structured method for determining the degree of agreement on a topic, selecting alternatives, or setting priorities. The technique uses questionnaires that are completed by participants on their own, in groups, or both. The questionnaires are structured to ask people to rate or rank the importance or validity of certain ideas. For example, Delphi participants might be asked to rate the importance of a particular program objective (1 = *definitely important* to 5 = *definitely not important*) and the likelihood that it might be achieved in a particular institution (1 = *definitely likely* to 5 = *definitely not likely*). The results of the ratings (Round 1) are sent back to the respondents, who are asked to review them and re-rate the items (Round 2).

In "mailed" Delphi's (regular mail, e-mail, or online), the participants are usually not known to one another. Anonymity is thought to encourage people to focus on the issues rather than on each other. In a Delphi variation in which Round 1 is mailed but Round 2 is a face-to-face meeting, the participants are known to each other, but their individual ratings are not. The idea behind a face-to-face discussion of the first round's results is that the dialogue increases attention to the subtleties of the issues and introduces new views into the rating process.

Example 2.2 describes an actual use of the Delphi method to identify the essential characteristics of cognitive-behavioral treatment manuals.

Example 2.2   Using Delphi by E-mail: What Do Experts Agree Should Be in a Cognitive Behavioral Treatment Manual? An Excerpt

---

Who Were the Delphi Participants?

All participants were experts who were defined as individuals who have published treatment manuals or have used them in published research. Potential participants' names were gathered primarily through an electronic search of the online literature.

(Continued)

Example 2.2 (Continued)

How Was Anonymity Guaranteed?

Twenty-nine prospective participants were e-mailed a pre-notification letter inviting them to participate in the study. A positive response was viewed as informed consent. The e-mail process enabled the mass mailing of all correspondence without individuals' knowledge of each other.

What Was the Study Plan?

Round 1. An e-mail, with attachment, was sent to the consenting sample. In the attachment, participants were asked to list their preferences for the contents of a good cognitive behavioral therapy treatment manual.

Round 2. Items generated from round 1 were thematically analyzed by the investigators and a colleague experienced in using treatment manuals. When initial disagreement regarding the categorization of items occurred, discussion took place until the investigator and his colleague reached agreement. Following analysis, a questionnaire was designed for the subsequent rounds. In order to facilitate completion, a 3-point rating scale was generated for each item:

E = Essential. Each manual must contain this item

D = Desirable. Inclusion of this item enhances the manual

I = Inappropriate. Not applicable to the manual

Round 3. The results of round 2 were collated, and the percentage agreement for each category was placed next to each item. The returned questionnaire included the participants' original responses, and participants were given the opportunity to amend their selections (if desired) in response to viewing the overall feedback.

How Was Consensus Defined?

As there is no agreement concerning the required degree of consensus in a Delphi study, the investigators set consensus levels at two-thirds of the responses.

What Did the Delphi Find to Be Essential?

Only 11 (13%) of the generated items were rated as essential:

General characteristics of treatment manuals

Appropriate for the problem addressed

Coherent and focused

Based on a clear theoretical model

A distinct feature of the Delphi technique is the anonymity of participants or responses. If participants are not known to one another, the method can be used to obtain agreement among groups and individuals that are normally hostile to one another. But Delphi participants may not be representative of the very group whose needs are being assessed, and this is a limitation. Participation requires the completion of written questionnaires through at least two rounds. Not everyone is survey savvy and can spend the required time. If the results are seen as nonrepresentative, then they might not be taken seriously. Further, no established definition of agreement or consensus exists, and this alone can make Delphi findings appear arbitrary for those who would use a different definition. Finally, the method tends to encourage a middle-of-the-road view, especially if average ratings or majority ratings are used.

The RAND/UCLA Appropriateness Method

The **RAND/UCLA Appropriateness Method (RUAM)** is used to determine the extent of agreement on controversial topics and topics for which the research base is poor or ambiguous (a mixture of positive and negative findings).

The RUAM was originally created to determine the appropriateness of certain medical procedures and surgical operations, such as gallbladder removals or coronary artery bypass surgery. Because the method has proved to be flexible, reliable, and valid (Shekelle, 2004), it has been adapted for use in a variety of other health and mental health contexts, including the creation of indicators of quality of care for children with attention deficit hyperactivity disorder, conduct disorder, and major depression (Zima et al., 2005) and the identification of indicators of quality care for elderly patients undergoing surgery (McGory et al., 2009).

The RUAM incorporates elements of the National Institutes of Health (NIH) consensus development process, the Delphi, and the nominal group techniques. It has the following characteristics:

- Six to 14 panelists are assembled. The panelists are well known in their fields and differ in their expertise.
- The study team compiles a state-of-the-art review of the literature for the panelists.
- The panelists participate in a two-round rating process using a 9-point scale.
- Round 1 is usually done by each panelist independently, before a group meeting.
- A highly skilled moderator conducts a meeting to discuss the ratings and clarify individual concerns. After discussion, the panelists do their ratings a second time; this constitutes the Round 2.

Example 2.3 (Continued)

Example of the Ratings for Round 1 Summarized

	1	2	2			1	2	1	2	
	1	2	3	4	5	6	7	8*	9	
	Very inappropriate			Uncertain			Very appropriate			

In this example, one (1) panelist rated the appropriateness as 1, two (2) rated it at 2, two (2) at 3, one (1) at 6, two (2) at 7, and two (2) at 9. This particular panelist rated the appropriateness as 8 because the 8 has an asterisk (*).

Disagreement/Agreement

Did the panelists agree with one another? A standard definition for disagreement is that it occurs if 3 or more panelists rate a statement in the high range (7–9) AND 3 or more rate it in the low range (1–3). Any other combination of ratings is considered agreement. In the example above, the panelists disagreed.

Round 2

Panelists were given the summary of the round 1 ratings. They then participated in a two-hour telephone conference to discuss the ratings, with particular emphasis on disagreement.

After discussion, the panelists re-rated the scenarios. Needs for services were recommended if, after the second round of ratings, a service received a rating of 7 or higher (very appropriate) and there was no disagreement.

Surveys

Surveys are usually used to gather information from large numbers of people. Several types are possible. A face-to-face interview may result in in-depth information but requires a skilled interviewer. Telephone surveys also require skilled interviewers, but it has become increasingly difficult to get people to agree to participate. People hanging up, the need to call back, and messages left on voice mail are costly.

Web-based or other electronically distributed surveys can reach large numbers of people. However, technical expertise is needed to design the survey, and you have to make certain that the people who are selected to participate can access the survey and complete it. Among the most difficult issues associated with electronic surveys is how to ensure privacy.

Mail surveys are in some ways the simplest because they do not require staff training (as do interviews) or technical expertise. The number of people who return questionnaires that are mailed to them, however, is often extremely low unless they are given an incentive to do so. The use of incentives in surveys may be costly and may boost the number of responses only slightly. Writing survey questionnaires requires a great deal of skill. Poorly designed questionnaires, those with poor instructions, hard-to-read questions, and inadequate response choices, typically result in low response rates. Low response rates mean invalid survey results.

An illustrative use of a survey to identify needs is given in Example 2.4. The purpose of the survey was to assess the nutritional needs of black women with type 2 diabetes as well as the barriers they encounter in meeting these needs.

Example 2.4   A Survey of the Needs of Women With Diabetes

Purpose. The purpose of this survey was to explore food purchasing, preparation, and consumption among black women with type 2 diabetes mellitus in an urban setting to assess barriers to medical nutrition therapy recommendations.

Methods. A telephone survey asked about shopping habits, the use of community resources for food supplementation, use of restaurant/fast-food establishments, dining habits, food purchasing and consumption, and food preparation methods. The survey contained 38 items.

Results. The respondents identified ways in which their participation in a culturally competent intervention of diabetes care and education helped them to change their dietary behaviors. The most common areas of change included purchasing, preparation, and portion size. The most commonly cited barriers to medical nutrition therapy included low income, time constraints, competing demands, and knowledge deficits.

Conclusions. Culturally sensitive diabetes interventions are an effective way to overcome some of the barriers to medical nutrition therapy. The results of the survey suggest that identification of more affordable healthy food resources in the community is needed. In addition, transportation to grocery stores should be on the public policy agenda. Finally, alternate sites for nutrition education, such as a supermarket forum, warrant further investigation.

SOURCE: Galasso, Amend, Melkus, & Nelson. (2005). Barriers to medical nutrition therapy in black women with type 2 diabetes mellitus. *Diabetes Educator, 31,* 719–725. Used with permission of Sage Publications, Inc.

Asset Mapping

Asset mapping aims to create an in-depth understanding of a community's needs by identifying and mapping local resources and gaps in services. An asset is a resource that improves the quality of community life. Examples include schools, hospitals, and churches; businesses that provide jobs; Neighborhood Watches or other citizen associations; and local private, public, and nonprofit institutions (*Section 1: Asset Mapping,* n.d.).

Asset mapping has five general steps:

1. Define the "community's" boundaries. This means defining the community: Is it everyone in the county? Subpopulations such as older people? New parents? The unemployed? Once the community is defined, select the streets or landmarks that define the geographic area in which the community can be found.

2. Identify and involve people in the community to work with you. They can help you define the geographic area and tell you the best way to identify the community's assets.

3. Identify the community's assets. Money and access to economic resources are the most obvious assets, but knowledge and skills, political know-how, and community acceptance are also important.

4. List the assets of groups and of individuals. Use the community partners to help assemble this list. Other sources of information about the community's assets include the Internet, the Yellow Pages, city directories, and neighborhood businesses. Consider doing a survey of individuals and businesses to find out about the resources they provide to the community.

5. Organize the placement of assets on a map. Maps are visual aids that enable you to see where there are gaps in services, where services overlap, and where services are most concentrated. Large projects should consider using asset mapping or geographic information system technology.

Asset mapping's advantages include identifying and building upon existing community resources. It is a participatory method that can raise awareness of a community's needs and bring people together to solve problems. However, it is a time-consuming and politically loaded process involving many people with competing interests. Some community resources may be difficult to identify, leading to a misinterpretation of needs. For instance, a cancer center may serve the community but not be located within its geographical borders. Asset mapping and geographical information system software are available, but they are expensive and require time to learn.

Example 2.5 describes a study that used asset mapping to identify and map the geographic distribution of available colorectal cancer screening resources.

Example 2.5   Using Asset Mapping to Identify and Map the Geographic Distribution of Colorectal Cancer Screening Resources (Gwede et al., 2010)

Objective. We sought to identify and map the geographic distribution of available colorectal cancer screening resources; following identification of this priority within a needs assessment of a local community-academic collaborative to reduce cancer health disparities in medically underserved communities.

Methods. We used geographic information systems (GIS) and asset mapping tools to visually depict resources in the context of geography and a population of interest. We illustrate two examples, offer step-by-step directions for mapping, and discuss the challenges, lessons learned, and future directions for research and practice.

Results. Our positive asset driven, community-based approach illustrated the distribution of existing colonoscopy screening facilities and locations of populations and organizations who might use these resources. A need for additional affordable and accessible colonoscopy resources was identified.

Conclusion. These transdisciplinary community mapping efforts highlight the benefit of innovative community-academic partnerships for addressing cancer health disparities by bolstering infrastructure and community capacity-building for increased access to colonoscopies.

Table 2.2 summarizes the objectives, characteristics, advantages, and limitations of some of the main community needs assessment methods.

Consensus Panels

The need to "do something" in situations of uncertainty is certainly characteristic of the health professions. In response, the NIH has supported the Consensus Development Program since 1977, the aim of which is to produce "state-of-the-science" reports (http://consensus.nih.gov). Although not yet widely implemented in the other helping professions, **consensus development conferences** are an integral part of evidence-based health care, and their methods can be usefully adapted to other

Table 2.2   Community Needs Assessment Methods

Name	Objectives	Implementation	Advantages	Limitations
Key informant	Gather views from members of the community who know the community from the "inside" because of their training or affiliations	Key informants (e.g., elected officials, religious and public services leaders, professionals, teachers, lawyers) are identified and then interviewed or surveyed.	Relatively inexpensive Provides perspectives from different viewpoints Can get "insider's" view	Limit on how many people can be included, so results may not be representative Cannot be sure that all "key" people are included
Public or community forum	Get views from a wide range of community residents in public meetings	A sponsoring agency puts on public forums. A list of discussion questions is generated by the sponsors.	Large number of views can be heard Enables people to participate in generating ideas about their community Relatively easy to implement Provides a quick view of community needs and preferences	Requires good leadership and advance organization Only some people might attend, so the views expressed may not be representative May generate more questions than answers
Focus group	Have a small group of up to 10 people answer no more than about five important questions in 2 hours	A trained moderator leads a discussion of each question in a "permissive" atmosphere (that is, "anything goes").	Provides answers to important questions in a relatively short period	Need a trained and experienced moderator Questions must be formulated so that they are important and answerable by the group within the time allotted May be costly because several groups are needed and each person must be compensated financially
Nominal group process	Hear all members' views in order to make	A moderator and a group of people are assembled.	Leads to definite conclusions Gives all participants	Need an experienced moderator who

Name	Objectives	Implementation	Advantages	Limitations
	decisions on competing alternatives	Ideas are put on paper. Discussion leads to listing ideas on a board. Ideas are voted on.	an equal opportunity to express their views	makes sure everyone is heard Results may not be representative because group size is relatively small
Delphi	Generate ideas and come to consensus	Respondents complete a questionnaire. The results are summarized and sent to participants. Participants review the summary and complete the questionnaire a second time. The process is repeated until general agreement is reached.	Participants are unknown to one another, which encourages frankness Conducive to independent thinking Can be used to reach agreement among groups that are hostile to each other because of the anonymity of participation	Participants may not be representative Tends to encourage a middle-of-the-road view Can be time-consuming because method requires several rounds Definition of agreement may be considered arbitrary
RAND/UCLA Appropriateness Method	Identify areas of agreement, disagreement, and uncertainty (not enough evidence to make a decision)	Panelists are given a review of the literature and sent a set of items to rate. On their own, they rate the appropriateness of each item using a standardized scale. Ratings are summarized and given to the panelists. Panelists meet face to face in a 1- to 2-day session to clarify ratings and discuss them. Panelists rate each of the items again.	Provides an opportunity to combine existing research with expert opinion Statistics on reliability and validity of the process are known and acceptable Process is flexible and can be used in a variety of settings and for a variety of topics Allows for uncertainty as well as providing a reliable portrait of current knowledge	Expert leader is essential Process is expensive because it is relatively lengthy Potential bias in choosing panelists whose views are likely to be accepted Does not force consensus

(Continued)

2. What are the patterns of co-occurrence of these factors?

3. What evidence exists on the safety and effectiveness of interventions for violence?

4. Where evidence of safety and effectiveness exists, are there other outcomes beyond reducing violence? If so, what is known about effectiveness by age, sex, and race/ethnicity?

5. What are the commonalities among interventions that are effective and those that are ineffective?

6. What are the priorities for future research?

The panelists had expertise in pediatrics, psychiatry, law, sociology, nursing, research methods, adolescent health, and social work. In their statement, they gave specific examples of programs that effectively reduced arrests or precursors to violence. They also discussed the characteristics shared by these programs, such as being derived from sound theoretical rationales, addressing strong risk factors, involving long-term treatments (lasting a year and sometimes much longer), working intensively with those targeted for treatment and often using a clinical approach, following a cognitive/behavioral strategy, being multimodal and multicontextual, focusing on improving social competency and other skill development strategies for targeted youth and their families, being developmentally appropriate, not being delivered in coercive institutional settings, and having the capacity to be delivered with fidelity.

The panelists also named specific programs that are not effective even though they are in use (in some cases widely) and cited reasons for the lack of success of these programs. These reasons included implementation protocols that are not clearly articulated, staff that are not well supervised or held accountable for outcomes, programs limited to scare tactics, programs limited to toughness strategies, and programs that consist largely of adults lecturing at youth.

The panelists concluded (among other things) that some interventions have been shown by rigorous research to reduce violence precursors, violence, and arrest. However, many interventions aimed at reducing violence have not been sufficiently evaluated or proven effective, and a few widely implemented programs have been shown to be ineffective and perhaps harmful. The panelists recommended sufficient funding to promote the dissemination of violence prevention programs that have been shown to be effective through rigorous randomized controlled trial research. Funding, they said, must include support for research, and monitoring must continue as these programs are more widely implemented.

NIH Consensus Development Conferences are the gold standard for developing agreement. And the NIH literature reviews that form the research base for these panel reviews are world class. Also, the speakers and panelists participating in NIH consensus development are internationally renowned. Of course, these characteristics encourage acceptance of the conference statements.

Online Program and Practice Databases: Where to Find and How to Evaluate Them

An outstanding website for evidence-based programs and practices is the one maintained by the Agency for Healthcare Research and Quality (AHRQ), a U.S. government agency dedicated to improving health care safety and quality (www.ahrq.gov/clinic/epcix.htm). The goal of its research is measurable improvements in health care gauged in terms of improved quality of life and patient outcomes, lives saved, and value gained for the amount of money spent. It is not surprising that the agency focuses on effectiveness, by which it means "improving health care outcomes by encouraging the use of evidence to make informed health care decisions."

AHRQ sponsors the Effective Health Care Program (www.effective healthcare.ahrq.gov), which funds individual researchers, research centers, and academic organizations to work with AHRQ to produce effectiveness and comparative effectiveness research for clinicians, consumers, and policy makers. It reviews and synthesizes published and unpublished scientific evidence, generates new scientific evidence and analytic tools, and compiles research findings that are synthesized and/or generated and translates them into useful formats for various audiences. The site provides a wealth of information and resources, including slide libraries, guides, reviews, and reports.

Another site for evidence-based preventive services, which includes glossaries and detailed explanations of methods for identifying best evidence, is the Guide to Community Preventive Services, prepared by the CDC (www.thecommunityguide.org). A portion of the first page is shown in Figure 2.4 (next page). You can see from the figure that the guide covers topics such as adolescent health, birth defects, and oral health—many significant major public health topics.

For a comprehensive list of promising practices, go to The Community Tool Box, created by the Work Group for Community Health and Development at the University of Kansas (http://ctb.ku.edu/en/promisingapproach/Databases_Best_Practices.aspx). A sample of the contents of the tool box is given in Figure 2.5 (p. 59).

Figure 2.4 Excerpt From the Centers for Disease Control's Guide to Community Preventive Services

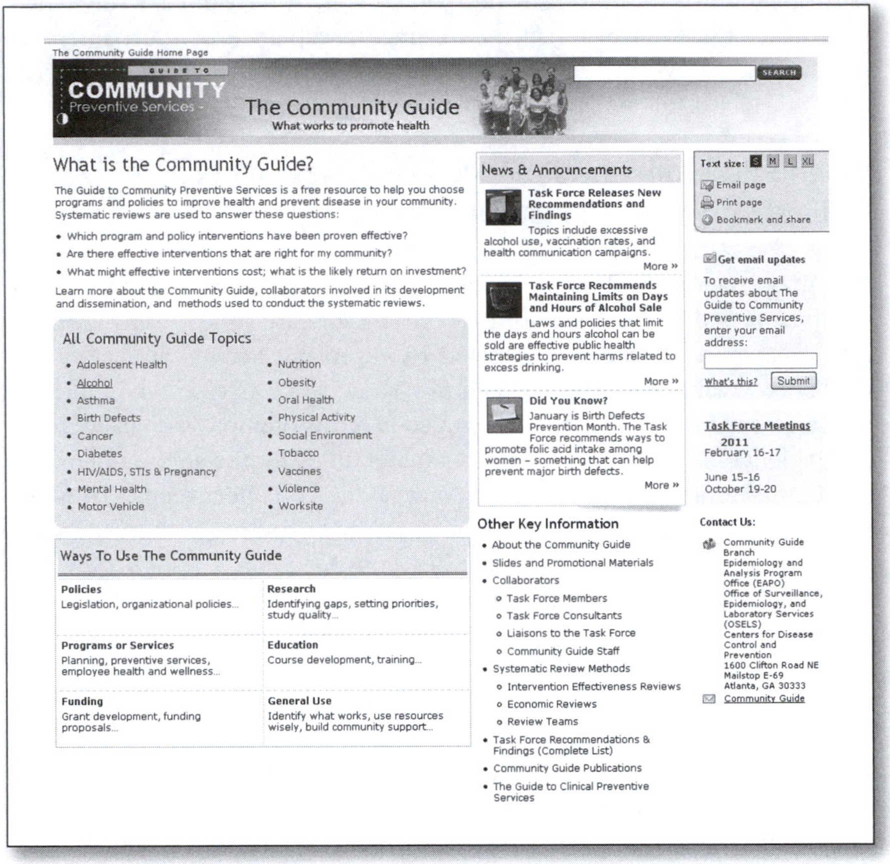

Search Engines and Online Health Information

One option for finding something (almost anything?) online is to use a search engine like Google or Bing. The problem with relying on search engines in general, as you probably have discovered already, is that the results you get almost always produce a mixture of very good and very bad information. Anyone can publish online and attract visitors, and frequent visits may move a bogus site to the first pages. Studies show that much health information online may be misleading, inaccurate, or even harmful (Berland et al., 2001; Siva, 2009).

Figure 2.5 A Portion of the Community Tool Box's Promising Approaches

Preventing Underage Drinking: Using Getting to Outcomes with the SAMSHA Strategic Prevention Framework to Achieve Results
For in-depth information on some Evidence-Based Environmental Strategies to prevent underage drinking, see p. 29-37 of this manual:

Preventing Underage Drinking: Using Getting to Outcomes with the SAMHSA Strategic Prevention Framework to Achieve Results. Imm P, Chinman M, Wandersman A, Rosenbloom D, Guckenburg S, Leis R. (2007). Preventing Underage Drinking: Using Getting to Outcomes with the SAMHSA Strategic Prevention Framework to Achieve Results, RAND, TR-403-SAMHSA. Santa Monica, CA: RAND Corporation.

SAMSHA's National Registry of Evidence-based Programs and Practices
The National Registry of Evidence-based Programs and Practices (NREPP) is a searchable database of interventions for the prevention and treatment of mental and substance use disorders. SAMHSA has developed this resource to help people, agencies, and organizations implement programs and practices in their communities.

VIOLENCE

Violence Prevention
The purpose of this website is to provide a violence prevention resource for policy makers, practitioners and others working to tackle and prevent violence. The website includes an Evidence Base (abstracts of systematically reviewed literature providing evidence of measures that can work to prevent violence), Resources (key publications and resources on violence and prevention), and other tools.

Corporation for National and Community Service Resource Center
This webpage offers tools and training for volunteer and service programs. Numerous effective practices are listed by topic.

A Seven-Step Empowerment Evaluation Approach For Violence Prevention Organization
This manual is designed to help violence prevention organizations hire an empowerment evaluator who will assist them in building their evaluation capacity through a learn-by-doing process of evaluating their own strategies. It is for state and local leaders and staff members of organizations, coalitions, government agencies, and/or partnerships working to prevent sexual violence, intimate partner violence, youth violence, suicide, and/or child maltreatment.

Blueprints for Violence Prevention
These Web pages provide information and resources from Blueprints for Violence Prevention, a project of the Center for the Study and Prevention of Violence at the University of Colorado, which identifies truly outstanding violence and drug prevention programs that meet a high scientific standard of effectiveness. In doing so, Blueprints serves as a resource for governments, foundations, businesses, and other organizations trying to make informed judgments about their investments in violence and drug prevention programs.

Therefore, it is helpful to consult the National Library of Medicine's tutorial for evaluating the quality of online health information (www.nlm.nih.gov/medlineplus/webeval/webeval.html). Although not directed specifically toward evaluating websites offering data on program effectiveness, the principles that the tutorial discusses apply to all websites aiming to effect public health. These principles are summarized in Table 2.4.

Table 2.4 Evaluating Health-Related Websites

1. Who runs the site?

   Any good health website should make it easy to learn who is responsible for the site and its information. On the U.S. Food and Drug Administration's (FDA) website, for example, the FDA is clearly noted on every major page, along with a link to the site's home (main) page, www .fda.gov. Information about who runs the site can often be found in an About Us or About This Web Site section, and there's usually a link to that section on the site's home page.

2. What is the site's purpose?

   Is the purpose of the site to inform? Is it to sell a product? Is it to raise money? If you can tell who runs and pays for the site, this will help you evaluate its purpose.

3. What is the original source of the information on the site?

   If the person or organization in charge of the site did not write the material, the original source should be clearly identified.

4. How is the information on the site documented?

   In addition to identifying the original source of the material, the site should identify the evidence on which the material is based. Medical facts and figures should have references (such as citations of articles in medical journals). Also, opinions or advice should be clearly set apart from information that is evidence-based.

5. How is information reviewed before it is posted on the site?

   Sites should give information about the credentials of the people who prepare or review the material.

6. How current is the information on the site?

   Sites should be reviewed and updated on a regular basis. It is particularly important that health and medical information be current and that the most recent update or review date be clearly posted. These dates are usually found at the bottom of the page. Even if the information has not changed, it is helpful to know that the site owners have reviewed it recently to ensure that the information is still valid. Click on a few links on the site. If there are a lot of broken links, the site may not be kept up to date.

7. How does the site choose links to other sites?

   Reliable sites usually have a policy about how they establish links to other sites. Some take a conservative approach and do not link to any other sites; some link to any site that asks or pays for a link; others link only to sites that have met certain criteria. Look for the website's linking policy, often found in a section titled About This Site.

8. What information about its visitors does the site collect, and why?

   Websites routinely track the path visitors take through their sites to determine what pages are being used. Some sites ask the visitor to subscribe or become a member. In some cases, this

Table 2.4 (Continued)

may be done so they can collect a fee or select relevant information for the visitor. In all cases, the subscription or membership will allow the site owners to collect personal information.

9. How does the site manage interactions with visitors?

   There should always be a way for visitors to contact the site owners with problems, feedback, and questions. If the site hosts a chat room or other online discussion areas, it should tell its visitors about the terms of using the service. Is the service moderated? If so, by whom, and why? It is always a good idea to spend time reading the discussion without joining in, in order to feel comfortable with the environment, before becoming a participant.

10. Can the accuracy of information received in an e-mail be verified?

    Carefully evaluate e-mail messages. Consider the origin of each message and its purpose. Some companies or organizations use e-mail to advertise products or attract people to their sites.

11. Is the information that is discussed online in social networks accurate?

    Assessing the reliability of health information that you come across in discussion groups is at least as important as it is for any online site. Most Internet service providers do not verify what is discussed in these groups, and you have no way of knowing the qualifications or credentials of the other people online.

SUMMARY OF CHAPTER 2: IDENTIFYING COMMUNITY NEEDS AND PROGRAMS

Words to Remember

administrative needs, asset mapping, behavioral needs, community needs, Consensus Development Conferences, Delphi technique, descriptor, educational needs, epidemiological needs, focus groups, genetic needs, Guide to Community Preventive Services, key informant, key word, Morbidity and Mortality Weekly Report (MMWR), needs assessment, nominal group process, online bibliographic or article databases, online or electronic journals, primary data collection, public or community forum, RAND/UCLA Appropriateness Method, secondary data analysis, social needs

A systematic effort to identify user needs and provide a context for them is called a *needs assessment*. Needs can be arranged into seven categories: social, communal or epidemiological, behavioral, environmental, educational, administrative, and genetic.

When consulting online program databases, be sure to check the date that the database was last updated. Anything more than 2 years old may be out of date. Also check the standards of evidence used to select programs in order to make sure that they agree with yours. Check the original evaluation articles and reports used to justify program choices. Make sure congruence exists between your highest priorities and the topics and approaches encompassed. All websites should be scrutinized for their sponsorship, accuracy, and privacy policy.

THE NEXT CHAPTER

Chapter 3 discusses how to do research literature reviews. It focuses on which databases to use and how to use them. It also discusses the practical screen through which you put articles and reports to make sure that that they are accessible, relevant, and ethically done. Chapter 3 gives an overview of the ethics of research and evidence-based public health.

EXERCISES

1. Name the assessment technique used in each of the following studies.

   a. Home Injury Hazard Risks and Prevention Methods for Young Children (Katcher et al., 2006)

   The Board requested a list of 5–7 injury hazards and 5–7 potential prevention behaviors and/or devices for children aged 1–5 years in each of the following areas of the home: bedroom/play area, kitchen/dining area, bathroom, living room, basement/ garage (including other outdoor areas such as the driveway), pool, stairs/hallway, and multiple rooms/general safety. We asked participants to develop their lists of hazards by considering the *frequency, severity,* and *preventability* of the potential injury from each hazard, as well as the *efficacy* and *feasibility* of each prevention method. Efficacy was defined as the ability of the behavior or the device, if implemented, to eliminate the hazard and/or to prevent the injury. Feasibility was defined as the likelihood of implementation of the behavior or the device (depending on acquisition, installation, utilization, and maintenance).

   Round 2 asked participants to *rate* each hazard and behavior/device listed in the responses submitted to survey 1 using a scale of 1 to 3 (with 3 being highest priority). Participants could also assign a score of zero (0) if they believed that an item should not remain on the list. In rating each item, the participants were instructed to consider the same factors used in the first round (for example, children aged 1–5 years;

frequency, severity, and preventability for the hazards; and efficacy and feasibility for the behaviors/devices). We calculated a mean score for each item by summing all ratings reported for a single item. Items were subsequently listed in descending order of priority.

The 47 hazards and 52 prevention methods with the highest mean scores were selected for inclusion in survey 3 based upon natural clusters, rather than just choosing the top 50 of each.

For the 99 selected items, the third round asked participants to *rate* each hazard using a Likert scale of 1 to 5 (with 5 being the most important) considering overall importance in an injury prevention program for preschool aged children, 3–5 years of age. This age group request differed from previous rounds as we sought to use the panel's findings for a future injury prevention program targeted at children aged 3–5 years.

b. Impact of Smoke-Free Residence Hall Policies: The Views of Administrators at Three State Universities (Gerson, Allard, & Towvim, 2005)

Interviews with XXX aimed to (1) explore staff interpretation of trends and data, (2) assess observed changes in campus constituent with attitudes and behaviors resulting from the policy change, and (3) determine the impact of the policy change on personnel workload. We designed questions tailored to each department to elicit information and to enrich understanding of the policy's impact. As appropriate, the interviewer requested additional existing documentation during interviews.

In total, we contacted 47 personnel for interviews. Thirty campus personnel contributed to the study through telephone interviews, e-mail correspondences, providing data, or a combination thereof. We conducted 27 telephone interviews: 10 at URI, 7 at MSU, and 10 at OSU. Three additional XXX answered questions by e-mail correspondence. At MSU and URI, personnel from all identified departments, except admissions, participated in the interviews. At OSU, personnel from all 7 departments participated. In some cases, we interviewed multiple personnel from a single department. The interviewer took copious notes during the interviews and then compiled them along with e-mail correspondence into an interview report.

Answers

a. Delphi

b. Key informant

Need	Definition
A. Social	1. Individual and communal lifestyles and beliefs that affect a community's well-being
B. Behavioral	2. Community's perceptions of its problems
C. Administrative	3. Problems that can be documented to affect a large number of people in the community
D. Communal/epidemiological	4. Social or physical factors that are external to an individual or a community
E. Physical	5. Policies and resources that exist in the organizations and institutions (e.g., school, hospital, business, nongovernmental organization) that might facilitate or hinder the adoption of a new program
F. Educational	6. Individual and community knowledge, attitudes, skills, and self-efficacy beliefs

2. Match each need with its appropriate definition.

    Answer:

    A-2

    B-1

    C-5

    D-3

    E-4

    F-6

3. The Healthy Aging Center has discovered a database that specializes in evidence-based programs to prevent elder abuse, a topic of special importance to the agency. The agency notes that the database is updated yearly, and the standards of evidence used to evaluate program effectiveness appear convincing. Before adapting any of the programs, the agency wants to check on the evaluations. Unfortunately, no links to the original evaluations can be found, although the site provides an extensive bibliography in PDF form. When the agency goes to check the sources online, free access is denied. The agency cannot afford to buy the access to many of the articles. What advice do you have for the agency?

    Answer:

    Contact the investigators in charge of maintaining the database ("About Us") or the first authors of the articles, and ask for copies of the evaluation results.

4. Which of the following is NOT necessarily characteristic of reliable information?

    a. Who runs the website

b. The original source of the information on the website

c. How information is reviewed before it is posted on the website

d. An address that is .org rather than .com

Answer:

   d. Just as you cannot tell a book by its cover, you cannot tell a website from its domain. Little supervision, if any, is available to guard against the use of .org or of website names that sound authentic.

REFERENCES

Berland, G. K., Elliott, M. N., Morales, L. S., Algazy, J. I., Kravitz, R. L., Broder, M. S., et al. (2001). Health information on the Internet: Accessibility, quality, and readability in English and Spanish. *Journal of the American Medical Association*, *285*, 2612–2621.

Curtis, A. C., Waters, C. M., & Brindis, C. (2011). Rural adolescent health: The importance of prevention services in the rural community. *Journal of Rural Health*, *27*, 60–71.

Galasso, P., Amend, A., Melkus, G. D., & Nelson, G. T. (2005). Barriers to medical nutrition therapy in black women with type 2 diabetes mellitus. *Diabetes Educator*, *31*, 719–725.

Gerson, M., Allard, J. L., & Towvim, L. G. (2005). Impact of smoke-free residence hall policies: The views of administrators at 3 state universities. *Journal of American College Health*, *54*, 157–165.

Gwede, C. K., Ward, B. G., Luque, J. S., Vadaparampil, S. T., Rivers, D., Martinez-Tyson, D., et al. (2010). Application of geographic information systems and asset mapping to facilitate identification of colorectal cancer screening resources. *Online Journal of Public Health Informatics*, *2*(1), 2893.

Janssens, A. C. J. W., Ioannidis, J. P. A., van Duijn, C. M., Little, J., & Khoury, M. J. (2011). Strengthening the reporting of genetic risk prediction studies: The GRIPS statement. *PLoS Medicine*, *8*(3), e1000420.

Katcher, M. L., Meister, A. N., Sorkness, C. A., Staresinic, A. G., Pierce, S. E., Goodman, B. M., et al. (2006). Use of the modified Delphi technique to identify and rate home injury hazard risks and prevention methods for young children. *Injury Prevention*, *12*, 189–194.

McGory, M. L., Kao, K. K., Shekelle, P. G., Rubenstein, L. Z., Leonardi, M. J., Parikh, J. A., et al. (2009). Developing quality indicators for elderly surgical patients. *Annals of Surgery*, *250*, 338–347.

Sartore, G., Hoolahan, B., Tonna, A., Kelly, B., & Stain, H. (2005). Wisdom from the drought: Recommendations from a consultative conference. *Australian Journal of Rural Health*, *13*, 315–320.

Section 1: Asset Mapping. (n.d.). Retrieved from http://partnerships.ucsf.edu/sites/partnerships.ucsf.edu/files/images/UCLA%20Center%20for%20Health%20Policy%20Research%20-%20Asset%20Mapping.pdf

Shekelle, P. (2004). The appropriateness method. *Medical Decision Making*, *24*, 228–231.

Siva, N. (2009). Search engines continue to advertise rogue online pharmacies. *British Medical Journal*, *339*, b3457.

Zima, B. T., Hurlburt, M. S., Knapp, P., Ladd, H., Tang, L., Duan, N., et al. (2005). Quality of publicly-funded outpatient specialty mental health care for common childhood psychiatric disorders in California. *Journal of the American Academy of Child Psychiatry*, *44*, 130–144.

- Use the PICO method to formulate questions to focus a literature review search
- Create search terms from the research questions to guide literature review
- Use Boolean operators (e.g., *and, or, not*) when searching the research literature
- Identify the components of the two practical literature review screens

1. Language, research design, the characteristics of the experimental and comparison programs, data collection dates and duration, and study sponsorship

2. Outcomes, participants, and settings

- Describe ethical issues that accompany research with human subjects
- Describe the characteristics of research misconduct
- Describe ethical concerns associated with evidence-based public health practice

❖ THE EVIDENCE AND THE RESEARCH LITERATURE

The foundation of evidence-based public health practice is confirmation of program effectiveness from high-quality published research, usually referred to as the *literature* or the *research literature.* Although it would be simpler to rely upon online program databases for research-based programs, this is impracticable because there are not enough sites or programs, and so, by default, evidence-based public health practice relies heavily on literature reviews.

A **research literature review** is different from a thorough reading of a journal article. It is a highly **systematic,** explicit, and reproducible method for identifying, evaluating, and synthesizing one or more studies or reports about programs.

When doing a research review, you systematically examine all sources and describe and justify what you have done. This enables someone else to duplicate your methods and to determine objectively whether to accept the results of the review. That way, when you state, "This program is effective and here are the reasons," someone else will be able to follow your logic.

Eight Literature Reviewing Tasks

A research literature review follows a very specific protocol and can be divided into eight tasks:

1. Choosing bibliographic and article databases

2. Framing research questions

3. Selecting databases, websites, and other sources

4. Choosing a search strategy

5. Applying practical criteria to retrieve articles that reviewers can efficiently obtain and evaluate

6. Applying methodological standards for evaluating a study's scientific quality and research ethics

7. Doing the review so that it can be reproduced by others

8. Synthesizing the results

Choosing an Online Bibliographic Database

Everyone with an Internet connection has access to much of the world's scientific, social scientific, technological, and medical literature—thanks to the U.S. government that supports it, the scientific community that produces it, and the schools and public and private libraries that purchase access to bibliographic databases and other sources of information. The U.S. National Library of Medicine at the National Institutes of Health (NIH), for example, maintains the best site for published medical research, PubMed (www.ncbi .nlm.nih.gov/pubmed), and access is free from any electronic device with access to the Internet. All original studies include structured abstracts of each study's objectives, design, and conclusions; many studies are also available in their entirety.

University and other libraries, including public libraries, usually provide free access to government, nongovernment, and some subscription bibliographic databases. Although most articles databases will provide free access to article abstracts, it is up to the journals themselves whether to grant free access to the entire article unless mandated to do so by the NIH or other research agencies. Table 3.1 lists four bibliographic databases commonly used in evidence-based public health practice.

Table 3.1 Databases Commonly Used in Evidence-Based Public Health Practice

	PubMed	PsycINFO	Web of Science	CINAHL Plus
Subject scope	Medicine, nursing, dentistry, veterinary medicine, the health care system, preclinical sciences	Psychology, psychiatry, education, business, medicine, nursing, pharmacology, law, linguistics, social work	Wide multidisciplinary coverage of the sciences and social sciences	Nursing, biomedicine, health sciences librarianship, alternative/complementary medicine, consumer health, allied health disciplines
Format scope	Journal articles	Journal articles, conference proceedings, books, reports, dissertations	Journal articles, reviews, corrections, discussions, letters, meeting abstracts, grant numbers	Journal articles, health care books, nursing dissertations, conference proceedings, standards of practice, educational software, audiovisuals, book chapters
Years covered	1948–present	1806–present	Science Citation Index: 1900–present Social Sciences Citation Index: 1956–present Arts and Humanities Citation Index: 1975–present	1937–present
Types of searches available	Key word, phrase, author, title, subject/medical subject headings (MeSH)	Exact phrase, all of the words, any of the words	Topic, author, title, address, key word, Boolean, exact phrase, words in same sentence	*Basic:* Standard (use Boolean operators), all of the words, any of the words, exact phrase
Search options	MeSH Browser, Single Citation Matcher, Batch Citation Matcher, Clinical Queries, Linkout, Explode	Advanced Search, Browse Indexes, Thesaurus Search, Search History/Alerts, Explode	Cited Reference, Topic, Author, Title, Address, Advanced, Combine Search Sets	*Advanced:* Limiters, Expanders (Full Text Search, Related Words), Search History/Combine Sets, Journal, Explode

How do you determine which online databases may be relevant in reviewing a particular research topic? Some, such as PsycINFO or PubMed, have names that describe their content (psychology and medicine, respectively). Others, such as TOXLINE (studies of air pollution and the biological and adverse effects of drugs, among other things), EMBASE (pharmaceutical literature), and CINAHL (nursing and allied health), have names that are not obvious. You need to check out the databases whose names are not familiar to you. Google Scholar also provides access to a broad range of articles that appear in the world's journals; as with other databases, it offers relatively easy access to abstracts, but full articles may only be available by subscription or for pay.

Each library usually has a list of databases by subject area, such as psychology or medicine. If you are unsure about the contents of a specific database, ask a librarian for information, or go directly to the site to find out what topics and resources it includes.

How do you select among bibliographic databases? It all depends on your topic and study questions. For example, if you are interested in finding out what the literature has to say about the best way to improve adolescent literacy, then a database listing research in education, such as ERIC, is an appropriate place to start. However, if you are interested in finding out about interactive programs to foster literacy, then a computer and information technology database may also be relevant. It helps to be precise about what you want and need to know so that you can choose all relevant databases.

Online Journals

An increasing number of journals or articles are appearing online without a print version. For example, the Public Library of Science (PLoS) is a nonprofit organization of scientists and physicians committed to making the world's scientific and medical literature a freely available public resource. Everything this group publishes is freely available online for reading, downloading, copying, distributing, and using (with attribution) any way you want.

The NIH Public Access Policy ensures that the public has access to the published results of NIH-funded research. It requires scientists to submit final peer-reviewed journal manuscripts that arise from NIH funds to the digital archive PubMed Central upon acceptance for publication. To help advance science and improve human health, the policy requires that these papers be accessible to the public on PubMed Central no later than 12 months after publication.

What Are Your Questions? PICO or Problem (Need), Interventions, Comparison, and Outcome

Did you ever use a search engine or bibliographic database to get information on a specific topic, only to find that the results included hundreds of pages and thousands of entries, some of which made no sense at all? Why does this happen? One reason is the methods required by librarians for search engine administrators to use in creating and organizing the listings. Another reason is that most people lack the special skills needed to perform efficient searches. Even though many search engines and most bibliographic databases are fairly user-friendly, most searches tend to be extremely broad, so the results include a great deal of related and unrelated information.

Searching begins with a request for information. This request is often referred to as a **research question**. For this purpose, a research question contains four components: the population or problem of concern; the intervention, practice, or program you hope to find; a comparison program; and the hoped-for outcomes. This formulation, called **PICO**, is derived from evidence-based medicine practices:

P = Problem/people targeted

I = Intervention (practice or program)

C = Comparison intervention

O = Outcome

Example 3.1 presents three relatively nonspecific and specific questions using the PICO formulation.

Example 3.1 Specific and Nonspecific Questions and the Use of PICO

Topic 1: Care for Diabetic Patients

Less specific
Research Question A: How can we improve care for diabetic patients?

More specific
Research Question B: How well does interactive computer education compare to written educational materials in improving quality of life when used as part of a comprehensive treatment plan for primary care patients with type 2 diabetes?

Comment
Question B is more specific because it specifies the population (patients with type 2 diabetes), the type of program being sought (interactive computer technology), a comparison program (written educational materials), and the desired outcomes (improved quality of life).

P = Primary care patients with Type 2 diabetes

I = Interactive computer education

C = Written educational materials

O = Improved quality of life

Topic 2: Preventing School Dropout

Less specific
Research Question A: Which programs successfully prevent students from dropping out of school?

More specific
Research Question B: When compared with one another, which dropout prevention programs prevent high school students from dropping out of school before they graduate?

Comment
Question B is more specific because it specifies the persons for whom a program is sought (high school students), describes the type of program being sought (dropout prevention), contains a comparison (programs are compared to one another), and specifies the hoped-for outcome (graduation).

P = High school students

I = Dropout prevention

C = Programs are compared to one another (the nature of the programs is not specified)

O = Graduation

Topic 3: Alcohol Use and Health

Less specific
Research Question A: Are programs available to reduce the risks of alcohol-related problems in adolescents?

More specific
Research Question B: When compared to physician education, how does patient education compare in reducing the risks of alcohol-related problems in adolescents (13–18 years of age)?

Comment
Question B is more specific because it defines the people being considered (adolescents), the type of program being sought (patient education), a comparison program (physician education), and the hoped-for outcome (reduction in risks of alcohol-related problems).

P = Adolescents (13–18 years of age)

I = Patient education

C = Physician education

O = Reduction in risks of alcohol-related problems

Research Questions, Descriptors, and Key Words

When you go to an online bibliographic database, you should be armed with a research question. When stated precisely, a research question has the benefit of containing the words the reviewer needs to begin an online search. These words or search terms are often referred to as **key words**, **descriptors**, **identifiers**, or operators.

Consider this question (Research Question 3B, Example 3.1): When compared to physician education, how does patient education compare in reducing the risks of alcohol-related problems in adolescents (13–18 years of age)? You can see that the important words—key words—include *physician education, patient education, risks of alcohol-related problems, adolescents (13–18 years of age)*.

What key words are suggested based on the wording of Questions 1B and 2B (Example 3.1)?

1B. *Primary care patients with Type 2 diabetes, interactive computer education, written educational materials, quality of life*

2B. *High school students, dropout prevention, graduate*

Just knowing the basic key words is a start, and a good one, but it is not always enough, unfortunately. For instance, suppose you are reviewing drop-out prevention programs to find out which afterschool programs work best to prevent high school students from dropping out before they graduate. You decide to use PsycINFO for your review because it is an online bibliographic database dealing with subjects in education and psychology. You also search the database using the exact phrase "dropout prevention" and are given a list of (at least) 210 articles. You find that the articles contain data on "graduation," but not all pertain to high school students. To narrow your search and reduce the number of irrelevant studies, you decide to combine "dropout prevention" with "high school graduation," which reduces the results to 36 articles. However, on further investigation, you find that not all of the 36 articles include data on effectiveness. So you decide to further narrow the search by adding a new term: "evaluation." This reduces the results to a mere 13 articles, which seems like a manageable number of articles to review. This story has a point: As you proceed with your search, you may have to do some refining.

However, fewer articles are not always optimal. If your search is very narrow, you may miss out on some important ideas. Your search may be overly restricted because you chose the key words based on your research question, but others who are interested in the same topic may have a different vocabulary.

More Search Terms:
Authors, Titles, Title Words, and
Journals and Then Some—Limiting the Search

Almost all bibliographic databases enable you to search for programs and studies by entering the author, article titles, words that you expect to be in the title (perhaps you forgot the exact title), and journal title. More specialized bibliographic databases (e.g., PubMed, Web of Science) have the capacity for very refined searches. You can narrow the search to type of research design (e.g., clinical trials, randomized trials), age groups (e.g., preschool child 2–5 years old, child 6–12 years old, adolescent 13–18 years old), language, date of publication, and gender.

Most bibliographic databases facilitate your work by providing menus and drop-down lists. For example, suppose you want to review the literature on programs to prevent alcohol misuse in adolescents. PubMed will let you limit the search by providing options for type of study design, language, age, and gender, among other concerns. Example 3.2 shows five articles that are the results of a PubMed search for alcohol misuse programs

Example 3.2   Five Articles Resulting From a PubMed Search for Alcohol Misuse Programs for Adolescents

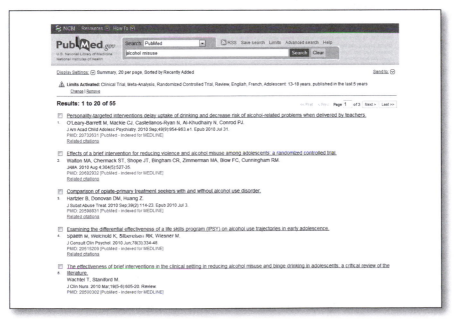

Example 3.4 (Continued)

AU: Cunningham RM

LA: eng

SI: ClinicalTrials.gov/NCT00251212

GR: L32 MD001870-01/MD/NCMHD NIH HHS/United States

GR: NIAAA 014889/PHS HHS/United States

GR: R01 AA014889-05/AA/NIAAA NIH HHS/United States

PT: Journal Article

PT: Randomized Controlled Trial

PT: Research Support, N.I.H., Extramural

PL: United States

TA: JAMA

JT: JAMA : the journal of the American Medical Association

JID: 7501160

SB: AIM

SB: IM

CIN: JAMA. 2010 Aug 4;304(5):575-7. PMID: 20682942

CIN: Evid Based Ment Health. 2011 Feb;14(1):20. PMID: 21266617

CIN: Evid Based Nurs. 2011 Jan;14(1):11-2. PMID: 21163789

MH: Adolescent

MH: Adolescent Behavior

MH: Aggression

MH: Alcoholism/*prevention & control

MH: Directive Counseling

MH: *Emergency Service, Hospital

MH: Female

MH: Humans

MH: Intervention Studies

MH: Male

MH: Michigan

MH: Single-Blind Method

MH: Trauma Centers

MH: Treatment Outcome

MH: Urban Population

MH: User-Computer Interface

MH: Violence/*prevention & control

EDAT: 2010/08/05 06:00

MHDA: 2010/08/10 06:00

CRDT: 2010/08/05 06:00

AID: 304/5/527 [pii]

AID: 10.1001/jama.2010.1066 [doi]

PST: ppublish

SO: JAMA. 2010 Aug 4;304(5):527-35.

Searching With Boolean Operators

Literature review searches sometimes are conducted by combining key words and other terms with words such as AND, OR, and NOT. These three words are called **Boolean operators**. Look at the three examples of the use of Boolean logic presented in Example 3.5.

Example 3.5   Examples of Boolean Logic

AND

depression AND *medication*: Use AND to retrieve a set of citations in which each citation contains all search terms. The terms can appear in any order—*medication* may appear before *depression*.

OR

medication OR *counseling*: Use OR to retrieve citations that contain at least one of the specified terms.

NOT

depression NOT *children*: Use NOT to exclude terms from your search. This search finds all citations containing the search term *depression* and then excludes from these citations all that contain the word *children*.

Be careful when using NOT because you may inadvertently eliminate important articles. As Example 3.5 shows, with reference to NOT, articles about children and depression are eliminated, but so are studies that include the word *children* as part of a general discussion about depression. If a study mentions children at all, it is omitted.

An advanced method of using AND, OR, and NOT involves enclosing an individual concept in parenthesis; the terms inside the parentheses, terms that are connected using the Boolean operators, will be processed as a unit.

Example 3.6 presents an efficient method of searching that is called *nesting*. The search engine will search for any articles on depression AND counseling as well as for any articles on depression AND medication. If both counseling and medication are studied in a single article about depression, the search engine will be able to identify it.

Example 3.6 Searching PubMed for Articles on Depression and Counseling or Depression and Medication

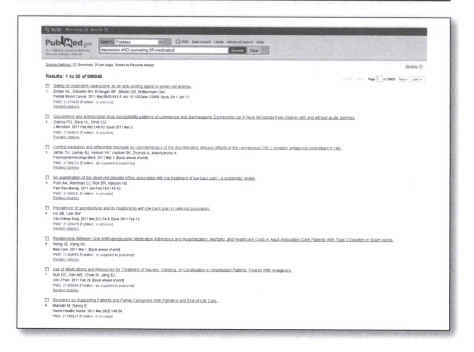

Not all bibliographic databases require you to capitalize AND, OR, and NOT. Check the Advance Search function to make certain you are using the correct syntax and punctuation. Each search engine has its own peculiarities. Also, many have other functions that are helpful in making a search more efficient. One such function, a "wildcard," often represented by an asterisk (*), is used to shorten the number of words with a common root. For example, the term *agoraphob** can be used to search for *agoraphobic* and *agoraphobia,* while the term **therapy* can be used to locate research dealing with *psychotherapy* and *pharmacotherapy.*

Initial key word searches can lead to hundreds of articles. In all probability, you will need to review the titles and abstracts of each article that you identify in this first pass in order to assess its potential relevance. Use the key words displayed in relevant articles to continue your search. Some bibliographic databases provide links to other articles; some of these may be pertinent and may offer clues to other key words.

You may find it useful to limit your use of key words to two or three at a time. Use the bibliographic database's advanced functions to restrict your initial search by language (e.g., English only), type of journal (e.g., clinical journal), and publication date (e.g., within the past year).

When your search is no longer fruitful, review your collection of literature. Check the entire list for quality and comprehensiveness. Get assistance from someone who is interested in the topic or has worked in the field. Ask questions: Are all important investigators or writers included on the list? Have any major studies been excluded?

Online Search

Is the following statement true or false?

An experienced literature reviewer only needs access to the Internet to do a comprehensive literature review.

False. Experienced literature reviewers must know how to locate databases and use the correct language and syntax to identify key words, subjects, titles, and so on in order to find pertinent studies. However, search processes are far from uniform or perfect. The databases and study authors may not use search terms uniformly (which is especially true with new topics), databases may differ in the journals they include, and even the most proficient reviewers may neglect to find one or more studies regardless of how careful they are. Additionally, a reviewer may, in actuality, have access to just a few databases. Also, some studies may be in progress and not yet ready for publication. Finally, some potentially important studies may never get published.

The following list summarizes the main reasons for supplementing computer searches of the literature with searches using other data sources:

- Evidence that many important studies are in progress or complete but not published
- Few acceptable studies are available
- Lack of uniformity across databases and fields in terminology
- Evidence that your electronic search is not comprehensive because you do not have access to all databases

Resources: Exclude all programs requiring training by the program developers or other specially trained in-service personnel

Program Duration: Include only programs that last 10 weeks or less

✓ Research Design

Research designs are typically divided into two categories: experimental and observational. **Experimental research designs** involve the collection of information to compare two or more groups, one of which participates in a new program while the other does not. An example of an experimental design is the randomized controlled trial in which the groups are constituted at random, which means that chance dictates which participants receive the experimental program. These designs rely on original data, that is, data collected for a specific study.

In **observational research designs**, the variables of interest are observed rather than controlled. An example of an observational design is the prospective cohort in which a large group of people (e.g., residents of Framingham, Massachusetts) is observed over a long time (e.g., since 1948). The purpose of the study is to describe, among other things, the effects of diet and exercise on heart disease.

Example of Practical Screening Criterion:
Research Design

Include only randomized trials

OR

Include randomized trials AND quasi-experimental designs

✓ Date of Publication

The publication date is important if you want to restrict your search to articles before or after a certain date.

Example of Practical Screening Criterion: Date of Publication

Include only studies published from January 1, 2011, to December 31, 2011

✓ Dates of Data Collection

Data collection refers to the information that is gathered to find out about the achievement of each outcome. For example, a survey of nutrition workers' job satisfaction is one type of data collection; a review of medical records to find out whether patients' health has improved is another type.

Some articles may be published within the past few years but rely on data from an earlier period. This can happen with epidemiological data in large databases.

Example of Practical Screening Criterion:
Dates of Data Collection

Include only studies that collected their data from 2009 to the present

Include only studies whose data are less than five years old from today's date

Exclude studies that do not give precise dates of data collection

✓ Duration of Data Collection

Some studies take place over a few weeks; others go on for years. If you are interested in identifying a program that lasts a relatively short time and for which limited effects can be expected, then you may be content with short data collection periods. Some study outcomes, such as quality of life or the costs of preventing violence or illness, take longer periods to assess, and you would expect longer data collection periods.

Example of Practical Screening Criterion:
Duration of Data Collection

Include only studies whose data collection continues for at least 12 months after completion of the program

✓ Content (Topics, Variables)

If the report or article does not specifically deal with your topic, you will probably want to exclude it from your review.

Example of Practical Screening Criterion: Content

Include only studies that focus on primary prevention of family violence

Exclude studies that focus on secondary or tertiary prevention of family violence

Exclude studies that focus on treatment

✓ Source of Financial Support

Research is funded by governments, philanthropic organizations, and private institutions and companies. If the funder has a stake in a study's outcomes, and the findings are positive, then the results may give the appearance of being compromised, or they may actually be compromised. A **conflict of interest** is a situation in which someone in a position of trust, such as a researcher, practitioner, or policy maker, has competing professional or personal interests. This competition can make it difficult to be impartial. Conflicts can be political, social, or economic. For example, a conflict of interest might occur if a researcher were related to someone on the funder's board of trustees, had previously done consultation work for the research funder, or had a proprietary interest in the program or intervention under study. Most reputable journals require investigators to indicate whether they have conflicts of interest and, if they do, to state what they are. Although a statement on its own does not eliminate the conflict, the information can be used as one factor in evaluating the credibility of the study's findings.

Example of Practical Screening Criterion:
Source of Financial Support

Exclude all studies in which conflict of interest information is missing

A literature review may use some or all types of practical screening criteria, as illustrated in Example 3.8.

Example 3.8   Practical Screening Criteria: Using Inclusion and Exclusion Criteria in a Hypothetical Review

---

Illustration 1: Quality of Life

To identify articles in English pertaining to measures of quality of life, we used PubMed and PsycINFO. We limited candidate articles to those having the term "quality of life" in their titles. From these candidate articles, we selected only those that were published from 2010 to the present and that also described or used at least one questionnaire. We excluded letters, editorials, and reviews because these are not really studies at all. We also excluded articles that were not written in English, French, Russian, Danish, or Spanish, all of which we had the resources to translate. We also excluded reports that dealt primarily with methodology or policy or whose principal investigator listed a conflict of interest pertaining to the study's funder. We then reviewed the list of articles and restricted our selection to 15 prominent journals. Here is a summary of the inclusion and exclusion criteria:

Inclusion criteria	Type
Term "quality of life" in titles	Content
Published from 2010 to the present	Publication date
Described or used at least one questionnaire or instrument	Content
English, French, Russian, Danish, and Spanish	Publication language
In 1 of 15 prominent journals (actual names given)	Journal
Exclusion Criteria	**Type**
Letters, editorials, review articles	Research design
Articles that deal with research design, measure development, or policy	Content
Articles whose principal investigator lists a conflict of interest with the study's funder	Source of financial support

Illustration 2: Child Abuse and Neglect

We examined evaluations of programs to prevent child abuse and neglect that were conducted from 2006 through 2011. In our selection, we did not distinguish between types of abuse (e.g., physical, emotional) and neglect (e.g., emotional, medical), intensity, or frequency of occurrence. Only evaluations of programs that were family based, with program operations focused simultaneously on parents and children, rather than just on parents, children, childcare professionals, or the community, were included. We excluded studies that aimed to predict the causes and consequences of abuse or neglect or to appraise the effects of programs to treat children and families after abuse and neglect had been identified. We also excluded essays on abuse, cross-sectional studies, consensus statements, and methodological research, such as the development of a new measure of abuse, and studies that did not produce judgments of program effectiveness. Here is a summary of the inclusion and exclusion criteria:

Inclusion Criteria	Type
Evaluations of programs to prevent child abuse and neglect	Content
Conducted from 2006 to 2011	Duration of data collection
Family-based programs: focus simultaneously on parents and children	Content
Exclusion Criteria	**Type**
Studies aiming to predict the causes and consequences of abuse or neglect	Content
Evaluations of programs to treat child abuse and neglect	Content
Essays on abuse, cross-sectional studies, consensus statements, and studies that do not produce judgments of effectiveness	Research design
Methodological research, such as the development of a new measure of abuse	Content

❖ THE PRACTICAL SCREEN, PART 2: OUTCOMES, POPULATION, COSTS, AND ETHICS

Outcomes are results of program participation. They include variables such as reductions in violence, improvements in health and quality of life, reductions in risk for heart disease, prevention of sexually transmitted diseases, and increases in health literacy. Outcomes are also called **dependent variables**.

Two programs may have similar methods but aim for different outcomes. For instance, one alcohol risk reduction program may aim to reduce drinking quantity and frequency, while another may aim to improve knowledge and self-efficacy. Both programs may use a similar method (e.g., motivational interviewing) to achieve their aim. The practical screen is used to rule out studies whose outcomes are not pertinent to the review.

You can only measure how effective a program is for a specific group of people, a defined population. The defined population is specified by the researcher (see Example 3.9). For instance, suppose your review uncovers an evaluation of a diet and exercise program that convinces you that program participants achieve desired exercise levels. You must then ask: Who are the participants? Suppose they are men and women between the ages of 21 and 65. If you plan to use the program with older (older than 65) or younger (20 years old and younger) people, you cannot be at all certain that the program will work for you.

Example 3.9 Population Matters (Ciampa et al., 2010)

Citations describing studies that implemented interventions targeted at preventing or reducing overweight or obesity in children younger than 2 years were selected by one of us (P. J. C.) for a full review. Additional studies were identified by a review of the reference lists of included articles. Studies included for this review article met the following inclusion criteria: (1) published in the English language, (2) targeted a population of children between birth and age 2 years, and (3) used a behavioral, educational, or quality improvement–based intervention designed to prevent obesity or to promote healthy nutrition and physical activity. Studies were excluded if they did not report original data.

In practice, if any doubt exists about a program's appropriateness, a **feasibility** or **pilot test** is necessary. A feasibility test is a scaled-down version of a study in which the primary aim is to find out if the program can be implemented in the community. Even though a feasibility test is usually much smaller than a full-scale study, it still must be done well to produce useful results.

Rather than conduct still more studies, many researchers and practitioners are taking to heart a more pragmatic approach in which more diverse groups of people are included in studies to maximize the studies' applicability to as many people and places as possible. **Practical evaluations** are also referred to as practical or pragmatic clinical trials (Glasgow, Magid, Beck, Ritzwoller, & Estabrooks, 2005; Tunis, Stryer, & Clancy, 2003). The idea is to develop programs that have effects in the real world, and that means evaluating programs and practices in real-world rather than lab and lab-like settings.

THE PRACTICAL SCREEN, PART 3: ETHICS   ❖

In recognition of the strong link between research and ethics, many journals require that the authors state in the text that their study protocol was reviewed and approved by an **ethics committee** or **institutional review board (IRB)**. In reviewing articles for best available evidence, a practical consideration (as well as a moral one) is that the evidence meet recognized standards for ethical research.

Research and the Institutional Review Board

An IRB or ethics committee is an administrative body whose purpose is to protect the rights and welfare of **human research subjects** who are recruited to participate in research activities. Research is defined by the U.S. Department of Health and Human Services (DHHS; 2004) as systematic investigation (including research development, testing, and evaluation) designed to develop or contribute to *generalizable knowledge*. The key point is that knowledge resulting from research must be presumed in advance to apply to other people in other settings.

According to the DHHS, a human subject is a living individual about whom an investigator (whether a professional or a student) conducting research obtains (a) data through intervention or interaction with the individual (e.g., in a counseling session, in a classroom) or (b) identifiable private information (e.g., birth date, medical record number).

The IRB is in charge of determining whether the research is structured to guarantee that each participant's privacy and rights are protected. If it is, the research can proceed. If it is not, the IRB will not allow any data collection. All major and reputable social, health, and welfare agencies (school districts, departments of mental health and social services, health departments, and so on) have ethics committees and protection requirements for human subjects. Research that receives any U.S. government support (e.g., from the National Institutes of Health, from the Agency for Healthcare Research and Quality) must formally be approved by an IRB or ethics committee that itself has been approved by the U.S. Office for Human Research Protections (OHRP; www.hhs.gov/ohrp). Many other countries are equally rigorous as the United States in applying human subject protection, and most of the principles are similar if not identical.

Three Guiding Principles of Ethical Research

According to the U.S. government, all IRB activities related to human subjects research should be guided by the ethical principles in *The Belmont Report: Ethical Principles and Guidelines for the Protection of Human Subjects of Research,* which was prepared by the National Commission for the Protection of Human Subjects of Biomedical and Behavioral Research in 1979 and is still the foundation for ethical research. Three major principles come from the Belmont Report.

Respect for Persons. Respect for persons requires investigators to obtain **informed consent** from research participants, to protect participants with impaired decision-making capabilities, and to maintain confidentiality.

Beneficence. This principle requires that the research design be scientifically sound and that the risks of the research be acceptable in relation to the likely benefits. The principle of beneficence also means that persons are treated in an ethical manner not only by respecting their decisions and protecting them from harm, but also by actively making efforts to secure their well-being.

Justice. Justice refers to the balance between receiving the benefits of research and bearing its burdens. For example, to ensure justice, the selection of research participants needs to be scrutinized in order to determine whether some classes (e.g., welfare recipients, persons in institutions) are being systematically selected simply because of their easy availability rather than for reasons directly related to the problems being studied.

U.S. government policy also mandates that an IRB must have at least five members, with varying backgrounds. When selecting members, the IRB must take into account racial and cultural heritage and be sensitive to community attitudes. In addition to possessing the professional competence necessary to review specific research activities, the IRB members must also be able to ascertain the acceptability of proposed research in terms of institutional commitments and regulations, applicable law, and standards of professional conduct and practice.

U.S. government policy requires that, if an IRB regularly reviews research that involves a vulnerable category of participants (e.g., children, prisoners, pregnant women, handicapped or mentally disabled persons), it must consider the inclusion of one or more individuals who are knowledgeable about and experienced in working with these participants. Also, the IRB must make every nondiscriminatory effort to ensure that it does not consist entirely of men or entirely of women.

Table 3.2 lists the major criteria used by IRBs and ethics committees in approving research protocols.

Table 3.2   Criteria Used by an Institutional Review Board (IRB) in Approving Research Protocols

Study Design: Many experts agree that an IRB should approve only research that is both valid and of value. The thinking is that a poorly designed study will necessarily lead to misleading results. Study design includes subject recruitment, selection, and assignment to groups; measure or instrument reliability and validity; and data analysis.

Risks and Benefits: IRBs evaluate whether the risks to participants are reasonable in relation to the anticipated benefits, if any, to the participants, and they asses the importance of the knowledge reasonably expected to result from the research.

Equipoise: The ethical basis for assigning treatment by randomization is the judgment that current evidence does not favor the superiority of the experimental over the control program.

Equitable Selection of Participants: The IRB usually considers the purpose and setting of the research and closely examines studies involving vulnerable populations, such as children, prisoners, participants with cognitive disorders, or economically or educationally disadvantaged people.

Identification of Participants and Confidentiality: The IRB is required to review the method for prospective identification of research participants. IRB members examine the researchers' means of identifying and contacting potential participants and the methods for ensuring the participants' privacy and confidentiality.

Participant Payment: Many medical and health-related studies provide financial and other incentives to study participants to compensate them for their time. Ethical concerns arise if the payment is high or too low. If the payment is high, some participants may be induced to take risks against their better judgment. If the payment is too low, some participants may not believe the study is worth their time.

Qualifications: The IRB examines the qualifications of the research team. In addition, the IRB considers the facilities and equipment used to conduct the research and to maintain the rights and welfare of the participants.

The Informed Consent Process: *Informed consent* means that participants who agree to participate in the research are knowledgeable about the risks and benefits of participation and the activities that comprise participation. They also agree to the terms of participation and are knowledgeable about their rights as research subjects.

Table 3.4 Problematic Behaviors in Research Leading to Charges of Misconduct

Problematic Behavior	Definition
Misconduct	Fabrication, falsification, or plagiarism
Questionable research practices	Actions that violate values of research and may be detrimental to the research process but do not directly threaten the integrity of the research record
	Examples include failing to retain research records for a reasonable period or using inappropriate statistics to enhance findings
Other misconduct, not pertaining to scientific integrity	Unacceptable behaviors subject to generally applicable legal and social penalties but that are not unique to research
	Examples include sexual harassment, misuse of funds, or violations of federal regulations
Other misconduct, pertaining to scientific integrity	Unacceptable behavior that does not directly affect the integrity of the research process but is nevertheless directly associated with misconduct in science
	Examples include cover-ups of scientific misconduct or reprisals against whistleblowers
Sloppiness	Negligent or irregular research practices that risk distortion of the research record but that lack the intent to do so

flawed, or unresponsive to important social and cultural needs. This raises ethical concerns for some practitioners:

1. Many important outcomes cannot be measured. Evidence-based practice aims to provide a simple, logical process for reasoning and decision making. But to make balanced decisions, all the relevant consequences of an action must be considered. Current measures of some outcomes (e.g., pain) are inadequate, while others (e.g., justice) may not be measurable. Further, other complex outcomes (e.g., quality of life) may not even be adequately definable (across cultures, generations, and over time). Often, researchers settle for imprecise measures or proximate outcomes.

2. Community needs may differ markedly from those of researchers and policy makers. The community—recipients of evidence-based practices—often has relatively little influence over the priorities and funding of research.

3. Because the large quantities of data required to meet the standards of evidence-based practice are available for relatively few interventions, a

systematic bias may be inevitable toward those interventions. The bias may ultimately result in the allocation of resources to those interventions for which there is rigorous evidence of effectiveness or toward those for which there are funds available to show effectiveness. This may be at the expense of other areas in which rigorous evidence does not currently exist or is not attainable (e.g., palliative care services). Allocating resources on the basis of evidence may therefore involve implicit value judgments, which is at odds with evidence-based practices that emphasize explicit objective criteria.

4. The application of cost-effectiveness measures to decisions about who does or does not receive services may adversely affect the position of the weaker groups in our society. People who are expected to benefit only slightly from particular programs, such as the elderly and the disabled, may be excluded from access to such programs, particularly when they are expensive. Many vulnerable people have been excluded from large-scale research because of the perceived (or real) difficulty of retaining and caring for them.

5. Use of the term *evidence-based* may be misleading (Steinberg & Luce, 2005). Program planners and policy makers, and others acting on the basis of recommendations labeled as being "evidence-based," should not blindly assume that the label truly applies. Evidence-based methods are often not applied consistently or interpreted properly. The potential exists for great variation in the validity of decisions and recommendations that claim to be evidence- based. In addition, evidence may be available for some but not all issues related to a decision or recommendation that has to be made, or the evidence that is available may not be directly relevant to the situation to which it is being applied.

Add the following considerations to the practical screen.

Checklist for Expanding the Practical Literature Review Screen

✓ Is this an evaluation report or something else?
✓ Does the report meet all the selected practical criteria?
✓ Are outcomes carefully defined?
✓ Are appropriate study outcomes compared?
✓ Are the study participants likely to be similar to the group of interest to my setting?
✓ Are the characteristics of the comparison group similar to those of the experimental group?

✓ Is information provided on costs, effectiveness, and benefits?

✓ Does the article tell whether the study had IRB or ethics board approval?

✓ Do the authors describe their conflicts of interest?

✓ Is the article "community-friendly"?

❖️ THE PRACTICAL SCREEN AND LIMITS

The practical screen is usually fairly easy to use because all online bibliographic databases provide mechanisms for refining (Web of Science) or limiting (PubMed) the search for articles. A search for child abuse prevention in Web of Science (Example 3.10) allows you to refine your search by subject areas, document types, authors, and so on.

Example 3.10   Refining a Search for Articles on Child Abuse Prevention (Web of Science)

The same search in PubMed, with limits actually applied, is given in Example 3.11. The limits are displayed at the top and include the type of study (randomized or clinical trials), publication data (in the past 2 years), language (English), and population (children 0–18 years old).

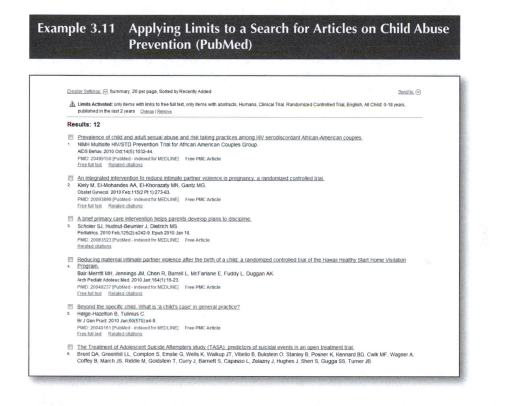

Example 3.11 Applying Limits to a Search for Articles on Child Abuse Prevention (PubMed)

SUMMARY OF CHAPTER 3: FINDING THE BEST AVAILABLE EVIDENCE: QUESTIONS, PRACTICAL CONCERNS, AND ETHICS

Words to Remember

beneficence, Boolean operator, conflict of interest, dependent variables, effectiveness evaluations, ethics committee, experimental research design, feasibility test, human research subjects, improvement evaluations, informed consent, institutional review board (IRB), justice, observational research design, outcomes, PICO, pilot test, population, practical screen, pragmatic clinical trial, research literature review, research misconduct

A research literature review is a highly systematic, explicit, and reproducible method for identifying, evaluating, and synthesizing one or more studies or reports that make up the existing body of completed and recorded work about programs, work produced by researchers, scholars, and practitioners.

Literature review searches begin with a request for information. This request is often referred to as *a research question.* For this purpose, a research question contains four components: the population or problem of concern; the intervention, practice, or program you hope to find; a comparison program; and the hoped-for outcomes. This formulation is called PICO:

P = **P**roblem/People targeted

I = **I**ntervention (another term for practice or program)

C = **C**omparison intervention

O = **O**utcome

When you go to an online bibliographic database, you should be armed with a research question. When stated precisely, this question has the benefit of containing the words the reviewer needs to begin an online search. These words or search terms are often referred to as *key words, descriptors,* or *identifiers.* Literature review searches often mean combining key words and other terms with words such as AND, OR, and NOT (Boolean operators).

The practical screen often consists of the article's or report's publication language; the study's author and design; the publication date; the dates and duration of data collection; and the program's outcomes, content, settings, participants, and ethics.

Evidence-based programs make differences in beneficial outcomes. An outcome is a measurable result such as quantity and frequency of alcohol use, self-efficacy, quality of life, health status, recidivism rate, symptoms of depression, and costs. Beneficial outcomes are improvements, for example, higher health literacy test scores or decreases in harmful alcohol use. Outcomes are dependent variables.

Research with human participants raises ethical concerns because people accept risks and inconvenience in order to contribute new knowledge and provide benefits to others. Evidence-based public health practice relies on the research of others. Its practitioners are not directly responsible for ensuring that research has been conducted in an ethical manner, but they can benefit greatly if they understand the characteristics of ethical research. Evidence-based public health practice is responsible for the use of research results, so it is important to learn about the limitations of depending upon them and how some of these limitations have ethical implications.

The Next Chapter

Chapter 4 deals with how to screen articles on the basis of their methodological quality, especially research design.

EXERCISES

1. Which of the following are typical research literature review tasks?

   a. Applying practical screening criteria

   b. Submitting a detailed protocol to an ethics committee

   c. Summarizing the findings in a protocol

   d. Evaluating the scientific quality of the review

   Answer:
   a, d

2. Read the list of topics below and name at least one article or bibliographic database that might provide you with information on that topic.

   a. Reducing risky health behaviors in adolescents

   b. Reducing symptoms of anxiety in older adults confined to wheelchairs

   c. Promoting health literacy

   Answers:
   Note: These answers are purely illustrative. Other articles databases may also be useful.

   a. PsycINFO, PubMed, Social Sciences Citation Index

   b. PubMed, PsycINFO

   d. PubMed

3. Frame questions for a literature review using the PICO method for each of the following topics.

   a. Preventing accidents in the home

      P = Older adults

      I = Web-based instruction

      C = Printed materials

      O = Fewer home-based falls

   b. Fostering parenting skills

      P = First-time parents

      I = Small-group sessions every week for 10 weeks

      C = Once-a-month home visits by a social worker for 5 weeks

      O = Better parenting skills (e.g., playing with child, learning what to do if child cries often)

   c. Enhancing community involvement in school activities

     P = Community leaders

     I = Ads on local television stations

     C = Electronic newsletter to community leaders

     O = Significant increase in membership in Parent–School Organization

   d. Improving health literacy

     P = People 75 years of age and older

     I = Pharmacist

     C = Clinic health educator

     O = Knowledge of name, dosage, and purpose of medications

Answers:

a. How does an online educational program compare to printed materials in reducing the number of home-based falls in older adults?

b. How do home visits and small-group sessions compare in fostering parenting skills in first-time parents?

c. Do ads on local television stations and e-mailed newsletters to community leaders increase parental involvement in the Parent–School Organization?

d. How do pharmacists and health educators compare in their ability to teach adults 75 years of age and older the names, dosages, and purposes of their medications?

4. Using each research question that you just created, select search terms or key words that can be used to guide a literature search.

Answers:

a. How does an online educational program compare to printed materials in reducing the number of home-based falls in older adults?

   Key words: online, web, Internet; aged 65+; printed materials; education; falls; program; evaluation; evaluation research; English

b. How do home visits and small-group sessions compare in fostering parenting skills in first-time parents?

   Key words: home visits; small groups; parenting; program evaluation; evaluation research; English

c. Do ads on local television stations and e-mailed newsletters to community leaders increase parental involvement in the Parent–School Organization?

Key words: advertisement; television; e-mail, electronic newsletter, e-news; community leaders; parents; program evaluation; evaluation research; English

d. How do pharmacists and health educators compare in their ability to teach adults 75 years of age and older the names, dosages, and purposes of their medications?

Key words: pharmacists; health educators; older adults, adults 75+; medications, medication use; health literacy; program evaluation; evaluation research; English

5. Use Boolean operators to conduct a search for literature to answer these research questions.

a. How does an online educational program compare to printed materials in reducing the number of home-based falls in older adults?

Key words: web; aged 65; printed materials; education; falls; program; evaluation; evaluation research; English

b. How do home visits and small-group sessions compare in fostering parenting skills in first-time parents?

Key words: home visits; small groups; parenting; program evaluation; evaluation research; English

Answers:

a. Aged 65+ AND education AND falls AND English

b. Parenting AND education AND program OR evaluation AND English

6. In addition to key words, what other terms can be used to guide a literature search?

Answer:

You can limit your search by author name, journal name, article title, date of publication, language, age group, gender, publication type, human or animal studies, and many more parameters. The limitations available depend on the database you are using.

7. Name three sources of information about programs and practices *not* including databases of articles or bibliographic citations and other web databases.

Answer:

a. Reference lists in high-quality studies

b. Colleagues and other experts (including authors of articles that interest you)

c. Government, university, and foundation websites

8. Describe the practical criteria used in this hypothetical review.
Does a Fetus Feel Pain?

This literature review examines whether a fetus feels pain and, if so, whether safe and effective techniques exist for providing direct fetal anesthesia or analgesia in the context of therapeutic procedures or abortion.

We systematically searched PubMed for English-language articles focusing on human studies related to fetal pain, anesthesia, and analgesia. Included articles studied fetuses of less than 30 weeks' gestational age or specifically addressed fetal pain perception or nociception. Articles were reviewed for additional references. The search was performed without date limitations and was current as of June 6, 2011.

Answer:

Practical criteria can include publication language, journal or origin of publication, program characteristics, program's theoretical foundation, research design, setting, data collection dates, duration of data collection, publication date, participants, content, and outcomes. Not all these criteria were discussed by the authors of the study on whether a fetus feels pain. The practical criteria that were used to select articles for this study were as follows:

Publication language: English

Publication dates: No restrictions on start date; last article reviewed was June 6, 2005

Participants: Human studies of fetuses of less than 30 weeks' gestational age

Content: Fetal pain, anesthesia, and analgesia; fetal pain perception or nociception

9. Match the following statement with the concept that supports or defines it.

1. In our RCT, we went to great trouble to ensure that the alternative program has not been proven superior to the experimental.	a. Informed consent
2. Participants in the research are knowledgeable about the risks and benefits of participation and the activities that comprise participation. They also agree to the terms of participation and are knowledgeable about their rights as research subjects.	b. Ethics committee or institutional review board (IRB)
3. U.S. government policy also mandates that it must have at least five members, with varying backgrounds. When selecting members, the committee must take into account racial and cultural heritage and be sensitive to community attitudes.	c. Equipoise
4. The selection of research participants needs to be scrutinized in order to determine whether some classes (e.g., welfare recipients, persons in institutions) are being systematically selected simply because of their easy availability rather than for reasons directly related to the problems being studied.	d. Justice

Answer:
1 = c; 2 = a; 3 = b; 4 = d

10. Which of these is characteristic of research misconduct? Circle all that apply.

a. Plagiarism

b. Falsification

c. Conflict of interest

d. Fabrication

Answer:
All (a–d) are characteristic of research misconduct.

11. Which of these is a potential ethical concern when considering the adaptation of evidence-based practices? Circle all that apply.

a. The application of cost-effectiveness measures to decisions about who does or does not receive services may adversely affect the position of the weaker groups in our society.

b. Many important outcomes cannot be measured.

c. Because the large quantities of data required to meet the standards of evidence-based practice are available for relatively few interventions, a systematic bias may be inevitable toward those interventions.

d. It may be impossible to decide between competing claims of different policy makers.

Answer:
All (a–d) are ethical concerns.

12. What is the primary reason that research with human participants raises ethical concerns? Circle one.

a. Participants are not always told why they are being asked to join a study.

b. Participants accept risks they might not otherwise agree to.

c. Participants frequently get paid for their participation.

d. Participants are rarely part of the ethics committee to approve the study protocol.

Answer:
b

13. Which of these is a defining characteristic of the ethical principal of beneficence? Circle one.

a. Scientifically sound research design

b. A balance between benefits and risks

c. Informed consent

Answer:
a

REFERENCES

Ciampa, P. J., Kumar, D., Barkin, S. L., Sanders, L. M., Yin, H. S., Perrin, E. M., et al. (2010). Interventions aimed at decreasing obesity in children younger than 2 years: A systematic review. *Archives of Pediatrics and Adolescent Medicine, 164,* 1098–1104.

Glasgow, R. E., Magid, D. J., Beck, A., Ritzwoller, D., & Estabrooks, P. A. (2005). Practical clinical trials for translating research to practice: Design and measurement recommendations. *Medical Care, 43,* 551–557.

National Commission for the Protection of Human Subjects of Biomedical and Behavioral Research. (1979). *The Belmont report: Ethical principles and guidelines for the protection of human subjects of research.* Retrieved from http://ohsr.od.nih.gov/guidelines/belmont.html

Steinberg, E. P., & Luce, B. R. (2005). Evidence-based? Caveat emptor! *Health Affairs, 24,* 80–92.

Tunis, S. R., Stryer, D. B., & Clancy, C. M. (2003). Practical clinical trials: Increasing the value of clinical research for decision making in clinical and health policy. *Journal of the American Medical Association, 290,* 1624–1632.

U.S. Department of Health and Human Services. (2004). *Guidelines for the conduct of research involving human subjects at the National Institutes of Health.* Washington, DC: Author. Retrieved from http://ohsr.od.nih.gov/guidelines/GrayBooklet82404.pdf

Wathen, C. N., & MacMillan, H. L. (2003). Interventions for violence against women: Scientific review. *Journal of the American Medical Association, 289,* 589–600.

CHAPTER 4

RESEARCH DESIGN, VALIDITY, AND BEST AVAILABLE EVIDENCE

The best available evidence on public health programs and policies comes from high-quality studies. A study's quality is dependent upon the strength of its methodology, including its research design, outcome measures, settings, participants, interventions, data collection strategies, and statistical techniques.

This chapter explores commonly used research designs and discusses how they affect a study's internal validity, external validity, and quality. Subsequent chapters discuss other components of study methodology.

CHAPTER OBJECTIVES ❖

After reading this chapter, you will be able to

- Describe the characteristics of commonly used research designs in studies to define and meet public health program needs, including
  - Randomized controlled trials with concurrent, parallel, or wait-list control groups and factorial designs
  - Quasi-experimental designs with concurrent or parallel control groups

Example 4.1 illustrates two randomized controlled trials with concurrent controls.

Example 4.1 Two Randomized Controlled Trials With Concurrent Controls

---

1. **Evaluating Home Visitation by Nurses to Prevent Child Maltreatment in Families Referred to Child Protection Agencies (MacMillan et al., 2005)**

Objective. Recurrence of child maltreatment is a major problem, yet little is known about approaches to reduce this risk in families referred to child protection agencies. Since home visitation by nurses for disadvantaged first-time mothers has proven effective in the prevention of child abuse and neglect, the researchers investigated whether this approach might reduce the recurrence of maltreatment.

Assessment for Eligibility. Families were eligible if they met the following criteria: (1) the index child was younger than 13 years, (2) the reported episode of physical abuse or neglect occurred within the previous 3 months, (3) the child identified as physically abused or neglected was still living with his or her family or was to be returned home within 30 days of the incident, and (4) families were able to speak English. Families in which the abuse was committed by a foster parent, or in [which] the reported incident included sexual abuse, were not eligible.

Evaluation Research Design. The evaluators randomly assigned 163 families to control or intervention groups. Control families received standard services arranged by the agency. These included routine follow-up by caseworkers whose focus was on assessment of risk of recidivism, provision of education about parenting, and arrangement of referrals to community-based parent education programs and other services. The intervention group of families received the same standard care plus home visitation by a public-health nurse every week for 6 months, then every 2 weeks for 6 months, then monthly for 12 months.

Findings. At 3-years' follow-up, recurrence of child physical abuse did not differ between groups. However, hospital records showed significantly higher recurrence of either physical abuse or neglect in the intervention group than in the control group.

2. **Evaluating Therapy for Depressed Elderly People: Comparing a Holistic Approach to Medication Alone (Nickel et al., 2005)**

Objective. To find out whether recovering the ability to function socially takes a different course with integrative, holistic treatment than it does with medication alone.

Assessment for Eligibility. To be included, participants had to be female; aged 65–75; living at home; and disturbed by symptoms such as sadness, lack of drive, and reclusion. Grounds for exclusion were the need for personal assistance in any of four key activities of daily living: Bathing, dressing, walking inside the house, and transferring from a chair; significant cognitive impairment with no available proxy; diagnosis of a terminal illness, psychosis, or bipolar disorder; the current use of antidepressants or psychotherapy; and plans to change of residence within next four months.

Findings. Both forms of therapy did afford a relatively rapid reduction of depressive symptoms. The integrative treatment not only led to a quicker reduction in depression, however, but was also the only one that led to a significant improvement in the ability to function socially.

3. **Evaluating a Health Care Program to Get Adolescents to Exercise (Patrick et al., 2006)**

   Objective. Many adolescents do not meet national guidelines for participation in regular, moderate, or vigorous physical activity; for limitations on sedentary behaviors; or for dietary intake of fruits and vegetables, fiber, or total dietary fat. This study evaluated a health care–based intervention to improve these behaviors.

   Assessment for Eligibility. Adolescents between the ages of 11 and 15 years were recruited through their primary care providers. A total of 45 primary care providers from 6 private clinic sites in San Diego County, California, agreed to participate in the study. A representative group of healthy adolescents seeing primary care providers was sought by contacting parents of adolescents who were already scheduled for a well-child visit and by outreach to families with adolescents. Adolescents were excluded if they had health conditions that would limit their ability to comply with physical activity or diet recommendations.

   Evaluation Research Design. After baseline measures but before seeing the provider, participants were randomized to either the Patient-Centered Assessment and Counseling for Exercise + Nutrition (PACE+) program or to a sun protection control condition.

   Findings. Compared with adolescents in the sun protection control group, girls and boys in the diet and physical activity program significantly reduced sedentary behaviors. Boys reported more active days per week. No program effects were seen with percentage of calories from fat consumed or minutes of physical activities per week. The percentage of adolescents meeting recommended health guidelines was significantly improved for girls for consumption of saturated fat and for boys' participation in days per week of physical activity. No between-group differences were seen in body mass index.

Wait-List Control: Do It Sequentially. With a wait-list control design, both groups are assessed for eligibility, but one is randomly assigned to be given the program now (experimental group) and the other is put on a waiting list (control group). After the experimental group completes the program, both groups are assessed a second time. Then the control group receives the program and both groups are assessed again (see Figure 4.2).

Figure 4.2 Randomized Controlled Trial Using a Wait-List Control

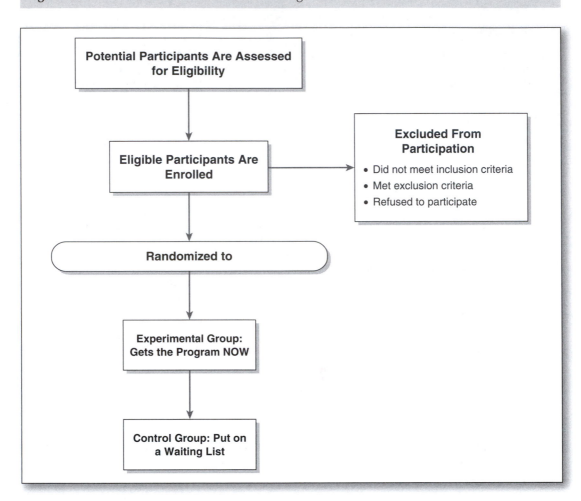

Here is how this design is used:

1. Compare Group 1 (experimental group) and Group 2 (control group) at baseline (the pretest). If random assignment has worked, the two groups should not differ from one another.

2. Give Group 1 the program.

3. Assess the outcomes for Groups 1 and 2 at the end of the program. If the program is working, expect to see a difference in outcomes favoring the experimental group.

4. Give the program to Group 2.

5. Assess the outcomes a second time. If the program is working, Group 2 should catch up to Group 1), and both should have improved in their outcomes (Figure 4.4).

Figure 4.3   Evaluating Effectiveness With a Wait-List Control

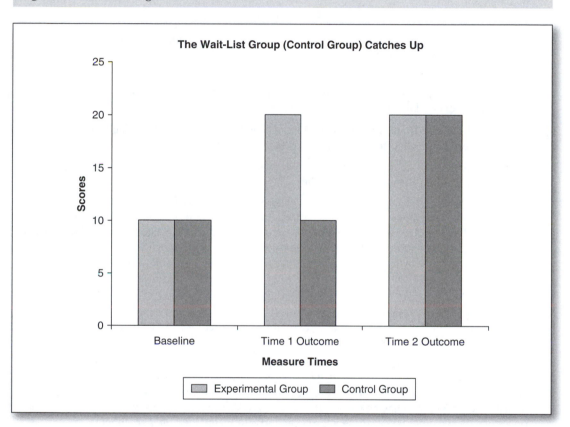

Example 4.2 has three illustrative wait-list control evaluation designs.

Example 4.2   Three RCTs With Wait-List Controls

1. Evaluating a Methadone Maintenance Treatment in an Australian Prison System (Dolan et al., 2003)

Objective. To determine whether methadone maintenance treatment reduced heroin use, syringe sharing, and HIV or hepatitis C incidence among prisoners.

(Continued)

Example 4.2 (Continued)

Assessment for Eligibility. Male inmates were eligible to participate if they (1) were assessed as suitable for methadone maintenance by a detailed interview with medical staff who confirmed they had a heroin problem; (2) were serving prison sentences longer than four months at the time of interview; and (3) were able to provide signed informed consent.

Evaluation Research Design. All eligible prisoners seeking drug treatment were randomized to methadone or a wait-list control group and followed up after four months.

Findings. Heroin use was significantly lower among treated than control subjects at follow-up. Treated subjects reported lower levels of drug injection and syringe sharing at follow-up. There was no difference in HIV or hepatitis C incidence.

2. **Evaluating Two Brief Treatments for Sleep Problems in Young Learning Disabled Children: A Randomized Controlled Trial (Montgomery, Stores, & Wiggs, 2004)**

   Objective. To investigate the efficacy of a media-based, brief behavioral treatment of sleep problems in children with learning disabilities.

   Assessment for Eligibility. The study included children aged 2–8 years with any form of severe learning disability, confirmed by a general practitioner. Severe sleep problems were defined according to standardized criteria as follows: (1) night waking occurring three or more times a week for more than a few minutes and the child disturbing the parents or going into their room or bed and/or (2) settling problems occurring three or more times a week with the child taking more than one hour to settle and disturbing the parents during this time. These problems needed to have been present for at least three months and not be explicable in terms of a physical problem such as pain.

   Evaluation Research Design. The parents of severely learning disabled children took part in a randomized controlled trial with a wait-list control group. Face-to-face delivered treatment was compared to usual care, and a booklet-delivered treatment was compared to usual care.

   Findings. Both forms of treatment (face-to-face and booklet) were almost equally effective compared with the controls. Two thirds of children who were taking over 30 minutes to settle five or more times per week and waking at night for over 30 minutes four or more times per week improved on average to having such settling or night waking problems for only a few minutes or only once or twice per week. These improvements were maintained after six months.

3. **Evaluating a Mental Health Intervention for Schoolchildren Exposed to Violence: A Randomized Controlled Trial (Stein et al., 2003)**

   Objective. To evaluate the effectiveness of a collaboratively designed school-based intervention for reducing children's symptoms of posttraumatic stress disorder (PTSD) and depression that has resulted from exposure to violence.

   Assessment for Eligibility. Sixth-grade students at two large middle schools in Los Angeles who reported exposure to violence and had clinical levels of symptoms of PTSD using standard measures.

Evaluation Research Design. Students were randomly assigned to a ten-session standardized cognitive-behavioral therapy (the Cognitive-Behavioral Intervention for Trauma in Schools) early intervention group or to a wait-list delayed intervention comparison group conducted by trained school mental health clinicians.

Findings. Compared with the wait-list delayed intervention group (no intervention), after three months of intervention, students who were randomly assigned to the early intervention group had significantly lower scores on symptoms of PTSD, depression, and psychosocial dysfunction. At six months, after both groups had received the intervention, the differences between the two groups were not significantly different for symptoms of PTSD and depression.

A wait-list control design (sometimes called *switching replications* or *delayed treatment* design) has the advantage of allowing the evaluator to compare experimental and control group performance on the same program. It is sometimes difficult to find or implement an alternative control program that is equal to or better than the new program. Also, the new program may be designed to fill a gap in the availability of programs, and no comparable program may actually be available at all. Finally, the nature of the design means that everyone receives the program, and, in some circumstances, this may be an incentive for everyone to participate fully.

Wait-list control designs are particularly practical when programs are repeated at regular intervals, as they are in schools with a semester system. For example, students can be randomly assigned to Group 1 or Group 2, with Group 1 participating in the first semester. Group 2 can then participate in the second semester. The design is especially efficient in settings that can wait for results.

Wait-list control designs are also reliant upon having the experimental group cease its improvement at the time of program completion. If improvement in the experimental group continues until the control group completes the program, then the effects of the program on the control group may appear to be less spectacular than they actually were. To avoid this confusion, some investigators advocate waiting for improvement in the experimental program to level off (a "wash out" period) and to time the implementation of the control program accordingly. However, the amount of time needed for the effect to wash out is usually unknown in advance.

Factorial Designs

Factorial designs enable researchers to evaluate the effects of varying the features of an intervention or practice to see which combination works best. In Example 4.3 the investigators are concerned with finding out if the response rate to web-based surveys can be improved by notifying prospective responders in advance by e-mail and/or pleading with them to respond. The investigators design a study to solve the response-rate problem using a two-by-two (2 × 2) factorial design in which participants are either notified about the survey in advance by e-mail or not prenotified, or they are pleaded with to respond or not pleaded with. The factors (they are also independent variables) are *pleading* (Factor 1) and *notifying* (Factor 2). Each factor has two levels: *plead* versus *don't plead* and *notify in advance* versus *don't notify in advance*.

		Factor 1: Pleading Status	
		Plead	Don't Plead
Factor 2: Notification Status	Notify in Advance		
	Don't Notify in Advance		

In a 2 × 2 design, there are four study groups: (1) prenotification e-mail and pleading invitation e-mail, (2) prenotification e-mail and nonpleading invitation, (3) no prenotification e-mail and pleading invitation, (4) no prenotification and nonpleading invitation. In the diagram above, the empty cells are placeholders for the number of people in each category (e.g., the number in the groups *plead* × *notify in advance* compared to the number in *plead* × *don't notify in advance*).

With this design, the researchers can study main effects (*plead* versus *don't plead*) or interactive effects (*prenotification* and *pleading*). The outcome in this study is always the response rate. If research participants are assigned to groups randomly, the study is a randomized controlled trial.

Example 4.3   Factorial Design (Felix, Burchett, & Edwards, 2011)

Improving Response Rate to Web Surveys

Objectives. To evaluate the effectiveness of pre-notification and pleading invitations in Web surveys by embedding a randomized controlled trial (RCT) in a Web-based survey.

Study Design and Setting. E-mail addresses of 569 authors of published maternal health research were randomized in a 2×2 factorial trial of a pre-notification vs. no pre-notification e-mail and a pleading vs. a non-pleading invitation e-mail. The primary outcome was completed response rate, and the secondary outcome was submitted response rate (which included complete and partial responses).

Results. Pleading invitations resulted in 5.0% more completed questionnaires, although this difference did not reach statistical significance [odds ratio (OR) 1.23; 95% confidence interval (CI): 0.86, 1.74; $P = 0.25$]. Pre-notification did not increase the completion rate (OR 1.04; 95% CI 0.73, 1.48; $P = 0.83$). Response was higher among authors who had published in 2006 or later (OR 2.07; 95% CI: 1.43, 2.98; $P = 0.001$). There was some evidence that pre-notification was more effective in increasing submissions from authors with recent publications ($P = 0.04$).

Conclusion. The use of a "pleading" tone to e-mail invitations may increase response to a Web-based survey. Authors of recently published research are more likely to respond to a Web-based survey.

Factorial designs may include many factors and many levels. It is the number of levels that describes the name of the design. For instance, in a study of psychotherapy versus behavior modification in outpatient, inpatient, and day treatment settings, there are two factors (*treatment* and *setting*), with one factor having two levels (*psychotherapy* versus *behavior modification*) and one having three levels (*inpatient, day treatment,* and *outpatient*). This design is a 2 × 3 factorial design.

Doing It Randomly

Randomization is considered to be the primary method of ensuring that participating study groups are probably alike at baseline, that is, before they participate in a program. The idea behind randomization is that if chance—which is what *random* means—dictates the allocation of programs, all important factors will be equally distributed between and among experimental and control groups. No single factor will dominate any of the groups, possibly influencing program outcomes. That is, each group will be as smart, as motivated, as knowledgeable, as self-efficacious, and so on as the other to begin with. As a result, any differences between or among groups that are observed later, after program participation, can reasonably be assigned to the program rather than to the differences that were there at the beginning. In researchers' terms, randomized controlled trials result in unbiased estimates of a program's or treatment's effects.

How does random assignment work? Table 4.2 describes a commonly used method and some considerations.

Table 4.2   Random Assignment

1. An algorithm or set of rules is applied to a table of random numbers, which are usually generated by computer (although tables of random numbers are sometimes used in small studies). For instance, if the research design includes an experimental group and a control group, and an equal probability of being assigned to each, then the algorithm could specify using the random number 1 for assignment to the experimental group and 2 for assignment to the control group— or vice versa. (Other numbers are ignored.)

2. As each eligible person enters the study, he or she is assigned one of the numbers (1 or 2).

3. The random assignment procedure should be designed so that members of the research team who have contact with study participants cannot influence the allocation process. For instance, random assignments to experimental or control groups can be placed in advance in a set of sealed envelopes by someone who will not be involved in opening them. Each envelope should be numbered (so that all can be accounted for by the end of the study). As a participant comes through the system, his or her name is recorded, the envelope is opened, and the assignment (1 or 2) is recorded next to the person's name.

4. It is crucial that researchers prevent interference with randomization. Who would tamper with assignment? Sometimes members of the research team may feel pressure to ensure that the most "needy" people receive the experimental program. One method of avoiding this is to ensure that tamper-proof procedures are in place. If the research team uses envelopes, they should ensure the envelopes are opaque (so no one can see through them) and sealed. In large studies, randomization is done off site.

Variations on how to conduct the random allocation of participants and programs certainly exist. As described in the checklist below, look for adherence to certain principles regardless of the specifics of the method reported in a particular evaluation study.

What Evidence-Based Public
Health Practice Should Watch For: A Checklist

✓ Study team members who have contact with participants were not part of the allocation process. Randomization can be done off-site.
✓ Assignment was not readily available to evaluation team members.
✓ A table of random numbers or a computer-generated list of random numbers was used.

Random Clusters

In some situations, it may be preferable for researchers to randomly assign **clusters** of individuals (e.g., families, communities) rather than individuals to the experimental or control groups. In fact, randomization by cluster may be the only feasible method of conducting an evaluation in many settings. Research that uses clusters to randomize is variously known as field trials, community-based trials, or cluster randomized trials.

Compared with individually randomized trials, cluster randomized trials are more complex to design and require more participants to obtain equivalent statistical power and more complex analysis. This is because observations on individuals in the same cluster (e.g., children in a classroom) tend to be interrelated by potentially **confounding** (confusing) **variables**. For example, students in a classroom are about the same age, may have the same ability, and will have similar experiences. Consequently, the actual sample size is less (one classroom) than the total number of individual participants (25 students). The whole is less than the sum of its parts!

Example 4.4 contains an example of random assignment by cluster. In this example, the cluster comprises colleges. Please note that data on the outcome (cessation of smokeless tobacco use in the previous 30 days) were collected from individual students, but randomization was done by college—not by student. Is this OK? The answer depends on how the study deals with the potential problems caused by randomizing with one unit (colleges) and analyzing data from another (students).

Example 4.4   A College-Based Smokeless Tobacco Program for College Athletes (Walsh et al., 1999)

Objective. The purpose of this study was to determine the effectiveness of a college-based smokeless tobacco cessation intervention that targeted college athletes. Effectiveness was defined as reported cessation of smokeless tobacco use in the previous 30 days.

Assessment for Eligibility. Current users of smokeless tobacco (use more than once per month and within the past month) were eligible for the study. A total of 16 colleges with an average of 23 smokeless tobacco users in each were selected from lists of all publicly supported California universities and community colleges. Half the participants were selected to be urban and half to be rural; all had varsity football and baseball teams. One-year prevalence of cessation among smokeless tobacco users was determined by self-report of abstinence for the previous 30 days.

Evaluation Research Design. The occurrence of smokeless tobacco use was calculated for each athlete using information from a questionnaire given to them at baseline. Colleges were then matched by pairs so that the level of smoking was approximately the same in each of the individual colleges paired. One college from each pair was randomized to receive the program, while the other college in the pair received no program.

Findings. In both groups, 314 students provided complete data on cessation. Cessation frequencies were 35% in the program colleges and 16% in the control colleges. The program effect increased with level of smokeless tobacco use.

❖ ENSURING BASELINE EQUIVALENCE: WHAT EVIDENCE-BASED PUBLIC HEALTH PRACTICE SHOULD WATCH FOR

When reviewing articles, be certain that researchers provide information as to whether baseline characteristics are balanced among clusters and individuals. The evaluators in Example 4.4 sought to achieve balance (i.e., equivalence) among universities (the clusters) by including only public universities and junior colleges in California. They aimed for equivalence in smoking levels among students within each university by pairing up universities in terms of their students' smoking levels and randomly assigning pair members to the experimental or the control group.

In addition to descriptive information on methods used to ensure equivalence, look for proof that the process worked and that, after it was over, the groups were indeed equivalent:

Of 273 children with asthma in this cohort, 42.1% were female, 41.7% were African-American, and the average age was 8.2 years. The baseline characteristics for Program and non-Program groups were quite similar in terms of demographics, enrollment, and asthma comorbidity. Compared with the Program group, the non-Program group had a significantly higher percentage of females and "other race" children, but significantly less Managed Care Organization enrollment and less allergy comorbidity.

Despite all efforts, chance may dictate that the two groups differ on important variables at baseline. Bad luck! Statistical methods may be used to "correct" for these differences, but it is usually better to anticipate the problem.

Improving on Chance

Small to moderate-sized RCTs can gain power to detect a difference between experimental and control programs (assuming one is actually present) if special randomization procedures are used to balance the numbers of participants in each (**blocked randomization**) and in the distribution of baseline variables that might influence the outcomes (**stratified blocked randomization**).

Why are special procedures necessary if random assignment is supposed to take care of the number of people in each group or the proportion of people in each with certain characteristics? The answer is that, by chance, one group may end up being larger than the other or differing in age, gender, and so on. Good news: This happens less frequently in large studies. Bad news: The problem of unequal distribution of variables becomes even more complicated when groups or clusters of people (e.g., schools, families) rather than individuals are assigned. In this case, the evaluator has little control over the individuals within each cluster, and the number of clusters (over which he or she does have control) is usually relatively small (e.g., five schools, 10 clinics). Some form of constraint such as stratification is almost always recommended in RCTs in which allocation is done by cluster.

Two commonly used methods for ensuring equal group sizes and balanced variables are blocked randomization and stratified blocked randomization as described in Table 4.3.

Table 4.3   Enhancing Chance: Blocked and Stratified Blocked Randomization

Blocking or Balancing the Number of Participants in Each Group	**Stratifying or Balancing Important Predictor (Independent) Variables**
Randomization is done in blocks of predetermined size. For example, if the block's size is 6, randomization proceeds normally within each block until the third person is randomized to one group, after which participants are automatically assigned to the other group until the block of 6 is completed. This means that in a study of 30 participants, 15 will be assigned to each group, and in a study of 33, the disproportion can be no greater than 18:15.	Stratification means dividing participants into segments. For example, participants can be divided into differing age groups (the stratum) or gender or educational level. In a study of a program to improve knowledge of how to prevent infection from HIV/AIDS, having access to reliable transportation to attend education classes is a strong predictor of outcome. It is probably a good idea to have similar numbers of people who have transportation (determined at baseline) assigned to each group. This can be done by dividing the study sample at baseline into participants with or without transportation (stratification by access to transportation) and then carrying out a blocked randomization procedure with each of these two strata.

Example 4.5 illustrates how these techniques have been applied in program evaluations.

Example 4.5   Enhancing Chance by Using Special Randomization Procedures

1. We randomly allocated families to control or intervention groups using a computer program sequence generated by our statistician, blocked after every eight allocations. We aimed to do secondary analyses within the intervention group, albeit with modest power, on the basis of the number of nurse visits. Therefore, to increase the numbers in the intervention group, toward the end of recruitment, we randomly allocated families using a 5-to-3 ratio (5 intervention families to 3 controls). Randomization was stratified by the age of the index child—i.e., younger than 4 years and 4 to 12 years—since evidence exists indicating that preschool children are at increased risk for recurrence of physical abuse and neglect. Group assignment was placed in numbered sequential sealed envelopes.

2. Group allocation was based on block randomization. A sequential list of case numbers was matched to group allocations in blocks of ten by randomly drawing five cards labeled "control" and five cards labeled "treatment" from an envelope. This procedure was repeated for each block of ten sequential case numbers. The list of case numbers and group allocation was held by a researcher not involved in recruiting or interviewing inmates. The trial nurses responsible for assessing, recruiting, and interviewing inmates had no access to these lists. Once an inmate had been recruited and interviewed, the study nurse contacted the Central Randomization System via a mobile telephone to ascertain the inmate's group allocation.

3. After the baseline period, patients meeting the inclusion criteria were randomly stratified by center (block size 12 not known to trial centers) in a 2:1:1 ratio (experimental program, an alternative program, waiting list) using a centralized telephone randomization procedure (random list generated with the Sample Software, version 8.0, Bronx, New York).

Blinding

In some randomized studies, the participants and investigators do not know which participants are in the experimental and control groups: This is the double-blind experiment. When participants do not know, but investigators do, this is called the **blinded** trial. Participants, people responsible for program implementation or assessing program outcomes, and statistical analysts are all candidates for being blinded.

Experts in clinical trials maintain that blinding is as important as randomization in ensuring valid study results. Randomization, they say, eliminates confounding variables, or confounders, before the program is implemented—at baseline—but it cannot do away with confounding variables that occur as the study progresses. A confounding variable is an extraneous variable in a statistical or research model that affects the dependent variables but has either not been considered or not been controlled for. For example, age, educational level, and motivation may be confounders in a study that involves adherence to a complicated intervention.

Confounders can lead to a false conclusion that the dependent variables are in a causal relationship with the independent or predictor variables. For instance, suppose research shows that drinking coffee (independent or predictor variable) is associated with heart attacks (dependent variable). One possibility is that drinking coffee causes heart attacks. Another is that having heart attacks causes people to drink more coffee. A third explanation is that some other confounding factor, such as smoking, is responsible for heart attacks and is also associated with drinking coffee.

Confounding during the course of a study can occur if participants get extra attention or the control group catches on to the experiment. The extra attention or changes in the control group's perceptions may alter the outcomes of a study. One method of getting around and understanding the biases that may result in unblinded studies is to standardize all program activities and to monitor the extent to which the program has been implemented as planned.

Pay special attention to the biases that may have occurred in randomized controlled studies without blinding. Expect the evaluator to report on how the program's implementation was monitored and the extent to which any deviations from standard program procedures may have affected the outcomes.

Example 4.6 contains examples of blinding used in RCTs.

Example 4.6   Blinding in RCTs

1. The Researcher Is Blinded

Seventy-five opaque envelopes were produced for the initial randomization and lodged with an independent staff member. Each contained a slip of paper with the word *conventional, booklet,* or *control* (25 each). The randomization was performed by this staff member selecting an envelope for each participant immediately after the initial assessment meeting with parents. For the re-randomization of the control crossover group, this process was repeated with a second batch of 26 envelopes, half each with the word *conventional* or *booklet*. The researcher conducting the study was therefore blind to the nature of the treatment allocated until after the posttreatment assessment. Following that point, both participant and researcher were aware of the treatment group to which they had been randomized.

2. Patients and Researchers Are Blinded

This study was a randomized, multicenter trial comparing acupuncture, sham acupuncture, and a no-acupuncture waiting-list condition. The additional no-acupuncture waiting list control was included because sham acupuncture cannot be substituted for a physiologically inert placebo. Patients in the acupuncture groups were blinded to which treatment they received. Analysis of headache diaries was performed by two blinded evaluators. The study duration per patient was 28 weeks: 4 weeks before randomization, the baseline; 8 weeks of treatment; and 16 weeks of follow-up. Patients allocated to the waiting list received true acupuncture after 12 weeks and were also followed up for 24 weeks after randomization (to investigate whether changes were similar to those in patients receiving immediate acupuncture).

RCTs are generally expensive, time-consuming, and tend to address very specific research questions. They should probably be saved for relatively mature programs and practices, that is, those that previous research suggests are likely to be effective. Previous research includes large pilot studies and other randomized trials.

Despite an important advantage over other types of research designs (specifically, their ability to establish that Program A is likely to have *caused* Outcome A), RCTs' requirement for control sometimes gives them a bad name. Some researchers and practitioners express concern over the fairness of excluding certain groups and individuals from participation or from receiving the experimental program. Others question the idea of regarding humans as fit subjects for an experiment and of obtaining good information from quantitative or statistically oriented research. To some extent, these are personal or ethical concerns and are not inherent weaknesses of the RCT design itself. Nevertheless, it is certainly reasonable to expect researchers to explain their choice of design in ethical as well as methodological terms. In Example 4.7, the evaluators of a program that provides respite care for homeless patients, a cohort study, defend themselves.

> **Example 4.7 Statement by the Evaluators of a Study of Respite Care for Homeless Patients Regarding the Ethics of Their RCT (Buchanan, Doblin, Sai, & Garcia, 2006)**

Finally, a randomized control trial is needed. Although the available demographic data, clinical variables, and baseline utilization data were similar in our respite care and usual care study groups, it is possible that unmeasured variables, including differential rates of substance use or psychiatric illness, may have confounded our results. Some might argue that a randomized trial would be unethical, given the obvious humanitarian virtues of respite care. But a randomized trial would be no less ethical than the current status quo in the United States, where respite care is available only to some, not all, homeless people. Now is the time for such a trial, given the results of the present study, the financial distress of many U.S. hospitals, and the unmet needs of our country's homeless people.

The evaluators understand that some people believe that if you have an intervention or program that is perceived to be humanitarian (e.g., respite care), you should not conduct an experiment in which some people are necessarily denied services. The investigators counter by arguing that some homeless people do not have access to respite care anyway. The evaluators also point out that evaluation research that takes the form of a randomized trial can help clarify the results of their study by providing information on unmeasured factors such as differential rates of substance use or psychiatric illness.

Quasi-Experimental Research Designs

Quasi-experimental research is characterized by nonrandomized assignment to groups or by conducting a series of measures over time on one or more groups.

Nonrandomized Controlled Trials: Concurrent Controls

Nonrandomized controlled trials are a type of quasi-experimental design. In fact, *quasi-experiment* is often synonymous with *nonrandomized control trial* and is defined as a design in which one group receives the program and one does not, the assignment of participants to groups is not controlled by the researcher, and assignment is not random.

Quasi-experimental, nonrandomized controlled trials rely on participants who volunteer to join the study, are geographically close to the study site, or conveniently turn up (e.g., at a clinic or a school) while the study is being conducted. As a result, people or groups in a quasi-experiment may self-select, and the evaluation findings may not be unbiased because they are dependent upon participant choice rather than chance.

Quasi-experimental researchers use a variety of methods to ensure that the participating groups are as similar to one another as possible (equivalent) at baseline or before "treatment." Among the strategies used to ensure equivalence is **matching**. Example 4.4 showed the matching approach applied to the randomized trial of a smokeless tobacco program for college athletes

Matching requires selecting pairs of participants or clusters of individuals who are comparable to one another on important confounding variables. For example, suppose a researcher was interested in comparing the acuity of vision among smokers and nonsmokers. One method of helping to ensure that the two groups are balanced on important confounders requires that, for every smoker, there is a nonsmoker of the same age, sex, and medical history.

Matching can effectively prevent confounding by important factors such as age and sex for individuals. The strategy's implementation can be relatively expensive, however, because finding a match for each study participant is sometimes difficult and often time-consuming.

Another technique for allocating participants to study groups in quasi-experiments include assigning each potential participant a number and using an alternating sequence in which every other individual (1, 3, 5, etc.) is assigned to the experimental group and the alternate participants (2, 4, 6, etc.) are assigned to the control. A different option is to assign groups in order of appearance; for example, patients who attend the clinic on Monday,

Wednesday, and Friday are in the experimental group, and those attending on Tuesday, Thursday, and Saturday are assigned to the control. To prevent certain types of patients (e.g., those who can only come on a certain day) from automatically being in one or the other of the groups, the procedure for assignment can be reversed after some number of days or weeks.

Illustrations of nonrandomized, quasi-experimental designs with concurrent groups are given in Example 4.8.

Example 4.8   Quasi-Experimental Design: Concurrent Groups

1. Reducing Injuries Among Teen Agricultural Workers (Reed & Kidd, 2004)

Objective. To test an agricultural safety curriculum [Agricultural Disability Awareness and Risk Education (AgDARE)] for use in high school agriculture classes.

Assessment for Eligibility. A total of 21 schools (1,138 agriculture students) from Kentucky, Iowa, and Mississippi participated in the program.

Research Design. Schools in each state were grouped geographically to improve homogeneity in agricultural commodities and production techniques and then assigned randomly to either one of two intervention groups (A or B) or the control group. Fourteen schools were assigned to the intervention arms, and seven schools were assigned to the control group.

Findings. Students who participated in AgDARE scored significantly higher in farm safety attitude and intent to change work behavior than the control group. School and public health nurses, working together with agriculture teachers, may make an effective team in reducing injuries among teen agricultural workers.

2. Contraceptive Practices Among Rural Vietnamese Men (Ha, Jayasuriya, & Owen, 2005)

Objective. To test a social-cognitive intervention to influence contraceptive practices among men living in rural communes in Vietnam.

Assessment for Eligibility. There were 651 married men from 12 villages in two rural communes (An Hong and Quoc Tuan) in the An Hai district of Hai Phong province in Vietnam. Interviewers visited each household in the selected villages and sought all married men aged 19–45 years who had lived with their wives in the same house during the three months prior to the study. The inclusion criteria were as follows: the wife was currently not pregnant, the couple did not plan to have a child in the next six months, they currently did not use condoms consistently for family planning, and the wives currently did not use the pill consistently for family planning.

Evaluation Research Design. Villages were chosen as the primary unit for intervention. From each of the two communes, three villages were chosen for intervention and three as controls. The intervention villages were separated from control villages by a distance of 2–3 km. Participants in both study groups were assessed, using interviewer-based questionnaires, prior to (baseline) and following the intervention (posttest).

Findings. There were 651 eligible married men in the 12 villages chosen. A significant positive movement in men's stage of readiness for IUD use by their wife occurred in the intervention group. There were no significant changes in the control group. Compared to the control group, the intervention group showed higher pros, lower cons, and higher self-efficacy for IUD use by their wife as a contraceptive method. Interventions based on social-cognitive theory can increase men's involvement in IUD use in rural Vietnam and should assist in reducing future rates of unwanted pregnancy.

Strong quasi-experimental designs have many desirable features. They can provide information about programs when it is inappropriate or too late to randomize participants. Another desirable characteristic of quasi-experiments is that, when compared to RCTs, their settings and participants may more accurately reflect the messiness of the real world. An RCT requires strict control over the environment, and to get that control the evaluator has to be extremely stringent with respect to the research question being posed and who is included and excluded from study participation. As a result, RCT findings may apply to a relatively small population in constrained settings.

Nonrandomized designs are sometimes chosen over randomized ones in the mistaken belief that they are more ethical than randomized trials. The idea behind the ethical challenge is that, if the evaluation researcher suspects that Program A is better than Program B, then how (in ethical terms) can he or she allocate Program B to innocent participants? In fact, evaluations are only ethical if they are designed well enough to have a strong likelihood of producing an accurate answer about program effectiveness. There are cases in which programs that were presumed effective turned out not to be so after all. We have to assume that the evaluator has no evidence that Program A is better than Program B to start with because, if he or she had proof, then the evaluation would be unnecessary.

Some researchers and practitioners also think that quasi-experiments are less costly than RCTs, but this has never been proven. Poor studies, whether RCTs or quasi-experiments, are costly when they result in misleading or incorrect information, which may delay or even prevent participants from getting needed services or education.

Good quasi-experiments are difficult to plan and implement and require the highest level of research expertise. Many borrow techniques from RCTs, including blinding. Many others use sophisticated statistical methods to enhance confidence in the findings.

The most serious potential flaw in quasi-experimental designs without random assignment is that the groups in the experimental and control groups may differ from one another at baseline so that the program cannot have a fair trial. Therefore, in evaluating quasi-experiments, it is absolutely crucial to find confirmation (usually done statistically) that either no difference in groups existed to begin with or the appropriate statistical methods were used to control for the differences.

Time-Series Designs

Time-series designs are **longitudinal studies** that enable the researcher to monitor change from one time to the next. They are sometimes called *repeated measures analyses*. Debate exists over whether time-series designs are research or analytic designs.

In a simple **self-controlled design** (also called **pretest-posttest design**), each participant is measured on some important program variable and serves as his or her own control. Participants are usually measured twice (at baseline and after program participation), but they may be measured multiple times afterward as well (see Example 4.9).

Example 4.9   Pilot Test of a Cognitive-Behavioral Program for Women With Multiple Sclerosis (Sinclair & Scroggie, 2005)

Objective. The purpose of this quasi-experimental study was to evaluate the effectiveness of a cognitive-behavioral intervention for women with multiple sclerosis (MS).

Assessment for Eligibility. Thirty-seven adult women with MS participated in a group-based program titled "Beyond MS," which was led by master's-prepared psychiatric nurses.

Research Design. Perceived health competence, coping behaviors, psychological well-being, quality of life, and fatigue were measured at four time periods: 5 weeks before the beginning of the intervention, immediately before the program, at the end of the 5-week program, and at a 6-month follow-up.

Findings. There were significant improvements in the participants' perceived health competence, indices of adaptive and maladaptive coping, and most measures of psychological well-being from pretest to posttest. The positive changes brought about by this relatively brief program were maintained during the 6-month follow-up period.

Pretest-posttest designs have many disadvantages from an evidence-based practice perspective. Participants may become excited about taking part in an experiment, and this excitement may help motivate performance; without a comparison group, you cannot control for the excitement. Also, between the pretest and the posttest, participants may mature physically, emotionally, and intellectually, affecting the program's outcomes. Finally, self-controlled evaluations may be affected by historical events, including changes in program administration and policy.

Because of their limitations, self-controlled time-series designs are not considered experimental designs (some researchers call them *pre-experimental* rather than *quasi-experimental*), and they are only appropriate for pilot studies or preliminary feasibility studies. Pretest-posttest designs are not useful for evidence of effectiveness, and they are not meant to be.

Historical Controls

Some researchers make up for the lack of a readily available control group by using a **historical control**. With traditional historical controls, investigators compare outcomes among participants who receive a new program with outcomes among a previous group of participants who received the standard program. An illustration of the use of historical controls is given in Example 4.10.

Time-series designs can also be improved by adding more measurements for a single group of participants before and after the program (in a single time-series design) and adding a control (in a multiple time-series design).

Example 4.10   Historical Controls: Use and Impact of an eHealth System by Low-Income Women With Breast Cancer (Gustafson et al., 2005)

Objective. To examine the feasibility of reaching underserved women with breast cancer and determine how they use the system and what impact it had on them.

Assessment for Eligibility. Participants included women recently diagnosed with breast cancer whose income was at or below 250% of the poverty level and were living in rural Wisconsin (n = 144; all Caucasian) or Detroit (n = 85; all African American).

Evaluation Research Design. Historical Control: A comparison group of patients (n = 51) with similar demographics was drawn from a separate recently completed randomized clinical trial.

Findings. When all low-income women from this study are combined and compared with a low-income control group from another study, the Comprehensive Health Enhancement Support System [CHESS]) group was superior to that control group in 4 of 8 outcome variables at both statistically and practically significant levels (social support, negative emotions, participation in health care, and information competence). We conclude that an eHealth system like CHESS will have a positive impact on low-income women with breast cancer.

Interrupted or Single Time-Series Designs

The **interrupted** or **single time-series** design without a control group (hence, the "single") involves repeated measurement of a variable (e.g., reported crime) over time, encompassing periods both before and after implementation of a program. The goal is to evaluate whether the program has interrupted or changed a pattern established before the program's implementation. For instance, an evaluation using an interrupted times-series design may collect quarterly arrest rates for drug-related offenses in a given community for 2 years before and 2 years following the implementation of a drug enforcement task force. The data analysis would focus on changes in patterns before and after the introduction of the program. In a multiple time-series design, multiple interrupted observations are collected before and after a program is launched. The "multiple" means that the observations are collected in two or more groups.

Time-series designs are complex research designs requiring many observations of outcomes and, in the case of multiple time-series designs, the participation of many individuals and even communities. Their complex analysis has led some researchers to take the position that they are really data analytic strategies.

Observational Designs

In **observational designs**, researchers conduct studies with existing groups of people or use existing databases. They do not intervene, which is to say, they do not introduce programs. Among the observational designs that are used in evaluation research are cohorts, case controls, and cross-sectional surveys.

Cohort Designs

A **cohort** is a group of people who have something in common and who remain part of a study group over an extended period of time. In public health research, cohort studies are used to describe and predict the risk factors for a disease and the disease's cause, incidence, natural history, and prognosis. They tend to be extremely large studies.

Cohort studies may be **prospective** or **retrospective**. With a prospective design, the direction of inquiry is forward in time; with a retrospective design, the direction is backward in time.

Example 4.11 contains abstracts of two cohort studies. The first is an abstract of the National Treatment Improvement Evaluation Survey, a longitudinal study (a prospective study that takes place over several years) of a national sample of substance abuse treatment programs that had received federal treatment improvement demonstration grants in 1990–1991 (the cohort). Treatment programs and their clients across 16 states completed highly structured lay-administered interviews between July 1993 and November 1995. Administrative interviews elicited information from senior program administrators that focused on program finances and staff configuration, including the primary measure of interest and whether the program had staff designated as case managers.

The second abstract in Example 4.11 is of a study to examine detection rates of depression in primary care. The investigators used data collected from a prospective cohort study of 1,293 consecutive general practice attendees in the United Kingdom.

Example 4.11   Two Cohort Studies

---

1. Prospective Cohort Design: Case Managers as Facilitators of Medical and Psychosocial Service Delivery in Addiction Treatment Programs (Friedmann, Hendrickson, Gerstein, & Zhang, 2004)

   Objective. To examine whether having designated case management staff facilitates delivery of comprehensive medical and psychosocial services in substance abuse treatment programs.

   Assessment for Eligibility. Clients from long-term residential, outpatient, and methadone treatment modalities.

   Research Design. A prospective cohort study of 2,829 clients admitted to selected substance abuse treatment programs.

   Findings. Availability of designated case managers increased client-level receipt of only two of nine services, and exerted no effect on service comprehensiveness compared to programs that did not have designated case managers. These findings do not support the common practice of designating case management staff as a means to facilitate comprehensive services delivery in addiction treatment programs.

2. A Prospective Cohort Design: Recognition of Depression in Primary Care: Does it Affect Outcome? The PREDICT-NL Study (Kamphuis et al., 2011)

   Background. Detection rates of depression in primary care are < 50%. Studies showed similar outcome after 12 months for recognized and unrecognized depression. Outcome beyond 12 months is less well studied.

(continued)

Example 4.11 (Continued)

Objective. We investigated recognition of depression in primary care and its relation to outcome after 6, 12 and 39 months.

Methods. Data were used from a prospective cohort study of 1,293 consecutive general practice attendees (PREDICT-NL), who were followed up after 6 ($n = 1236$), 12 ($n = 1179$) and 39 ($n = 752$) months. We measured the presence and severity of major depressive disorder (MDD) according to DSM-IV criteria and Patient Health Questionnaire 9 (PHQ-9) and mental function with Short Form 12 (SF-12). Recognition of depression was assessed using international classification of primary care codes (P03 and P76) and Anatomical Therapeutic Chemical (N06A) codes from the GP records (6 months before/after baseline).

Results. At baseline, 170 (13%) of the participants had MDD, of whom 36% were recognized by their GP. The relative risk of being depressed after 39 months was 1.35 [95% confidence interval (CI) 0.7–2.7] for participants with recognized depression compared to unrecognized depression. At baseline, participants with recognized depression had more depressive symptoms (mean difference PHQ-9 2.7, 95% CI 1.6–3.9) and worse mental function (mean difference mental component summary −3.8, 95% CI −7.8 to 0.2) than unrecognized depressed participants. After 12 and 39 months, mean scores for both groups did not differ but were worse than those without depression.

Conclusions. A minority of patients with MDD is recognized in primary care. Those who were unrecognized had comparable outcome after 12 and 39 months as participants with recognized depression.

High-quality prospective or **longitudinal** studies are expensive to conduct, especially if the researcher is concerned with outcomes that are relatively rare or hard to predict. Studying rare and unpredictable outcomes requires large samples and numerous measures. Also, researchers who do prospective cohort studies have to be on guard against loss of subjects over time, or **attrition** (also called **loss to follow-up**). For instance, longitudinal studies of children are often beset by attrition because, over time, children lose interest, move far away, change their names, or are otherwise unavailable. If a large number of people drop out of a study, the sample that remains may be very different from the one that was originally enrolled. The remaining sample may be more motivated or less mobile than those who left, for example, and these factors may be related in unpredictable ways to any observed outcomes.

When reviewing prospective cohort studies, make sure that the researchers address how they handled loss to follow-up or attrition. Ask these questions: How large a problem was attrition? Were losses to follow-up handled in the analysis? Were the study's findings affected by the losses?

Because of the difficulties and expense of implementing prospective cohort designs, many cohort designs reported in the literature tend to be retrospective. Retrospective cohort designs use existing databases to identify cohorts; they may do an analysis of the data that already exist in the database or collect new data. A sample retrospective cohort design that identifies the cohort and collects new data is illustrated in Example 4.12.

Example 4.12   Retrospective Cohort Design: Tall Stature in Adolescence and Depression in Later Life (Bruinsma et al., 2006)

Objective. To examine the long-term psychosocial outcomes for women assessed or treated during adolescence for tall stature.

Assessment for Eligibility. Women assessed or treated for tall stature identified from the records of Australian pediatricians were eligible to participate.

Research Design. Retrospective cohort study in which women treated for tall stature were traced using electoral rolls and telephone listings. Once found, the women were contacted by mail and invited to complete a postal questionnaire and computer assisted telephone interview. Psychosocial outcomes were measured using the depression, mania, and eating disorders modules of the Composite International Diagnostic Interview (CIDI), the SF-36, and an index of social support.

Findings. There was no significant difference between treated and untreated women in the prevalence of 12 month or lifetime major depression, eating disorders, or scores on the SF-36 mental health summary scale or the index of social support. However, compared with the findings of population-based studies, the prevalence of major depression in both treated and untreated tall girls was high.

Retrospective cohort designs have the same strengths as prospective designs. They can establish that a predictor variable (e.g., being in a treatment program) precedes an outcome (e.g., depression). Also, because data are collected before the outcomes being assessed are known with certainty, the measurement of variables that might predict the outcome (e.g., being in a program) cannot be biased by prior knowledge of which people are likely to develop a problem (e.g., depression).

Case-Control Designs

Case-control designs are generally retrospective. They are used to explain why a phenomenon currently exists by comparing the histories of two different groups, one of which is involved in the phenomenon. For example, a case-control design might be used to help understand the social, demographic, and attitudinal variables that distinguish people who, at the present time, have been identified with frequent headaches from those who do not currently have frequent headaches. The researchers in a case-control study like this want to know which factors (e.g., dietary habits, social arrangements, education, income, quality of life) distinguish one group from the other.

The cases in case-control designs are individuals who have been chosen on the basis of some characteristic or outcome (e.g., frequent headaches). The controls are individuals without the characteristic or outcome. The histories of cases and controls are analyzed and compared in an attempt to uncover one or more characteristics that are present in the cases and not in the controls.

How can researchers avoid having one group decidedly different from the other (e.g., healthier, smarter)? Some methods include randomly selecting the controls, using several controls, and carefully matching controls and cases on important variables.

Example 4.13 uses a sophisticated sampling strategy to compare the role of alcohol use in boating deaths.

Example 4.13   Alcohol Use and Risk of Dying While Boating (Smith et al., 2001)

Objective. To determine the association of alcohol use with passengers' and operators' estimated relative risk of dying while boating.

Assessment for Eligibility. A study of recreational boating deaths among persons aged 18 years or older from 1990–1998 in Maryland and North Carolina (n = 221) provided the cases, which were compared with control interviews obtained from a multistage probability sample of boaters in each state from 1997–1999 (n = 3,943). Persons aged 18 years or older from 1990–1998 in Maryland and North Carolina (n = 221) were compared with control interviews obtained from a multistage probability sample of boaters in each state from 1997–1999 (n = 3,943).

In this study, a complex random sampling scheme was employed to minimize bias among control subjects and maximize their comparability with cases (e.g., deaths took place in the same location).

Epidemiologists often use case-control designs to provide insight into the causes and consequences of disease and other health problems. Reviewers of these studies should be on the lookout for certain methodological problems, however. First, cases and controls are often chosen from two separate populations. Because of this, systematic differences (e.g., motivation, cultural beliefs) may exist between or among the groups that are difficult to anticipate, measure, or control, and these differences may influence the study's results.

Another potential problem with case-control designs is that the data often come from people's recall of events, such as asking women to discuss the history of their physical activity or asking boaters about their drinking habits. Memory is often unreliable, so the results of a study that depends on memory may result in misleading information.

Cross-Sectional Designs

Cross-sectional designs result in a portrait of one or many groups at one period of time. They are sometimes called *descriptive* or *pre-experimental* designs. Following are three illustrative uses of cross-sectional designs

The most common use of cross-sectional designs is to describe the study sample. The tabular description of results is sometimes called Table 1 because it is often the first table in a study report or article. Example 4.14 shows an example Table 1.

Example 4.14	Sociodemographic Characteristics, Substance Abuse History, and History of Violence: Low-Income Women Seeking Emergency Care in the Bronx, NY, 2001–2003 (El-Bassel, Gilbert, Vinocur, Chang, & Wu, 2011)		
	Total (N = 241)	**Participants Not Meeting PTSD Criteria (n = 169)**	**Participants Meeting PTSD Criteria (n = 72)**
Sociodemographic characteristics			
Age, y, mean (SD)	33 (10)	33 (10)	33 (10)
Race/ethnicity, no. (%)			
Latina	119 (49)	81 (48)	38 (53)
African American	105 (44)	75 (44)	30 (42)
Other	17 (7)	13 (8)	4 (6)
High school diploma, no. (%)	127 (53)	93 (55)	34 (47)
Employed in past 6 mo., no. (%)	111 (46)	86 (51)	25* (35)
Homeless in past 6 mo., no. (%)	38 (16)	23 (14)	15 (21)

(continued)

Example 4.14 (Continued)

	Total (N = 241)	Participants Not Meeting PTSD Criteria (n = 169)	Participants Meeting PTSD Criteria (n = 72)
Substance abuse in past 6 mo., no. (%)			
Heavy episode drinking	57 (24)	30 (18)	27** (38)
Illicit drug use	104 (43)	61 (36)	43** (60)
History of violence, no. (%)			
Childhood sexual abuse (before age 16 y)	99 (41)	50 (30)	49** (68)
Lifetime sexual IPV	167 (69)	107 (63)	60** (83)
Lifetime physical or injurious IPV	165 (68)	103 (61)	62** (86)

NOTE: IPV = intimate partner violence; PTSD = posttraumatic stress disorder.

$*P < 0.05; **P < 0.01$

The major limitation of cross-sectional studies is that, on their own and without follow-up, they provide no information on causality; they only provide information on events at a single, fixed point in time. For example, suppose a researcher finds that girls have less knowledge of current events than do boys. The researcher cannot conclude that being female somehow causes less knowledge of current events. The researcher can only be sure that, in *this* survey undertaken at *this* particular time, girls had less knowledge than boys did.

To illustrate this point further, suppose you are doing a literature review on community-based exercise programs. You are specifically interested in learning about the relationship between age and exercise. Does exercise decrease with age? In your search of the literature, you find the report presented in Example 4.15.

Example 4.15   A Report of a Cross-Sectional Survey of Exercise Habits

In March of this year, Researcher A surveyed a sample of 1,500 people between the ages of 30 and 70 to find out about their exercise habits. One of the questions he asked participants was, "How much do you exercise on a typical day?" Researcher A divided his sample into two groups: People 45 years of age and younger and people 46 years and older. Researcher A's data analysis revealed that the amount of daily exercise reported by the two groups differed with the younger group reporting 15 minutes more exercise on a typical day.

Based on this summary, does amount of exercise decline with age? The answer is that you cannot get the answer from Researcher A's report. The decline seen in a cross-sectional study like this one can actually represent a decline in exercise with increasing age, or it may reflect the oddities of this particular sample. The younger people in this study may be especially sports minded, while the older people may be particularly adverse to exercise. As a reviewer, you need to figure out which of the two explanations is better. One way you can do this is to search the literature to find out which conclusions are supported by other studies. Does the literature generally sustain the idea that amount of exercise always declines with age? After all, in some communities the amount of exercise done by older people may actually increase because, with retirement or part-time work, older adults may have more time to exercise than do younger people.

Observational Designs and Controlled Trials: Compare and Contrast

Observational data can be useful adjuncts to randomized controlled trials and quasi-experiments. They can assist the researcher in determining whether effectiveness under controlled conditions translates into effective treatment in routine settings. Also, some problems simply do not lend themselves to a randomized controlled trial. For instance, when they studied the effects of cigarette smoking on health, it was impossible for researchers to randomly assign some people to smoke while assigning others to abstain. The only possible design was an observational one, albeit one that involved decades of observing hundreds of thousands of people all over the world.

The case for observational studies over RCTs is suggested in a study reported in the *British Medical Journal*:

> The investigators in the study aimed to determine whether "parachutes are effective in preventing major trauma related to gravitational challenge." To find out, they reviewed all the randomized controlled trials they could find in Medline [PubMed], Web of Science, EMBASE, and the Cochrane Library databases. They also reviewed appropriate Internet sites and citation lists. To be included, a study had to discuss the effects of using a parachute during free fall. The effects were defined as death or major trauma, defined as an injury severity score > 15.
>
> Despite their diligence and scientific approach to the review, the investigators were not able to find any randomized controlled trials of the effectiveness of parachute intervention. They concluded that as with many interventions intended to prevent ill health, the effectiveness of

parachutes has not been subjected to rigorous evaluation by using randomized controlled trials. The investigators point out that this is a serious problem for hard-line advocates of evidence-based medicine who are adamantly opposed to the adoption of interventions evaluated by using only observational data. To resolve the problem, the investigators recommend that the most radical protagonists of evidence-based medicine organize and participate in a double blind, randomized, placebo controlled, crossover trial of the parachute. They further conclude that individuals who insist that all interventions need to be validated by a randomized controlled trial need to come down to earth with a bump.

❖ THE BOTTOM LINE: INTERNAL AND EXTERNAL VALIDITY

Internal validity refers specifically to whether an experimental program makes a difference and whether there is sufficient evidence to support the claim. A study has internal validity when you can confidently say that Program A causes Outcome A. A study has **external validity** if it is **generalizable** because its results are applicable to other programs, populations, and settings.

Internal Validity Is Threatened

Just as the best-laid plans of mice and men (and women) often go awry, evaluation research no matter how well planned loses something in the execution. Randomization may not produce equivalent study groups, for example, or people in one study group may drop out more often than will people in the other. Factors such as less-than-perfect randomization and attrition can threaten or compromise an evaluation's validity. There are at least eight common threats to internal validity.

1. **Selection of participants.** This threat occurs when biases result from the selection or creation of groups that are not equivalent. Either the random assignment did not work or attempts to match groups or control for baseline confounders were ineffective. As a result, groups can be distinguished by being more affected by a given policy, more mature, and more affected by differential administration and content of the baseline and postprogram measures. Selection can interact with history, maturation, and instrumentation.

2. **History.** Unanticipated events occur while the evaluation is in progress, and this history jeopardizes internal validity. A change in policy

or a historical event may affect participants' behavior while they are in the program. For instance, the effects of a school-based program to encourage healthier eating may be affected by a healthy eating campaign on a popular children's television show.

3. **Maturation.** Processes (e.g., physical and emotional growth) occur within participants inevitably as a function of time, threatening validity. Children in a 3-year school-based physical education program mature physically, for example.

4. **Testing.** This threat can occur because taking one test has an effect on the scores of a subsequent test. For instance, after a 3-week program, participants are given a test. They recall their answers on the pretest, and this influences their responses to the second test. The influence may be positive (they learn from the test) or negative (they recall incorrect answers).

5. **Instrumentation.** Changes in a measuring instrument or changes in observers or scorers cause an effect that can diminish validity. For example, Researcher A makes slight changes between the questions asked at baseline and those asked after the conclusion of the program. Or Researcher B administers the baseline measures, but Researcher A administers the posttest measures.

6. **Statistical regression**. This effect operates when participants are selected on the basis of extreme scores and regress or go back toward the mean (e.g., average score) of that variable. Only people at great risk are included in the program, for example. Some of them inevitably regress to the mean or average score. Regression to the mean is a statistical artifact (i.e., due to some factor or factors outside of the study).

7. **Attrition (dropout)** or **loss to follow-up.** This threat to internal validity is the differential loss of participants from one or more groups on a nonrandom basis. For instance, participants in one group drop out more frequently than do participants in the others or are lost to follow-up. The resulting two groups, which had similar characteristics at baseline, no longer do.

8. **Expectancy.** A bias is caused by the expectations of the evaluator, the participants, or both. Participants in the experimental group expect special treatment, for example, while the evaluator expects to give it to them (and sometimes does). Blinding is one method of dealing with expectancy. A second is to ensure that a standardized process is used in delivering the program.

External Validity Is Threatened

Threats to external validity are most often the consequence of the way in which participants or respondents are selected and assigned. For example, respondents in an experimental situation may answer questions atypically because they know they are in a special experiment; this is called the **Hawthorne effect**. External validity is also threatened whenever respondents are tested, surveyed, or observed. They may become alert to the kinds of behaviors that are expected or favored. There are at least four relatively common sources of external invalidity.

1. **Interaction effects of selection biases and the experimental treatment.** This threat to external validity occurs when an intervention or program and the participants are a unique mixture, one that may not be found elsewhere. The threat is most apparent when groups are not randomly constituted. Suppose a large company volunteers to participate in an experimental program to improve the quality of employees' leisure time activities. The characteristics of the company (some of which, like leadership and priorities, are related to the fact that it volunteered for the experiment) may interact with the program so that the two together are unique; the particular blend of company and program can limit the applicability of the findings.

2. **Reactive effects of testing.** These biases occur when a baseline measure interacts with the program, resulting in an effect that will not generalize. For example, two groups of students participate in an ethics program evaluation. Group 1 is given a test before watching a film, but Group 2 just watches the film. Group 1 performs better on a posttest because the pretest sensitizes them to the program's content, and they pay more attention to the film's content.

3. **Reactive effects of experimental arrangements** or **the Hawthorne effect.** This threat to external validity can occur because participants know that they are participating in an experiment. This threat is caused when people behave uncharacteristically because they are aware that their circumstances are different. (They are being observed by cameras in the classroom, for instance, or they have been chosen for an experiment.)

4. **Multiple program interference.** This threat results when participants are in other complementary activities or programs that interact. For example, participants in an experimental mathematics program are also taking physics class. Both teach differential calculus.

External validity is dependent upon internal validity. Research findings cannot be generalized to other populations and settings unless we first know if these findings are due to the program or to other factors.

Randomized controlled trials with double blinding have the greatest chance of being internally valid—assuming that their data collection and analysis are also valid. As soon as the researcher begins to deviate from the strict rules of an RCT, threats to internal validity begin to appear. Example 4.16 illustrates a sample of the threats to internal and external validity found in evaluation reports.

Example 4.16   Threats to Internal and External Validity: Reducing Confidence in the Evidence of the Effectiveness of Four Programs

---

1. Evaluating a Health Care Program to Get Adolescents to Exercise (Patrick et al., 2006)

An additional concern in interpreting results is the potential impact on our findings of measurement reactivity in which self-reported behavior is influenced by the measurement process itself. Repeated assessments of the target behaviors as well as extensive surveys on thoughts and actions used to change behaviors (not described in this article) could have motivated and even instructed adolescents in both conditions to change behaviors, and control participants reported improvements in several diet and physical activity behaviors [reactive effects of testing]. Measurement effects have been demonstrated in studies promoting physical activity through primary care settings, and this also may occur with diet assessment.

2. Evaluating a Mental Health Intervention for Schoolchildren Exposed to Violence: A Randomized Controlled Trial (Stein et al., 2003)

The CBITS [Cognitive Behavioral Intervention for Trauma in Schools] intervention was not compared with a control condition such as general supportive therapy, but rather with a wait-list delayed intervention. As a consequence, none of the informants (students, parents, or teachers) were blinded to the treatment condition. It is possible that the lack of blinding [expectancy] may have contaminated either the intervention or assessments. School staff and parents may have provided more attention and support to students who were eligible for the program while they were on a waiting list; alternatively, respondents may have been more likely to report improvement in symptoms for those students whom they knew had received the intervention.

3. HIV-Risk-Reduction Intervention Among Low-Income Latina Women (Peragallo et al., 2005)

Individuals lost to follow-up (n = 112) differed from those who received at least one session of the intervention (n = 292) [attrition, generalizability] with respect to age (younger), ethnicity (Puerto Rican), years in the United States (slightly more years in United States), education (completed 1 more year), marital status (less likely to be married), insurance source (more likely to have insurance), and acculturation (more non-Hispanic acculturation) [selection].

(continued)

Example 4.16 (Continued)

4. Tall Stature in Adolescence and Depression in Later Life (Bruinsma et al., 2006)

Another possibility is that the assessment or treatment procedures predisposed women to depression either because it medicalized the issue of their height or because of the intrusiveness of the assessment and treatment [reactive effects of testing and of experimental arrangements] and its effect on adolescent girls. In this study, there was evidence that women who reported a negative experience of assessment or treatment procedures were significantly more likely to have a history of depression than women who did not, which is consistent with other studies.

A high-quality research article will always describe threats to its validity, sometimes called *limitations*, in the discussion or conclusions section.

The following checklist consists of questions to ask when evaluating a study's internal and external validity.

What Evidence-Based Public Health Practice Should Watch For: A Checklist for Evaluating a Study's Internal and External Validity

✓ If the research has two or more groups, is information given on the number of people in each group who were eligible to participate?

✓ If the research has two or more groups, is information given on the number in each group who agreed to participate?

✓ If the research has two or more groups, is information given on the number in each group who were assigned to groups?

✓ If the research has two or more groups, is information given on the number in each group who completed all of the program's activities?

✓ Were reasons given for refusal to participate among participants (including personnel)?

✓ Were reasons given for not completing all program or data collection activities?

✓ Did any historical or political event occur during the course of the study that may have affected its findings?

✓ In long-term studies, was information given on the potential effects on outcomes of physical, intellectual, and emotional changes among participants?

✓ Was information provided on concurrently running programs that might have influenced the outcomes?

✓ Was there reason to believe that taking a preprogram measurement affected participants' performance on a postprogram measurement?

This problem might arise in evaluations of programs that take a few weeks or require only a few sessions.

✓ Was there reason to believe that changes in measures or observers may have affected the outcomes?

✓ Did the researchers provide information on whether observers or people administering the measures (e.g., tests, surveys) were trained and monitored for quality?

✓ If participants were chosen because of special needs, did the researchers discuss how they dealt with regression toward the mean?

✓ Did the researchers provide information on how staff ensured that the program was delivered in a standardized manner?

✓ Were participants or researchers blinded to the intervention? If not, did the researchers provide information on how the outcomes were affected?

THE PROBLEM OF INCOMPARABLE PARTICIPANTS: ❖ STATISTICAL METHODS TO THE RESCUE

Randomization is designed to reduce disparities between experimental and control groups by balancing them with respect to all characteristics (e.g., participants' age, sex, or motivation) that might affect a study's outcome. With effective randomization, the only difference between study groups is whether or not they are assigned to receive an experimental program. The idea is that, if discrepancies in outcomes are subsequently found by statistical comparisons (e.g., the experimental group improves significantly), they can be attributed to the fact that some people received the experiment while others did not.

In observational and nonrandomized studies, the researcher cannot assume that the groups are balanced before they receive (or do not receive) a program or intervention. In observational studies, for example, measured participant characteristics are obtained before, during, and after program participation, and it is often difficult to determine exactly which characteristics are baseline variables. Also, there frequently are unmeasured characteristics that are not available, inadequately measured, or unknown. But if the participants are different, then how can the evaluator who finds a difference between experimental and control outcomes separate the effects of the intervention from differences in study participants? One answer is to consider taking care of potential confounders during the data analysis phase using statistical methods such as analysis of covariance and propensity score methods.

Analysis of Covariance

Analysis of covariance (ANCOVA) is a statistical procedure that results in estimates of intervention or program effects adjusted for participants' background (and potentially confounding) characteristics or **covariates** (e.g., age, gender, educational background, severity of illness, type of illness, motivation). The covariates are included explicitly in a statistical model.

Analysis of covariance adjusts for the confounder by assuming (statistically) that all participants are equally affected by the same confounder, say, age. That is, the ANCOVA can provide an answer to this question: If you balance the ages of the participants in the experimental and control groups so that age has no influence on one group versus the others, how do the experimental and control groups compare? The ANCOVA removes age as a possible confounder at baseline.

The choice of covariates to include in the analysis comes from the literature, preliminary analysis of study data, and expert opinion on which characteristics of participants might influence their willingness to participate in and benefit from study inclusion.

Example 4.17 illustrates the use of ANCOVA in a study **protocol** or plan to improve work task performance in young adults with Down syndrome.

Example 4.17   Excerpt From Study Protocol of a Randomised Controlled Trial to Investigate if a Community-Based Strength Training Programme Improves Work Task Performance in Young Adults With Down Syndrome

---

Aim. The aim of this study is to investigate if a student-led community-based progressive resistance training programme can improve these outcomes in adolescents and young adults with Down syndrome.

Methods. A randomised controlled trial will compare progressive resistance training with a control group undertaking a social programme. Seventy adolescents and young adults with Down syndrome aged 14–22 years and mild to moderate intellectual disability will be randomly allocated to the intervention or control group using a concealed method.

The intervention group will complete a 10-week, twice a week, student-led progressive resistance training programme at a local community gymnasium. The student mentors will be undergraduate physiotherapy students. The control group will complete an arts/social programme with a student mentor once a week for 90 minutes also for 10 weeks to control for the social aspect of the intervention.

Work task performance (box stacking, pail carry), muscle strength (1 repetition maximum for chest and leg press) and physical activity (frequency, duration, intensity over 7 days) will be assessed at baseline (Week 0), following the intervention (Week 11), and at 3 months post intervention (Week 24) by an assessor blind to group allocation.

Data will be analysed using ANCOVA with the baseline score added as the covariate with an alpha level of .05. Separate ANCOVAs will be completed to determine if the intervention group improved more than the control group at the end of training (at Week 11), and to determine if the intervention group had improved more than the control group after training had stopped for 3 months (at Week 24). The mean difference within group and the mean difference between groups and the associated 95% confidence intervals will also be calculated.

SOURCE: Shields, N., Taylor, N., & Fernhall, B. (2010). A study protocol of a randomized controlled trial to investigate if a community based strength training programme improves work task performance in young adults with Down syndrome. *BMC Pediatrics, 10*(1), 17.

Propensity Score Methods

The propensity score for an individual is the probability of being given the experimental intervention or program depending upon the individual's background characteristics. Put another way, the propensity score is a measure of the likelihood that an individual would have been given the experimental program based on his or her background characteristics. Mathematically, the propensity score is the probability (between 0 and 1) that a participant is in the experimental group given his or her background characteristics.

A propensity score is frequently estimated by using logistic regression in which the experimental program variable (e.g., participated yes or no) is the outcome, and the background characteristics (e.g.,15 years of age and under, 16 years and older), not the study outcomes (e.g., improved workplace literacy, better quality of life), are the independent or predictor variables in the model. The model would then include age as a predictor of participation. For example, a propensity score analysis could be used to find out if participants who are 15 years of age and under are more or less likely to be in the experimental program than participants who are 16 years and older.

The goal of a **propensity score analysis** is to create subgroups of study participants who are similar across a broad range of confounding variables or covariates and then to test the program effect within those groups. That is, within homogenous subgroups (e.g., all older participants, all teens at risk for school dropout) the evaluator compares the outcomes of those who did and did not receive the program. For example, using a propensity score analysis, the evaluator of a school dropout prevention program's effectiveness could compare the dropout rate among high-risk students who participated in the program with the rate of high-risk students who did not.

The advantage of the technique is that the evaluator can include all relevant covariates, no matter how many are identified. Unfortunately, identifying the covariates is not always easy because although it is axiomatic that there are always many of them, no one knows exactly how many and what they are.

An example of the use of propensity score analysis is given in Example 4.18.

Example 4.18   Evaluating SAFE Homes for Children With the Help of Propensity Score Analysis (DeSena et al., 2005)

Objective. To evaluate the SAFE Homes (SH) program, a short-term group care program for children between 3 and 12 years of age who enter care for the first time. The program aims to improve case outcomes by consolidating resources to facilitate assessment and treatment planning.

Assessment for Eligibility. Children were included in the sample if (a) the removal was the first placement for the child; (b) they entered out-of-home care between the dates (inclusive) of April 1, 1999, and December 31, 2000; and (c) they were between the ages of 3 and 12 years old at the time of entry into care. Children were excluded from the sample if (a) their case record was incomplete; (b) access to the case record was denied for security reasons because the case involved relatives of department employees; or (c) foster care children (FC) had siblings that had previously gone through SH services in another community.

Evaluation Research Design. Propensity score matching to control for hidden bias in treatment group assignment. The one-year outcomes of 342 children who received SAFE Home services and 342 matched foster care (FC) control children were compared. The 684 subjects were selected from a larger pool of 909 subjects using propensity score matching. An original cohort of 909 subjects was divided into five groups according to propensity score quintile to create five groups of subjects with similar risk and maltreatment history profiles. When there was an excess of children from one group included in a quintile, subjects from the other group were randomly removed so that the final sample included an equal number of SH and FC cases in each quintile. This resulted in a reduction of the original cohort of 909 to a sample of 684 propensity score matched subjects, with the two groups now statistically indistinguishable on each of the 16 case characteristics included in the propensity score.

Findings. Prior to the initiation of the SAFE Homes program, 75% of the children who entered care in the state experienced three or more placements in the first year. The outcomes of both the SH and FC cases were significantly improved over pre–SAFE Home state statistics. The FC group, however, had comparable or better outcomes on most variables examined. In addition, the total cost for out-of-home care for the children in FC was significantly less, despite the fact that the two groups spent similar amounts of time in care (average time in care: 7 months).

As a rule, it is better for researchers to account for confounders when they are designing the study than to wait until after the study is complete and they are doing the statistical analysis. For instance, researchers can use matching techniques (described earlier) to create groups. Of course, matching has problems, too, including difficulties in finding matches. Unfortunately, however, statistical methods such as ANCOVA may not be the answer to the problem of confounders either; studies have shown that these methods may not be able to remove all the confounders adequately.

SUMMARY OF CHAPTER 4: RESEARCH DESIGN, VALIDITY, AND BEST AVAILABLE EVIDENCE

Words to Remember

analysis of covariance, ANCOVA, attrition, baseline, blinding, blocked randomization, case-control study, cluster, cohort, concurrent controls, confounding variables, control group, covariates, cross-sectional, dependent variable, evaluation research design, experimental design, experimental group, external validity, factor, factorial designs, Hawthorne effect, historical analysis, independent variable, instrumentation, interactive effects of selection bias, internal validity, interrupted time-series design, longitudinal, loss to follow-up, matching, multiple program interference, nonrandomized controlled trials, outcomes, posttest, power, predictor, pretest, pretest-posttest design, propensity score, prospective, quasi-experimental design, random allocation, random assignment, randomization, randomized controlled trial, RCT, reactive effects of experimental arrangements, reactive effects of testing, retrospective, statistical regression, stratified blocked randomization, summative evaluation, threats to internal and external validity, time-series design, true experiments, wait-list controls

Randomized controlled trials can provide evidence that programs cause results. Strict rules regarding randomization and blinding must be followed. When using quasi-experimental design, the research must provide evidence that participating groups do not differ before program implementation. Statistical methods (e.g., propensity score analysis) may help to compensate for the inability to randomize. Observational designs are sometimes used to provide information on events that have already occurred (e.g., retrospective cohorts) and on current status (e.g., prospective cohorts). A study must be internally valid to be generalizable or externally valid.

THE NEXT CHAPTER

Chapter 5 covers the methods researchers use to collect information on participants and outcomes. These methods include surveys, record reviews, and physical examinations. The chapter also discusses what the public health practitioner needs to watch out for in studies that use each of these measures and how to assess the data collection's reliability and validity.

EXERCISES

1 Find the following two articles. For each one, describe the main objective, describe how participants were assessed for inclusion and exclusion, name the evaluation research design, and briefly summarize the findings.

   a. Guo, J. J., Jang, R., Keller, K. N., McCracken, A. L., Pan, W., & Cluxton, R. J. (2005). Impact of school-based health centers on children with asthma. *Journal of Adolescent Health*, *37*, 266–274.

   b. Linde, K., Streng, A., Jurgens, S., Hoppe, A., Brinkhaus, B., Witt, C., et al. (2005). Acupuncture for patients with migraine: A randomized controlled trial. *Journal of the American Medical Association*, *293*, 2118–2125.

Answer:

   a. Impact of School-Based Health Centers on Children With Asthma

   Objective. To assess the impact of school-based health centers (SBHCs) on hospitalization and emergency department (ED) visits for children with asthma.

   Assessment for Eligibility. Children with asthma with at least two years of continuous enrollment who had medical claims for asthma diagnosis and anti-asthmatic medications were selected. Two comparison (non-SBHC) school districts (six schools) were selected to reflect students with similar characteristics to those in SBHC schools based on Ohio census data from local education departments, including information on rural/urban setting, percentage of student body that was nonwhite, and percentage of students eligible for free or reduced-price lunch.

   Evaluation Research Design. The study was conducted at four SBHC intervention school districts and two comparable non-SBHC school districts in Greater Cincinnati, Ohio. A longitudinal, quasi-experimental, time-series repeated measures design was used.

   Findings. Asthma was one of the major diseases for SBHC encounters. After the opening of the SBHC, relative risks of hospitalization and ED visits in the SBHC group decreased. The cost of hospitalization per child decreased significantly over time for children in SBHC schools. Costs of ED visits for children in SBHC schools were significantly lower than for children in non-SBHC schools.

   b. Acupuncture for Patients With Migraine: A Randomized Controlled Trial

   Objective. To investigate the effectiveness of acupuncture compared with sham acupuncture and with no acupuncture in patients with migraine.

   Assessment for Eligibility. Patients with migraine headaches (based on International Headache Society criteria) who were treated at 18 outpatients centers in Germany over a nine-month period.

   Evaluation Research Design. Three-group, randomized controlled trial with patients participating in one of three programs: acupuncture, sham acupuncture, or waiting-list control.

Results. Between baseline and weeks 9 to 12, the mean number of days with headache of moderate or severe intensity decreased by 2.2 days from a baseline of 5.2 days in the acupuncture group compared with a decrease to 2.2 days from a baseline of 5.0 days in the sham acupuncture group, and by 0.8 days from a baseline of 5.4 days in the waiting list group. No difference was detected between the acupuncture and the sham acupuncture groups, while there was a difference between the acupuncture group compared with the waiting list group. Acupuncture was no more effective than sham acupuncture in reducing migraine headaches although both interventions were more effective than a waiting list control.

2. Read the following baseline information, and write a paragraph describing the findings:

Baseline Characteristics of Smokeless Tobacco (ST) Users by Group

	Control (*N* = 166)		Intervention (*N* = 141)	
	n	%	*n*	%
Years in high school				
Senior	46	27.7	41	29.1
Junior	57	34.3	57	40.4
Sophomore	48	28.9	24	17.0
Freshman	15	9.0	19	13.5
Smoking status				
Current	20	12.1	15	10.7
Former	33	20.0	28	20.0
Never	112	67.9	97	69.3
Confidence in ability to quit				
None/a little	65	39.4	49	35.5
Somewhat	27	16.4	31	22.5
Very	73	44.2	58	42.0
Frequency of ST use				
Daily	77	46.4	54	39.1
Weekly	56	33.7	45	32.6
Monthly	33	19.9	39	28.3

(Continued)

uncommon) problem. Invalid measures do harm to any study no matter how carefully it is designed. That is, a brilliantly designed randomized controlled trial with an invalid test or other measure will produce inaccurate results.

4. Describe the advantages and limitations of these commonly used research designs:
   - Randomized controlled trials with concurrent and wait-list control groups
   - Quasi-experimental or nonrandomized designs with concurrent control groups
   - Time-series designs
   - Observational designs, including cohorts, case controls, and cross-sectional surveys

   Answer:

   RCTs and wait-list controls guard against most biases. They produce the most internally and externally valid results. In their purest forms, they may be somewhat complex to implement. It is often difficult, if not impossible, to blind evaluation participants, for example.

   Quasi-experimental designs are often more realistic designs for clinical and other real-world settings. However, preexisting differences in groups may interfere with the results so that you cannot be certain whether group differences or programs are responsible for outcomes.

   Time-series designs can provide (or refute) evidence of impact. However, their implementation requires a justifiable and often relatively long period of time for outcomes to be visible.

   Observational designs are convenient because the researcher does not have to develop and implement a research protocol—complicated activities, to say the least. At the same time, the researcher may have little control over data collection or the assignment of participants.

5. List the covariates reported in the excerpts taken from this study.

   The Effectiveness of a Community-Based Intervention for Parents to Help Reduce Conduct Problems in Clinically Referred Children (Gardner et al., 2006)

   Design. Randomised controlled trial, follow-up at 6, 18 months, assessors blind to treatment status.

   Participants. 76 children referred for conduct problems, aged 2–9, primarily low-income families, randomised to treatment vs. 6-month wait-list group. Retention was 93% at 6 months, 90% at 18 months.

   Interventions. Webster-Stratton Incredible Years video-based 14-week group programme, teaches cognitive-behavioural principles for managing behaviour, using a collaborative, practical, problem-solving approach.

   Primary Outcomes. Child problem behaviour by parent-report and home-based direct observation; secondary outcomes include observed positive and negative parenting; parent-reported parenting skill, confidence, and depression.

   Analysis. *T*-tests for continuous, and chi-sq for categorical, variables revealed no significant differences between groups at baseline on demographic factors, parent-reported parenting skills, depression, or child behaviour problems. However, since there was some variation between groups, particularly on observational measures, we controlled for baseline scores when analysing intervention effects, using ANCOVA, with baseline scores as covariates for each corresponding post-intervention score.

Answer:

The covariates are the baseline scores on the primary outcome measures: (1) child problem behavior and (2) positive and negative parenting skill, confidence, and depression.

6. List the variables used in the propensity score analysis discussed in the excerpts from the following research report.

A Propensity Score Analysis of Brief Worksite Crisis Interventions After the World Trade Center Disaster (WTCD): Implications for Intervention and Research (Boscarino, Adams, Foa, & Landrigan, 2006)

Because our study was a population-based observational design, we statistically controlled for selection bias as the result of observable factors by matching intervention cases to controls using a propensity score method. In this study, variables for the propensity score were those potentially related to receiving worksite interventions and included demographic factors, exposure to WTCD events, residential location, treatment history, etc. . . . To control for potential bias, study matching variables in our study included age, gender, marital status, level of education, household income, race/ethnicity, immigrant status, language spoken, borough of residence, exposure to WTCD events, history of mental health treatment, history of depression, and having experienced a peri-event panic (PEP) attack during the WTCD.

Answer:

The variables used in the propensity score analysis were as follows: age, gender, marital status, level of education, household income, race/ethnicity, immigrant status, language spoken, borough of residence, exposure to WTCD events, history of mental health treatment, history of depression, and having experienced a peri-event panic attack during the WTCD.

REFERENCES

Boscarino, J. A., Adams, R. E., Foa, E. B., & Landrigan, P. J. (2006). A propensity score analysis of brief worksite crisis interventions after the World Trade Center disaster: Implications for intervention and research. *Medical Care, 44*, 454–462.

Bruinsma, F. J., Venn, A. J., Patton, G. C., Rayner, J. A., Pyett, P., Werther, G., et al. (2006). Concern about tall stature during adolescence and depression in later life. *Journal of Affective Disorders, 91*, 145–152.

Buchanan, D., Doblin, B., Sai, T., & Garcia, P. (2006). The effects of respite care for homeless patients: A cohort study. *American Journal of Public Health, 96*, 1278–1281.

DeSena, A. D., Murphy, R. A., Douglas-Palumberi, H., Blau, G., Kelly, B., Horwitz, S. M., et al. (2005). SAFE Homes: Is it worth the cost? An evaluation of a group home permanency planning program for children who first enter out-of-home care. *Child Abuse & Neglect, 29*, 627–643.

Dolan, K. A., Shearer, J., MacDonald, M., Mattick, R. P., Hall, W., & Wodak, A. D. (2003). A randomised controlled trial of methadone maintenance treatment versus wait list control in an Australian prison system. *Drug and Alcohol Dependence, 72*, 59–65.

El-Bassel, N., Gilbert, L., Vinocur, D., Chang, M., & Wu, E. (2011). Posttraumatic stress disorder and HIV risk among poor, inner-city women receiving care in an emergency department. *American Journal of Public Health, 101*, 120–127.

Felix, L. M., Burchett, H. E., & Edwards, P. J. (2011). Factorial trial found mixed evidence of effects of pre-notification and pleading on response to Web-based survey. *Journal of Clinical Epidemiology*, *64*, 531–536.

Friedmann, P. D., Hendrickson, J. C., Gerstein, D. R., & Zhang, Z. W. (2004). Designated case managers as facilitators of medical and psychosocial service delivery in addiction treatment programs. *Journal of Behavioral Health Services & Research*, *31*, 86–97.

Gardner, F., Burton, J., & Klimes, I. (2006). Randomised controlled trial of a parenting intervention in the voluntary sector for reducing child conduct problems: Outcomes and mechanisms of change. *Journal of Child Psychology and Psychiatry*, *47*, 1123–1132.

Guo, J. J., Jang, R., Keller, K. N., McCracken, A. L., Pan, W., & Cluxton, R. J. (2005). Impact of school-based health centers on children with asthma. *Journal of Adolescent Health*, *37*, 266–274.

Gustafson, D. H., McTavish, F. M., Stengle, W., Ballard, D., Hawkins, R., Shaw, B. R., et al. (2005). Use and impact of eHealth system by low-income women with breast cancer. *Journal of Health Communication*, *10*(Suppl 1), 195–218.

Ha, B. T. T., Jayasuriya, R., & Owen, N. (2005). Increasing male involvement in family planning decision making: Trial of a social-cognitive intervention in rural Vietnam. *Health Education Research*, *20*, 548–556.

Kamphuis, M. H., Stegenga, B. T., Zuithoff, N. P. A., King, M., Nazareth, I., de Wit, N. J., et al. (2011). Recognition of depression in primary care: Does it affect outcome? The PREDICT-NL study. *Family Practice*. Advance online publication. doi:10.1093/fampra/cmr049

Linde, K., Streng, A., Jurgens, S., Hoppe, A., Brinkhaus, B., Witt, C., et al. (2005). Acupuncture for patients with migraine: A randomized controlled trial. *Journal of the American Medical Association*, *293*, 2118–2125.

MacMillan, H. L., Thomas, B. H., Jamieson, E., Walsh, C. A., Boyle, M. H., Shannon, H. S., et al. (2005). Effectiveness of home visitation by public-health nurses in prevention of the recurrence of child physical abuse and neglect: A randomised controlled trial. *Lancet*, *365*, 1786–1793.

Montgomery, P., Stores, G., & Wiggs, L. (2004). The relative efficacy of two brief treatments for sleep problems in young learning disabled (mentally retarded) children: A randomised controlled trial. *Archives of Disease in Childhood*, *89*, 125–130.

Nickel, M. K., Nickel, C., Lahmann, C., Mitterlehner, F. O., Tritt, K., Leiberich, P. K., et al. (2005). Recovering the ability to function socially in elderly depressed patients: A prospective, controlled trial. *Archives of Gerontology and Geriatrics*, *41*, 41–49.

Patrick, K., Calfas, K. J., Norman, G. J., Zabinski, M. F., Sallis, J. F., Rupp, J., et al. (2006). Randomized controlled trial of a primary care and home-based intervention for physical activity and nutrition behaviors: PACE+ for adolescents. *Archives of Pediatrics and Adolescent Medicine*, *160*, 128–136.

Peragallo, N., Deforge, B., O'Campo, P., Lee, S. M., Kim, Y. J., Cianelli, R., et al. (2005). A randomized clinical trial of an HIV-risk-reduction intervention among low-income Latina women. *Nursing Research*, *54*, 108–118.

Reed, D. B., & Kidd, P. S. (2004). Collaboration between nurses and agricultural teachers to prevent adolescent agricultural injuries: The agricultural disability awareness and risk education model. *Public Health Nursing*, *21*, 323–330.

Sinclair, V. G., & Scroggie, J. (2005). Effects of a cognitive-behavioral program for women with multiple sclerosis. *Journal of Neuroscience Nursing*, *37*, 249–257, 276.

Smith, G. S., Keyl, P. M., Hadley, J. A., Bartley, C. L., Foss, R. D., Tolbert, W. G., et al. (2001). Drinking and recreational boating fatalities: A population-based case-control study. *Journal of the American Medical Association, 286,* 2974–2980.

Smith, G. S., & Pell, J. P. (2003). Parachute use to prevent death and major trauma related to gravitational challenge: Systematic review of randomised controlled trials. *British Medical Journal, 327,* 1459–1461.

Stein, B. D., Jaycox, L. H., Kataoka, S. H., Wong, M., Tu, W., Elliott, M. N., et al. (2003). A mental health intervention for schoolchildren exposed to violence: A randomized controlled trial. *Journal of the American Medical Association, 290,* 603–611.

Walsh, M. M., Hilton, J. F., Masouredis, C. M., Gee, L., Chesney, M. A., & Ernster, V. L. (1999). Smokeless tobacco cessation intervention for college athletes: Results after 1 year. *American Journal of Public Health, 89,* 228–234.

Zun, L. S., Downey, L., & Rosen, J. (2006). The effectiveness of an ED-based violence prevention program. *American Journal of Emergency Medicine, 24,* 8–13.

CHAPTER 5

WANTED! VALID AND MEANINGFUL DATA AS PROOF OF BEST AVAILABLE EVIDENCE

The best available evidence comes from reliable and valid data. This chapter discusses the data collection methods typically used in studies of program effectiveness and describes methods for assessing their reliability and validity. The chapter also gives suggestions on how to evaluate the methods researchers use to improve their study's validity in case of incomplete or missing data and to distinguish between statistical and practical significance.

Valid measures should accurately reflect community or population-based health care needs and beliefs. Researchers often use health behavior change models to guide program development and the choice of variables to measure about program effectiveness. Health behavior change models provide a framework for understanding which variables need to be influenced in order to get people to modify their health habits. There is no guarantee that the models researchers choose accurately reflect a given community's values or behavior, and what works in one community may not be appropriate in another. This chapter discusses the foundations of commonly used health behavior change models, such as the Health Belief Model, Social Cognitive Theory, and the Socio-Ecological Model.

Example 5.1 (Continued)

Well-Being at School

Students' well-being at school was measured with items that were initially developed by the Finnish National Board of Education (Metsämuuronen & Svedlin, 2004), including general liking of school (e.g., "My school days are generally nice"), academic self-concept (e.g., "Learning brings me joy"), classroom climate (e.g., "There is a good climate in our class"), and school climate (e.g., "I feel safe at school"). Students responded to 14 items on a 5-point scale (0 = I disagree completely, 4 = I agree completely). All items loaded highly on one factor and thus were combined into one scale by averaging the item scores (Cronbach's $\alpha = .88$).

2. Obesity Prevention in African American Girls (Klesges et al., 2010)

Objective. To determine the efficacy of a 2-year obesity prevention program in African American girls.

Selected Measures
Anthropometric, Bioelectrical Impedance, and Sexual Maturation Measurements

Height, weight, and waist circumference were measured twice while girls were barefoot and wore lightweight clothing. A stadiometer (Shorr Productions, Olney, Maryland) and electronic scale (model 5602; Scale-Tronix, White Plains, New York) were used to measure height and weight, respectively. Waist circumference was measured at the level of the umbilicus at end expiration with a physician's tape measure (Moore Medical, Farmington, Connecticut). The BMI percentiles were calculated using the Centers for Disease Control and Prevention growth charts. Three measurements of triceps skinfold thickness were obtained (Harpenden Skinfold Caliper, model C-136; Creative Health Products, Inc, Plymouth, Michigan). The mean of all measurements was determined.

Dietary Assessment

Trained interviewers obtained 24-hour dietary recall information (Nutrition Data System for Research, version 4.05-33; University of Minnesota, Minneapolis) on 3 nonconsecutive days (including 1 weekend day) and analyzed the information according to 3-day means. The first 24-hour recall occurred face to face, and the subsequent 2 recalls were conducted by telephone. Standardized methods were used, and quality control procedures included a multiple-pass approach and probes.

Physical Activity Monitoring

A validated accelerometer (Actigraph version 2.2; Manufacturing Technologies Inc, Pensacola, Florida) was used to assess physical activity for 3 consecutive days, typically including 1 weekend day; the mean of these measurements was determined. The number of minutes spent in moderate to vigorous physical activity was calculated, defined as 3000 counts or more per minute.

Data collection or measurement has two main components. The first is the form the measure takes, such as interviews with research participants or use of an accelerometer to assess physical activity for 3 days. The second measurement component is the validity of the collected information. A measure will produce inaccurate information if it is not appropriate (difficult to access or read), difficult to administer (instructions are unclear), or poorly constructed (program will not let participants move from one screen to the other without a special code).

Self-Administered Survey Questionnaires

Self-administered survey questionnaires are among the most commonly used of all measurement formats. They ask participants to answer questions or respond to **items** in writing (paper and pencil) or online. Some paper-and-pencil surveys are mailed to participants, and others are completed on site (e.g., at a clinic or school).

Survey questionnaire items may be **open-ended**, enabling the **respondent** to give the answer in her or his own words (Example 5.2).

Example 5.2   Open-Ended Question: Respondents Answer in Their Own Words

---

How courteous are the people who answer the telephone?

Survey items may take the form of statements or questions that give respondents choices for their answers (Example 5.3). This survey item type is referred to as **forced-choice** or multiple-choice.

Example 5.3   Closed Question: Respondents Reply to a Set of Choices

---

The people who answer the phone are courteous.

Circle one choice

Definitely agree	1
Agree	2
Disagree	3
Definitely disagree	4

- Tests are the often the best method of measuring knowledge.
- Multiple-choice tests are relatively easy to score and interpret.

What Evidence-Based Public Health Practice Should Watch For

- Multiple-choice tests are not appropriate for measuring higher levels of knowledge, understanding, attitudes and values, actual behavior, or skills.
- Not all programs are geared to standardized tests or existing measures. Developing new questions requires skill and costs money.
- Each test question must be carefully tested to ensure that it measures the concept it is supposed to measure. Some test questions measure ability to read rather than ability to reason thoughtfully about the correct answer.
- Some people are philosophically opposed to multiple-choice tests because they believe that they are misused and that they measure superficial knowledge. These people may refuse to answer some or all questions.
- Multiple-choice achievement tests are designed to measure knowledge. The relationship of improved knowledge to desirable changes in attitudes and behavior is far from linear.

Record Reviews

Record reviews are analyses of an individual's documented behavior. The documentation may be in print, online, or in audio or video form.

Records come in two types. The first consists of those that are already in place (e.g., a medical record). The second form of record is one that the researcher may ask participants to develop specifically for a given program. For example, an evaluator of a nutrition education program may ask participants to keep a diary of how much food they consumed over a 1-month period after they have completed their study participation.

Researchers also use data from existing records because doing so reduces the burden that occurs when people are required to complete surveys or achievement tests. In other words, existing records are **unobtrusive measures**. Why ask people to spend their time answering questions when the answers are already available in their records? Birth date, gender, place of birth, and other demographic variables are often found in accessible records and need not be asked directly of people.

Records are also relatively accurate repositories of behavior. For example, evaluators interested in the effects of a program on school attendance can ask students, teachers, or parents about attendance. But school records are probably more reliable because they do not depend on people's recall, and they are updated regularly. For the same reason, records are also good places to find out about actual practices. Which treatments are usually prescribed? Check a sample of medical records. How many children were sent to which foster families? Check the foster agency files.

The main problems with records are that they are not always accessible or understandable—even when electronic. If an evaluation uses more than one site (e.g., two hospitals, four states), the study team may have to learn how to access the data in each system and then create a mechanism for linking the data across systems. Also, coding practices vary, and it takes time to learn them.

Diaries are a special type of record in which people are specifically asked to record (e.g., in writing, on video) certain activities. Diaries are typically used in evaluations of programs involving diet, sleep, substance abuse, and alcohol use. People are notoriously inaccurate when asked to recall how much they ate or drank, but keeping a diary improves the quality of their information.

Example 5.5 describes the use of diaries in an evaluation of a combined dietary, behavioral, and physical activity program to treat childhood obesity. The researchers asked obese children to keep 2-day food records.

Example 5.5   Food Diaries and Obese Children (Nemet et al., 2005)

This evaluation examined the short and long term effects of a 3-month program among an experimental and control group of obese children. All children were instructed on how to keep a 2-day food record and were evaluated for understanding and accuracy through administration of a 24-hour recall before initiation of the study. Children kept three 2-day food records (at baseline, at the end of the 3-month program, and 1 year later). The food record data were reviewed by the project nutritionist and checked for omissions (for example, whether dressing was used on a salad listed as ingested with no dressing) and errors (for example, inappropriate portion size). All children completed the baseline, 3-month, and 1-year food records.

Why Researchers Use Records

- Obtaining data from existing records can be relatively unobtrusive because daily activities in schools, prisons, clinics, and so on need not be disturbed.

Why Researchers Use Observations

- Observations provide an opportunity to collect firsthand information.
- Observations can provide information that cannot be anticipated because the researcher is present when the unforeseen occurs.

*What Evidence-Based Public
Health Practice Should Watch For*

- A very structured format and extensive training are required for dependable observations. Otherwise, it is possible that two people may witness the same event, but interpret it differently. Be sure the evaluation report describes the format and training.
- The observer (camera or human) can influence the environment being studied, and people can act different than usual because they are being "watched." The best observations are ones in which people have consented to be watched but, as time passes, become unaware of the observer.
- People sometimes see what they look for. When reviewing studies using data from observations, check that at least two trained observers were present.
- All episodes to be observed have to be selected carefully so that they typify the phenomenon being observed. Does the evaluation report describe how the episodes were selected?

Interviews

Interviews are conducted in person (with or without the assistance of a computer), on the telephone, and via electronic methods. They are particularly useful in studies involving people who have difficulty completing self-administered questionnaires because they have trouble seeing, writing, or reading. Some researchers use interviews when they want the in-depth information that personalizing a survey can bring. Because interviews involve direct personal contact, interviewers need to be carefully screened, trained, and monitored, and these are costly activities. In evaluation research, interviews almost always rely on preset questions and extensive interviewer training.

Example 5.7 is an excerpt from a sample telephone interview form.

Example 5.7   Excerpted Portions of a Telephone Interview Form

Instructions: The purpose of this telephone interview is to determine to what extent the health care facility implements the Clinical Practice Guideline on Treating Tobacco Use and Dependence. Read the Introduction and survey questions as they are written. Circle the appropriate response to each question. Do not read aloud items in capital letters. For questions that ask for additional detail, please write the response clearly.

Introduction

Hello. My name is _____ (first and last name) and I am a volunteer for the _____ Drug Free Coalition. We are talking with health care clinic administrators and providers about steps clinics are taking to implement the clinical practice guideline to treat drug use and dependence. Could I please speak with _____, or an administrator or a provider who is familiar with staff training and current clinical practice?

APPROPRIATE PERSON ANSWERS THE CALL

Hello. My name is _____ (first and last name) and I volunteer for the _____ Drug Free Coalition. Our coalition has worked with your facility in the past to help implement the Clinical Practice Guideline to treat alcohol use and dependence. We are talking with clinics to understand whether the guideline is being implemented. This interview should not take more than 10 minutes. Do you have time now to answer a few questions about the Clinical Practice Guideline?

IF NO: Can I make an appointment to call you back?

IF YES: Great. Thank you. Before I ask the first question, I would like to confirm the following: (GO THROUGH EACH ITEM [BELOW] AND EITHER CONFIRM THE INFORMATION ALREADY WRITTEN DOWN OR ASK FOR IT WITH THE INDIVIDUAL YOU ARE SPEAKING WITH.)

1. **Clinic Name**

2. **Contact Name/Position**

3. Does your clinic have a dedicated staff member, cessation champion or team that treats alcohol abuse and dependence?

     YES   1
     NO   2
     DON'T KNOW   3

4. Do providers at your facility receive formal training to implement the clinical practice guideline on treating alcohol abuse use and dependence?

     YES   1
     NO   2
     DON'T KNOW   3

PROBE IF YES: Please describe the type of formal training your providers receive:

_____

_____

_____

_____

Why Researchers Use Interviews

- Interviews allow researchers to ask about the meaning of questions.
- Interviews can be useful in collecting information from people who may have difficulty reading or seeing.

What Evidence-Based Public Health Practice Should Watch For

- Interviewers require extensive training and monitoring if they are to elicit accurate information in a timely manner. Is the training adequately described in the article?
- Self-reported data, the type that results from interviews, may not reflect actual behavior.

Vignettes

A **vignette** is a short scenario that is used in collecting data in "what if" situations. Example 5.8 describes how a group of researchers explored the impact of a doctor's ethnicity, age, and gender on patients' judgments. Study participants were given one of eight photos of a "doctor" who varied in terms of ethnic group, age, and gender. Six general practices in South West London (England) took part, and 309 patients rated the doctor.

Example 5.8   Vignettes: Influence of Physicians' Ethnicity, Age, and Gender (Shah & Ogden, 2006)

The researchers used a factorial design involving photographs of a doctor who varied in terms of ethnicity (White versus Asian), age (old versus young), and gender (male versus female). This required eight separate photographs. The age groups were defined broadly with "young" being doctors aged between 25 and 35 and "old" being doctors aged between 50 and 65. Patients were asked to rate the photograph in terms of expected behavior of the doctor, expected behavior of the patient, and patient ease with the doctor. Eight individuals were identified that fitted the required ethnicity, age, and gender criteria. Background features, lighting, hairstyle, expression, make up, etc. were kept as consistent as possible. Photographs were taken using a digital camera.

Participants were presented with one of the eight photographs followed by this statement: "Imagine that you have been feeling tired and run down for a while; you see this doctor for the FIRST time." They were then asked to rate the picture (doctor), using scales ranging from "not at all" [1] to "extremely" [5] in terms of three broad areas: expected behavior of the doctor, expected behavior of the patient, and expected ease of the patient.

Why Researchers Use Vignettes

- Vignettes can be fun for participants.
- Vignettes can be efficient. They enable the researcher to vary important factors (e.g., age, gender) one factor at a time. Not every research participant has to review a scenario with every factor as long as all participants review some factors and all factors are reviewed.

What Evidence-Based Public Health Practice Should Watch For

- Producing vignettes requires technical and artistic (writing) skill if the results are to be convincing. Review the scenarios to determine how convincing the vignettes are.
- Sampling can get complicated when varying factors and participants.
- Vignettes are hypothetical. The scenarios they describe may never occur in the evaluation participant's life, and even if they do, the participant may not act as indicated in the hypothetical setting. Vignettes are self-reports, not actual behavior.

Physical Examinations

Physical examinations are sometimes used in evaluations of drug and alcohol programs (e.g., urine tests), in programs to prevent violence in families and communities, and in programs to improve medical outcomes such as a reduction in blood pressure for people with hypertension. Many physical tests are reliable and have norms, or standards against which to compare experimental and nonexperimental group performance. Check to see if the evaluation report or article discusses who conducted the tests, which instruments were used, and who interpreted the findings.

THEORIES OF HEALTH BEHAVIOR CHANGE: ❖ MEASUREMENT AND PROGRAM PLANNING GUIDES

Evidence-based public health practice uses the best available evidence to identify programs that effectively promote and improve health and well-being. Putting a new program in place almost always means changing the behavior of individuals and communities so that their current health practices are replaced with better ones.

Changing health behaviors is an extremely complex process involving interactions among individual, social, and economic values, resources, and constraints. **Health behavior change models** provide a framework for understanding which variables need to be influenced in order to get people to modify their health habits.

The **Health Belief Model (HBM)** is one of the most frequently used health behavior change models, and it has a long history (Figure 5.1). The HBM was developed in the 1950s as part of an effort by social psychologists in the U.S. Public Health Service to explain the lack of public participation in health screening and prevention (Becker, 1974; Rosenstock, 1996).

According to the HBM, the likelihood that people will take action to prevent illness depends on their perception that they are personally vulnerable to a particular condition, that the consequences of the condition can be serious, that if they take precautions the condition will be prevented, and that the benefits of reducing the threat of the condition exceed the costs. These four factors, which are influenced by modifying variables (including

Figure 5.1 The Health Belief Model

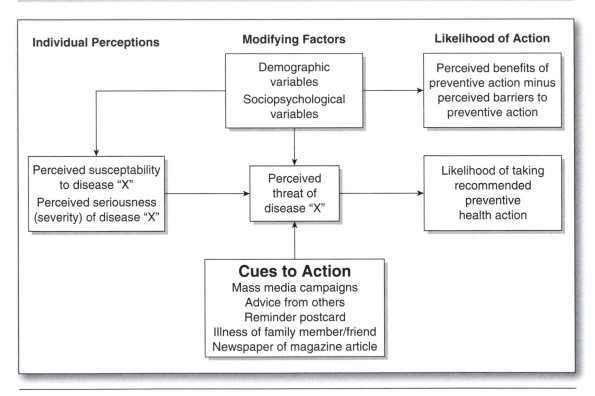

SOURCE: Barch, 1996

demographic variables and health messages or cues to action), indirectly influence the probability that someone will perform the protective health behaviors. Recent formulations of the HBM have added self-efficacy to the model. Self-efficacy is key component of social cognitive theory.

According to Social Learning/Social Cognitive Theory (Bandura, 2001), behavior change is affected by environmental influences, personal factors, and attributes of the behavior itself. Each may affect or be affected by either of the other two. A central tenet of Social Cognitive Theory is the concept of self-efficacy. A person must believe in his or her capability to perform the behavior (i.e., the person must possess self-efficacy) and must perceive an incentive to do so (i.e., the person's positive expectations from performing the behavior must outweigh the negative expectations). Additionally, a person must value the outcomes or consequences that he or she believes will occur as a result of performing a specific behavior or action.

Outcomes may be classified as having immediate benefits (e.g., feeling energized following physical activity) or long-term benefits (e.g., experiencing improvements in cardiovascular health as a result of physical activity). But because these expected outcomes are filtered through a person's expectations or perceptions of being able to perform the behavior in the first place, self-efficacy is believed to be the single most important characteristic that determines a person's behavior change.

Self-efficacy can be increased in several ways, among them by providing clear instructions, providing the opportunity for skill development or training, and modeling the desired behavior. To be effective, models must evoke trust, admiration, and respect from the observer; models must not, however, appear to represent a level of behavior that the observer is unable to visualize attaining.

The Theory of Reasoned Action and Theory of Planned Behavior (Ajzen & Fishbein, 1980; Montaño, Kasprzyk, & Taplin, 1997) presumes that individual performance of a given behavior is primarily determined by a person's intention to perform that behavior. This intention is affected by the person's attitude toward the behavior (beliefs about the outcomes of the behavior and the value of these outcomes) and the influence of the person's social environment or subjective norms (beliefs about what other people think the person should do, as well as the person's motivation to comply with the opinions of others).

The Theory of Planned Behavior adds to the Theory of Reasoned Action the concept of perceived control over the opportunities, resources, and skills necessary to perform a behavior. The concept of perceived behavioral control is similar to the concept of self-efficacy—a person's perception of his or her ability to perform the behavior. Perceived behavioral control over opportunities, resources, and skills necessary to perform a behavior is believed to be a critical aspect of behavior change processes (Figure 5.2).

Example 5.9   The Effect of Mere Measurement of Cognitions on Physical Activity Behavior: A Randomized Controlled Trial Among Overweight and Obese Individuals (Godin, Belanger-Gravel, Amireault, Vohl, & Perusse, 2011)

Background. The promotion of physical activity among an overweight/obese population is an important challenge for clinical practitioners and researchers. In this regard, completing a questionnaire on cognitions could be a simple and easy strategy to increase levels of physical activity. Thus, the aim of the present study was to test the effect of completing a questionnaire based on the Theory of Planned Behavior (TPB) on the level of physical activity.

Methods. Overall, 452 overweight/obese adults were recruited and randomized to the experimental or control group. At baseline, participants completed a questionnaire on cognitions regarding their participation in leisure-time physical activity (experimental condition) versus a questionnaire on fruit and vegetable consumption (control condition). The questionnaires assessed the TPB variables that are beliefs, attitude, norm, perception of control, intention and a few additional variables from other theories. At three-month follow-up, leisure-time physical activity was self-reported by means of a short questionnaire. An analysis of covariance with baseline physical activity level as covariate was used to verify the effect of the intervention.

Results. At follow-up, 373 participants completed the leisure-time physical activity questionnaire. The statistical analysis showed that physical activity participation was greater among participants in the experimental condition than those in the control condition ($F(1,370) = 6.85$, $p = .009$, $d = 0.20$).

Conclusions. Findings indicate that completing a TPB questionnaire has a significant positive impact on subsequent participation in physical activity. Consequently, asking individuals to complete such a questionnaire is a simple, inexpensive and easy strategy to increase the level of physical activity among overweight/obese adults.

Reliability and Validity: A Team Approach

Much of the vocabulary that is associated with measurement comes from the field of **psychometrics**. Psychometrics is the discipline that is concerned with the theory and technique of psychological measurement, which includes the measurement of knowledge, abilities, attitudes, and personality traits. In recent years, psychometric methods have been applied to the panoply of measures found in evaluations of programs to improve health, education, and social welfare.

Because of the complexity of developing measures that result in "truth," the use of any measure is accompanied by error. **Measurement error** is a term used to describe the discrepancy between responses to a measure and the true value of the concept. Best evidence comes from measures that maximize truth and minimize error. Developing and finding such measures, as you can well imagine, is a big deal and requires hard work.

A reliable measure is a consistent one. A measure of quality of life, for example, is reliable if, on average, it produces the same information from the same people today and 2 weeks from now. You need a measure to be reliable—to give you consistent results—but reliability alone is not enough. For instance, if the needle of a scale is 5 pounds away from 0 at its start point (before there is any weight on the scale), I will always overreport my weight by 5 pounds. Is the measurement consistent? Yes, but it is consistently wrong! Is the measurement valid? No! In fact, it is incorrect. A measurement's validity refers to the degree to which it accurately measures the characteristic it is supposed to measure (e.g., my weight). A valid measure is also an accurate and consistent—or reliable—one. So to understand validity, it helps to learn first about reliability.

Reliability

A reliable measure is reproducible and precise: Each time it is used, it produces the same value. A beam scale can measure body weight precisely, but a questionnaire about good citizenship is likely to produce values that vary from person to person and even from time to time. A measure (e.g., of good citizenship) cannot be perfectly precise if its underlying concept is imprecise (e.g., because of differing definitions of good citizenship). This imprecision is the gateway to **random** (chance) **error**. Error comes from three sources: variability in the measure itself, variability in the respondents, and variability in the observer.

A measure can itself produce unreliable data if it is difficult to complete or improperly designed. For example, if a test's scoring boxes are difficult to fill in (e.g., too small, too hard to see) or the scanning software is deficient, then unreliable data will result. Respondents may be the source of error if they are especially tired, not very motivated, or extremely anxious. If people in a dental clinic expecting a root canal are asked to complete a questionnaire, the responses they give about their current mood are likely to differ somewhat from the responses they might have given under less strained circumstances. Finally, the observer or administrator of the measure can also introduce error. An interviewer who treats respondents differently from day to day or does not follow a strict interviewing protocol, for example, can produce unreliable data because he or she is inconsistent.

How do you know if a measure is reliable and not subject to error? Researchers assess the reliability of measures in four ways, as illustrated in Table 5.1.

Table 5.1 Four Ways of Assessing Reliability

Type of Reliability	How Assessed
Within measure	Test-retest, internal consistency, split-half
Between measures	Alternate form
Between observers	Inter-rater

Within-Measure Reliability

Test-Retest Reliability. A measure has test-retest reliability if the correlation or reliability coefficient between the scores obtained each time the measure is used is high. A correlation is a numerical index that reflects the linear relationship (described by a straight line) between two numerical measurements made on the same group of people. A correlation coefficient (r) ranges from −1 to +1, with 0 indicating no relationship. The absolute value of the coefficient reflects the strength of the correlation so that a correlation of −.60 is stronger than a correlation of −.50.

Suppose students are tested twice, first in April and then in May. If the test is reliable, and no special program to change behavior was introduced, on average the test scores should be pretty much the same both times. Their relationship should be nearly perfect, or 1.0 (+1). But perfection is not possible, and two variables tested over time will differ to some extent because people differ from time to time (e.g., they are more tired at one time than at another) and the measures are not perfect to begin with. To find out the exact r, statisticians compute a **Pearson product-moment correlation coefficient**. Researchers have set standards for interpreting the strength of the relationship between test and retest reliability (Landis & Koch, 1977; see Table 5.2).

Table 5.2 Standards for Test-Retest Reliability

Correlation Obtained Between Test and Retest	Strength of Relationship
.00 to .20	Poor
.21 to .40	Fair
.41 to .60	Moderate
.61 to 1.0	Almost perfect

In your review, look for substantial or almost perfect test-retest reliability.

Another concern in estimating test-retest reliability is the number of people who should be tested. In general, researchers have agreed that between 25 and 100 people is an acceptable sample size, especially when the sample is part of a larger study. It is not uncommon for expert researchers to study and report on how a given measure performs with the participants in their study who, after all, are not usually identical to the participants with whom the measure was originally tested. This special testing is done to make certain that the measure is reliable in the evaluation's setting.

Researchers usually discuss and justify measures in the Methods section of their reports and articles. Sometimes you will find a section devoted to "instruments" or to "main measures." Example 5.10 contains two slightly modified examples of how researchers describe test-retest reliability.

Example 5.10   Establishing Test-Retest Reliability

---

1. **An Instrument That Describes the Diverse Problems Seen in Milder Forms of Pervasive Developmental Disorder (PDD) (Hartman, Luteijn, Serra, & Minderaa, 2006)**

   To examine test-retest reliability, 59 mothers completed the Children's Social Behavior Questionnaire (CSBQ) for the second time after an interval of approximately four weeks. The average age of their children was 9.03, with a standard deviation of 2.87. Test-retest reliability was established by means of Pearson r. For all scales, test-retest reliability was good (actually almost perfect) total score (r = .90); "not optimally tuned to the social situation" (r = .89); "reduced contact and social interest" (r = .88); "orientation problems in time, place, or activity" (r = .82); "difficulties in understanding social information" (r = .80); "stereotyped behavior" (r = .80); and "fear of and resistance to changes" (r = .83).

2. **Development of a Short Form of the Workstyle Measure (Feuerstein & Nicholas, 2006)**

   Test-retest reliability was assessed by examining the correlation of the baseline short form total workstyle score with the short form total workstyle score from the surveys completed 3 weeks after the baseline assessment. This analysis indicated stable test-retest reliability with a correlation coefficient of r = 0.88, P < 0.01.

Internal Consistency Reliability. Internal consistency is an indicator of the cohesion of the items in a single measure. That is, all the items in an internally consistent measure actually assess the same idea or concept. One example of internal consistency might be a test of two questions. The first statement says, "You almost always feel like smoking." The second question says, "You almost never feel like smoking." If a person agrees with the first and disagrees with the second, the test has internal consistency.

When reviewing evaluation reports that discuss internal consistency, you will come across terms such as **Cronbach's alpha** and **Kuder-Richardson** (see Table 5.3).

Table 5.3 Internal Consistency: Cronbach's Alpha and Kuder-Richardson

Term	Explanation
Cronbach's Alpha	Cronbach's alpha reflects the extent to which a set of test items can be treated as measuring a single latent variable. Latent variables, as opposed to observable variables, are those that cannot be directly observed but are rather inferred from other variables that can be observed and directly measured. Examples of latent variables include attitudes toward school, self-efficacy, and quality of life. Cronbach's alpha can range between 0 and 1. A measure with an alpha .61 and above is usually considered to be internally consistent.
Kuder-Richardson	This reflection of internal consistency is like Cronbach's alpha except that it is used for measures in which questions can be responded to in only one of two ways (e.g., true/false, yes/no). Like alpha, Kuder-Richardson reliability can range from 0 to 1. An internally consistent measure would have a Kuder-Richardson reliability of .61 or above.

Example 5.11 gives excerpted samples of how researchers justify the internal consistency of the measures included in their study.

Example 5.11 Justifying Measures' Internal Consistency

1. **Secondary Prevention of Intimate Partner Violence (McFarlane, Groff, O'Brien, & Watson, 2006)**

   The Severity of Violence against Women Scale (SAVAWS) is a 46-item instrument designed to measure threats of physical violence (19 items) and physical assault (27 items). Examples of behaviors that threaten physical violence are threats to destroy property, hurt the woman, or harm other family members. Examples of behaviors that represent physical violence are kicking, choking, beating up, and forced sex. For each item, the woman responds using a 4-point scale to indicate how often the behavior occurred (0 = never, 1 = once, 2 = 2–3 times, 3 = 4 or more times). The possible range of scores was 0 to 57 for the threats of abuse and 0 to 81 for physical assault. Internal consistency reliability estimates for abused women have ranged from .89 to .91 for threats of abuse and .91 to .94 for assault. . . . For the present study, reliability, as measured by Cronbach's alpha, was .92 for both threats of abuse and physical assault.

   The Employment Harassment Questionnaire is an 8-item instrument taken from a recent report to Congress . . . using studies of worksite harassment of women by intimate partners. The questions are answered as yes or no. Items include repeated calls and/or visits to the worksite and preventing the woman from going to work. The range of scores was 0 to 8. The instrument has a reported internal consistency of .76. . . . For the present study, reliability, as measured by Cronbach's alpha, was .87.

2. The Self-Injury Questionnaire (Santa Mina et al., 2006)

The Self-Injury Questionnaire (SIQ) is a 30-item, self-report instrument, conceptualized from the trauma literature and tested initially in a community sample. The SIQ, based on . . . classification of self-injury, measures intentions for self-harm per method (overdose, cut, hang, etc.) across all four subscales (i.e., body alterations, indirect self-harm, failure to care for self, and overt self-injury). It measures the frequency, type, and functions of self-harm behaviors and their associations with histories of childhood trauma. The items represent eight conceptual themes for self-injurious behavior: regulation of feelings, regulation of realness, safety, communication with self, communication with others, fun, social influence, and regulation of body sensations. Cronbach alphas were also adequate for each of five subscales.

Note: If the alphas are "adequate," they must be .61 and above.

Split-Half Reliability. To estimate split-half reliability, the researcher divides a measure into two equal halves (e.g., by choosing all odd-numbered questions to be in the first half and all even-numbered questions to be in the second half). Then, using a technique called the **Spearman-Brown prediction formula**, the researcher calculates the correlation between the two halves. A correlation coefficient of .61 and above is considered acceptable for split-half reliability.

Example 5.12 gives an example of how split-half reliability is written up.

Example 5.12   Writing Up the Results of Split-Half Reliability

---

Note on Psychometric Properties of Playfulness Scales With Adolescents (Fix & Schaefer, 2005)

In total, 105 female and 85 male high school students completed two scales designed to measure playfulness, the Playfulness Scale for Adults and the Adult Playfulness Scale, and two scales designed to measure creativity, the Similes Test and the Franck Drawing Completion Test. The playfulness scales exhibited high internal consistency and good construct validity. Cronbach alpha was .84 for the Playfulness Scale for Adults and .88 for the Adult Playfulness Scale, and split-half reliability was .79 (Spearman-Brown) and .79 (Guttman a variation of the Spearman-Brown) for the Adult Playfulness Scale and .87 (Spearman-Brown) and .86 (Guttman) for the Playfulness Scale for Adults. The 2-week test-retest reliability for the Playfulness Scale for Adults was .89, which compared favorably to the test-retest reliability of .84 previously reported for the Adult Playfulness Scale.

Measurement validity is not the same thing as either internal validity or external validity, which we discussed in connection with evaluation research design (Chapter 4). Internal validity is the extent to which the design and conduct of an evaluation are likely to have prevented bias, so we can have confidence in the accuracy of the findings. External validity refers to the extent to which evaluation results provide a correct basis for generalizations to other people and circumstances. Measurement validity refers to the extent to which a measure or instrument provides data that accurately represent the concepts of interest.

Measurement validity is often thought of as having four dimensions: content, predictive, concurrent, and construct.

Content Validity

Content validity refers to the extent to which a measure thoroughly and appropriately assesses the skills or characteristics it is intended to measure. A depression scale may lack content validity if it only assesses the affective dimension of depression but fails to take into account the behavioral dimension. The trick in developing a measure with content validity is to be extremely knowledgeable regarding the theories underlying the concept being measured (e.g., depression) as well as regarding what research says about it.

Another dimension of validity is how a measure appears on the surface: Does it seem to cover all the important domains? Ask all the needed questions? This dimension is called **face validity**. It is established by experts in the field who are asked to review a measure and comment on its coverage. Face validity is the weakest type because it does not have theoretical or research support.

Criterion validity refers to the degree to which a measure correlates with an external criterion of the phenomenon being investigated. You can understand criterion validity better if you see that the term is a coverall term for predictive and concurrent validity.

Predictive Validity

Predictive validity refers to the extent to which a measure forecasts future performance (the criterion). A graduate school entry examination that predicts who will do well in graduate school (as measured, for example, by grades) has predictive validity.

Concurrent Validity

Concurrent validity is demonstrated when a new measure compares favorably with one that is already considered valid (the criterion). For example, to establish the concurrent validity of a new aptitude test, the researcher can administer the new and the older validated measure to the same group of people and compare the scores. Or the researcher can administer the new test and then compare the scores to experts' judgment. A high correlation between the new test scores and the criterion measure's—the older validated test—means the new test has concurrent validity. Establishing concurrent validity is useful when a new measure is created that claims to be shorter, cheaper, or fairer than an older one.

Construct Validity

Construct validity is established experimentally to demonstrate that a measure distinguishes between people who do and do not have certain characteristics. For example, a researcher who claims construct validity for a measure of competent teaching will have to prove that teachers who do well on the measure are competent whereas teachers who do poorly are incompetent.

Construct validity is commonly established in at least two ways:

1. The researcher hypothesizes that performance on the new measure correlates with performance on one or more measures of a similar characteristic (**convergent validity**) and does not correlate with performance on measures of dissimilar characteristics (**discriminant validity**). For example, a researcher who is validating a new quality-of-life measure might posit that it is highly correlated ("converges") with another quality-of-life measure, a measure of functioning, and a measure of health status. At the same time, the researcher would hypothesize that the new measure does not correlate with (but rather "discriminates" against) selected measures of social desirability (the tendency to answer questions so as to present yourself in a more positive light) and of hostility.

2. The researcher hypothesizes that the measure can distinguish one group from another on some important variable. For example, a

measure of compassion should be able to demonstrate that people who are high scorers are more compassionate than low scorers, who are less compassionate. This requires translating a theory of and research on compassionate behavior into measurable terms, identifying people who are compassionate and who are unfeeling (according to the theory and research), and proving that the measure consistently and correctly distinguishes between the two groups.

When you review evaluation reports to assess the adequacy of their measures' approach to validity, you will find information on both reliability and validity, as in the illustrations in Example 5.15.

Example 5.15   Write-Ups of Reliability and Validity

1. Validating an Anger Scale in Sweden (Lindqvist, Daderman, & Hellstrom, 2005)

In this study, the internal reliability and construct validity of the recently adapted Swedish version of the Novaco Anger Scale (NAS-1998-S), as well as its scale correlations with demographic and criminality variables, were investigated. Construct validity was established by assessing the correlation pattern of the scales of NAS-1998-S with concurrent scales of similar and distinct constructs. Ninety-five male violent prisoners, ranging in age from 18 to 67 years, participated. The results demonstrated good internal reliability, consistent intra-scale relationships, and appropriate construct validity of NAS-1998-S.

2. Comparing Three Measures of Violence (Chen, Rovi, Vega, Jacobs, & Johnson, 2005)

A four-item brief instrument, HITS (Hurt, Insulted, Threatened with harm, and Screamed at) is compared with two other previously validated measures: the Woman Abuse Screening Tool (WAST) and the Index of Spouse Abuse-Physical Scale (ISA-P). Cronbach's alpha was 0.76, 0.80, and 0.78 for the English version of HITS, ISA-P, and WAST, respectively. The Spanish version of HITS had lower internal consistency than ISA-P and WAST (0.61, 0.77, 0.80, respectively). However, when administered first and analyzed alone, the Spanish version of HITS had a reliability of 0.71. For the total sample, all three instruments showed good reliability.

The English interviews had similar reliability of all instruments regardless of whether participants completed HITS and WAST or ISA-P first. The Spanish interviews revealed that both presentations were similar in the reliability of ISA-P and WAST. However, compared to those who first answered the ISA-P, the reliability of HITS was higher for those who first answered HITS and WAST (Cronbach's alpha = 0.71 and 0.49, respectively). Presentation method was not significantly associated with total scores of HITS, ISA-P, and WAST, after controlling for demographic characteristics.

Sensitivity and Specificity

Sensitivity and *specificity* are two terms that are used in connection with screening and diagnostic tests and measures to detect disease.

Suppose you are interested in finding an effective program to prevent hazardous alcohol use. You might come across a statement such as this in your literature review: "The Alcohol-Hazardous Drinking Index (AHDI) was 89% sensitive and 93% specific in identifying at-risk drinkers." **Sensitivity** refers to the proportion of people with disease who have a positive test result. Said another way, a sensitive measure will correctly detect disease (e.g., alcohol-related risk) among people who have the disease. A sensitive measure is a valid measure. What happens when people without the disease get a positive test anyway, as sometimes happens? That is called a **false positive**. Insensitive, invalid measures lead to false positives.

Specificity refers to the proportion of people without disease who have a negative test result. Measures with poor specificity lead to **false negatives**. They invalidly classify people as not having a disease (e.g., alcohol-related risk) when in fact they actually do.

A third term associated with sensitivity and specificity is **positive predictive value (PPV)**. The PPV of a test is the probability that a person has the disease when restricted to those patients *who test positive* (as compared to those who have the disease). Finally, there is the **negative predictive value (NPV)**, which is defined as the probability that the patient will not have the disease when restricted to all patients who test negative.

Examples of how these terms are used in evaluation reports are given in Example 5.16.

Example 5.16 Sensitivity, Specificity, and Predictive Value

---

1. **The Postpartum Bonding Questionnaire (Brockington, Fraser, & Wilson, 2006)**

   Scale 1 (a general factor) had a sensitivity of 0.82 for all mother-infant relationship disorders. Scale 2 (rejection and pathological anger) had a sensitivity of 0.88 for rejection of the infant, but only 0.67 for severe anger. The performance of scale 3 (infant-focused anxiety) was unsatisfactory. Scale 4 (incipient abuse) selected only a few mothers, but was of some value in identifying those at high risk of child abuse. Revision of the thresholds can improve sensitivity, especially of scale 2, where a cut-off point of 12 = normal, 13 = high better identifies mothers with threatened rejection. These new cut-off points would need validation in another sample.

(Continued)

Example 5.16 (Continued)

2. The Alcohol Use Disorders Identification Test—French Version (Gache et al., 2005)

In total, 1,207 patients presenting to outpatient clinics (Switzerland, n = 580) or general practitioners' (France, n = 627) successively completed CAGE, MAST, and AUDIT self-administered questionnaires and were independently interviewed by a trained addiction specialist. AUDIT showed a good capacity to discriminate dependent patients (with AUDIT >= 13 for males, sensitivity 70.1%, specificity 95.2%, PPV 85.7%, NPV 94.7% and for females sensitivity 94.7%, specificity 98.2%, PPV 100%, NPV 99.8%); and hazardous drinkers (with AUDIT >= 7, for males sensitivity 83.5%, specificity 79.9%, PPV 55.0%, NPV 82.7% and with AUDIT >= 6 for females, sensitivity 81.2%, specificity 93.7%, PPV 64.0%, NPV 72.0%).

3. The Childhood Experience of Care and Abuse Questionnaire (CECA.Q) (Bifulco, Bernazzani, Moran, & Jacobs, 2005)

When sensitivity and specificity of these higher cut-off scores were determined against the CECA interview, higher overall correct classification was achieved (average 80%) than with the previous cut-offs, and higher specificity or true negative rate (average 87%) but lower sensitivity or true positive rate (average of 60%).

❖ NEEDING IT ALL OR JUST NEEDING SOME OF IT: RELIABILITY, VALIDITY, SENSITIVITY, AND SPECIFICITY

Research articles can be overwhelming to plough through under the best of circumstances, and you may be tempted to just accept the researchers' word on the quality of their measures' reliability and validity. As you go through a research article or report, make certain that the measures are concerned with the same outcomes that you are; that you agree with the researchers in terms of their definitions of the outcomes; and that, if given the choice, you would measure them in the same way. Measures of self-confidence, anger, quality of life, and so on are defined and measured differently depending on their theoretical foundations and research base. When in doubt about a measure's background and theoretical and empirical rationales, go to the researchers' cited references.

You should also make sure that the article presents the exact statistical results (e.g., the test-retest correlation coefficient = 0.80) for each important measure. Do not accept statements such as "The interclass correlation was high" or "The construct validity was good when compared to the ABC Measure." If the language about a measure's validity is vague or unclear, or you are uncertain as to the adequacy of the evidence for choosing it for the evaluation, go to the original source (the one cited by the researcher) and make your own judgment.

Reviewers sometimes assume that if a researcher uses previously validated measures, then that should suffice. Unfortunately, it may not, and there are two reasons for this. First, the measure may have been validated among people and in a setting that differ from the evaluator's. Second, the setting may have little to do with the reviewer's community. It is important to make certain that the psychometric properties of all measures are appropriate.

Data Collection, Data Analysis, Statistical and Practical Significance

Evidence-based public health knowledge relies on randomized or non-randomized control trial research designs to test the effectiveness of a new program or practice against an alternative. Researchers compare data collected from experimental and control groups to examine whether a meaningful difference exists between the groups after program participation. But what constitutes a meaningful difference? Often, *meaningful* is equated with *statistical*: a difference that is unlikely to have occurred by chance alone.

In statistics, a result is called **statistically significant** if it is unlikely to have occurred by chance. The amount of evidence required to accept that an event is unlikely to have arisen by chance is known as the *significance level,* or critical P-value.

Researchers start with an assumption that there are no differences between the groups in their experiment (the **null hypothesis**). They use statistical tests to challenge the assumption, hoping that there really is difference favoring the experimental group. The idea is that when the research data are analyzed, the statistical tests will be used to determine the P-value or the probability of seeing an effect as big as or bigger than that occurring in the study by chance, if the null hypothesis (no differences) were true. The null hypothesis is rejected in favor of its alternative if the P-value (the probably of a difference) is less than some predetermined level, traditionally 1% (0.01) or 5% (0.05). This predetermined level is α (alpha), or the level of statistical significance.

For example, suppose an evaluation compares Programs A and B in terms of their ability to improve functional status in older adults. The researcher starts off with the assumption that the two programs are equally effective (the null hypothesis) and sets alpha at 0.05. That means the researcher has set 5% as the maximum chance of incorrectly rejecting the null hypothesis (that there is no difference). This 5% is the level of reasonable

Because of the pragmatic nature of almost all the research on which evidence-based public health relies, none is immune to methodological flaws. The researcher's challenge is to design and implement a study that results in findings and conclusions that are more accurate than they would have been with another sampling strategy, research design, outcome measure, or analytic method. The research's strengths must be demonstrably greater than its limitations.

What Evidence-Based Public Health Practice Should Watch For

When reviewing the data analysis and results section of research reports and articles:

- Check to see that if P-values are used, the exact P-value is given
- Look for CI rather than P-values
- Look for a discussion of the practical significance of the statistical results
- Check to see if an explanation can be found discussing how the evaluation's strengths outweigh its limitations so that it has public health relevance

Missing: Where Are the Data?

Researchers collect data at numerous points throughout their study. Screening or assessment measures are used to determine who is and is not eligible to participate. Baseline information is collected, and then the performance of the program is monitored by assessing progress and outcomes. Progress can be measured twice (e.g., by comparing baseline performance and performance at the end of a program) or several times (e.g., at baseline, 6 months after baseline, a year after baseline, at the end of program participation, and a year after that). Whether data are collected a few or many times, opportunities arise for program participants to refuse to, or be unable to, complete some or all of a study's measures. That is, they drop out.

Researchers will tell you that complete data are rarely if ever obtained on all participants. In fact, experienced researchers will also tell you that they always anticipate that important data may be missing for some participants (especially in large and longitudinal evaluations). In practice, this means that researchers know that the possibility exists that participants who remain in the study and complete all data collection tasks may very well differ from the dropouts and refusers. They may be more motivated to stay in for any number of reasons. For example, they may be healthier, enjoy participating in research, have the time to participate, be grateful for the attention or the services, or be more highly educated.

What happens if people drop out of the study and complete little or even none of the required data collection measures? Consider two alcohol misuse prevention programs, one of which is effective and the other isn't.

- People in the effective program reduce their drinking and stay in the study.
- In the ineffective program, some people reduce drinking anyway and stay in the study.

Those who fail to reduce their drinking are more likely to drop out, perhaps to try something else. This will make the ineffective program look better than it really is—and, by comparison, the effective program looks worse than it really is—because the only people who remain in the study following the ineffective program are those who reduced their drinking!

Some researchers compensate by using statistical methods to make up for loss of data, or **attrition**. One commonly used method is the **last observation carried forward** (LOCF), which uses the last value observed before the participant left, regardless of when the dropout occurred. LOCF makes the probably unrealistic assumption that participants who drop out would continue responding precisely as they did at the time of dropout. Because of this assumption, LOCF has fallen somewhat out of favor.

Newer methods are increasingly being used, thanks to the availability of sophisticated statistical software that can handle the newer methods' complexity. These methods have the advantage of using all the data from all time points available for all participants. They allow for nonconstant correlations among the time points by estimating responses after dropout using data prior to dropout. Thus, they use all the data and can reduce bias due to dropout. Researchers can fit models in which each participant is allowed his or her own regression line (or curve) over time, so that when a participant drops out, his or her curve is projected to the end of the study, rather than simply holding at whatever the last value was, as in LOCF.

Another method of handling missing data is to fill in a "reasonable" value such as an average score for each participant who did respond. Suppose Participant A did not answer a survey question about his annual household income. To fill in the blank with a reasonable value, the researcher

Figure 5.4 Data Collection Flow Chart: Who Is Eligible and Who Provides Data for Analysis?

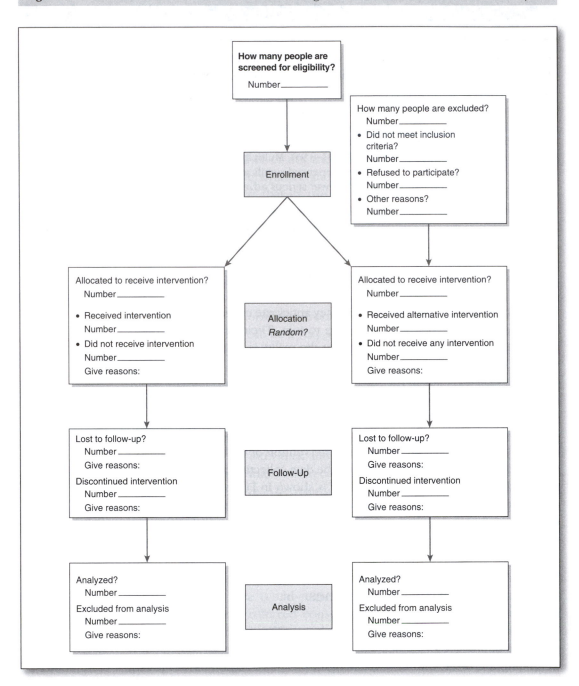

such lofty goals requires long-term and large studies. Although these are often the ideal, they may not always be possible to conduct. In practice, it is not uncommon for program developers and researchers to find that programs accomplish one or a few **proximate outcomes** rather than the hoped-for ultimate outcomes. Proximate outcomes are intermediate outcomes. They are chosen because they are meaningful in themselves and because previous research and clinical insight suggest that they are associated with the hoped-for outcomes. For example, a reduction in the quantity and frequency of alcohol use can be considered a proximate outcome in a program to reduce alcohol-related problems (the ultimate outcome).

Table 5.4 describes the relationship between hoped-for and proximate outcomes.

Table 5.4   Hoped-For Outcomes Versus Proximate Outcomes (Stein et al., 2003)

Hoped-for Outcome: Improvement in the quality of life

Program: Cognitive behavioral therapy

Participants: Children and adolescents who suffer frequent and severe headaches

Proximate Outcome Achieved by Program Participants: Decrease in symptoms of depression

Reason for Choice of Proximate Outcomes: Depression influences headache prevalence (Bandell-Hoekstra et al., 2000). Cognitive behavioral therapy is effective in treating recurrent headache (Eccleston et al., 2003) in children as well as in decreasing their symptoms of depression (Stein et al., 2003).

You must decide if proximate outcomes are compelling evidence of program effectiveness. You may consider using consensus techniques or focus groups to help you decide on the value of the proximate outcomes in your setting (Chapter 2).

DATA COLLECTION AND PUBLIC HEALTH PRACTICE   ❖

The following checklist is a guide for evaluating the quality of the measures used to collect evidence about program effectiveness.

EXERCISES

1. Locate the following evaluations, and name the types of measures used in each.

   a. King, C. A., Kramer, A., Preuss, L., Kerr, D. C. R., Weisse, L., & Venkataraman, S. (2006). Youth-nominated support team for suicidal adolescents (version 1): A randomized controlled trial. *Journal of Consulting and Clinical Psychology*, *74*, 199–206.

   b. Garrow, D., & Egede, L. E. (2006). Association between complementary and alternative medicine use, preventive care practices, and use of conventional medical services among adults with diabetes. *Diabetes Care*, *29*, 15–19.

   c. Lieberman, P., Morey, A., Hochstadt, J., Larson, M., & Mather, S. (2005). Mount Everest: A space analogue for speech monitoring of cognitive deficits and stress. *Aviation, Space, and Environmental Medicine*, *76*, 1093–1101.

   Answer:

   a. Self-administered questionnaires

   The Suicidal Ideation Questionnaire—Junior (SIQ-JR; Reynolds, 1988) is a 15-item self-report questionnaire used to assess the frequency of a wide range of suicidal thoughts.

   The Spectrum of Suicide Behavior Scale (Pfeffer, 1986) is a 5-point rating of the history of suicidality (none, ideation, intent/threat, mild attempt, serious attempt).

   Measures of internalizing symptoms include the Youth Self-Report (YSR; Achenbach, 1991) internalizing scale and the Reynolds Adolescent Depression Scale (RADS; Reynolds, 1987). The YSR consists of 119 problem behavior items that form internalizing and externalizing scales. The RADS is a 30-item self-report questionnaire that assesses frequency of depressive symptoms on a 4-point scale with endpoints of *almost never* and *most of the time*.

   The CAFAS (Hodges & Wong, 1996) assesses functional impairment in multiple areas, including moods/self-harm. On the basis of parent responses to a structured interview, a trained clinician rates level of functioning on a 4-point scale (0, 10, 20, 30) ranging from 0 (*minimal or no impairment*) to 30 (*severe impairment*).

   b. Large database

   The 2002 National Health Interview Survey (NHIS), a national household survey sponsored by the National Center for Health Statistics, was used to collect data on whether participants had a diagnosis of diabetes or other illness, the use of complementary and alternative medicine, demographic and socioeconomic characteristics, preventive health care practices, and the use of conventional medical services.

   c. Audio records

   A computer-implemented acoustic voice measure was used to track slight as well as profound cognitive impairment.

2. A researcher's colleague decided to play a practical joke. The colleague came across a glossary of terms that the researcher had prepared for a class she was teaching and altered some of the definitions. Now the glossary contains some false statements and some true ones. You are the Good Samaritan and decide to correct the statements before the researcher finds out she is the victim of a joke. The following include some of the statements from the glossary that the colleague altered. Your job is to put in the correct terms.

A measure has internal consistency reliability if the correlation or reliability coefficient between scores recorded at different times is high.

A commonly used method for determining the agreement between observations and observers results in a statistic called *alpha,* defined as the agreement beyond chance divided by the amount of agreement possible beyond chance.

Content validity refers to the extent to which a measure thoroughly and appropriately assesses the skills or characteristics it is intended to measure.

Predictive validity is demonstrated when two measures agree with one another, or a new measure compares favorably with one that is already considered valid.

Construct validity is established experimentally to demonstrate that a measure distinguishes between people who do and do not have certain characteristics, such as fear of flying or good quality of life.

A sensitive measure will correctly detect disease (e.g., alcohol-related risk) among people who have the disease.

Specificity refers to the proportion of people without disease who have a negative test result.

Some researchers refer to the use of multiple measures as triangulation.

A Type II error is analogous to a false positive in that the evaluator concludes that a difference exists when one does not.

The null hypothesis postulates that no difference exists between experimental and control program participants.

With intention to treat analysis, outcomes between study groups are compared with every participant analyzed according to his or her randomized group assignment regardless of whether he or she received the assigned intervention or produced any data, under most circumstances. In per protocol analysis, only participants who complete the entire study are counted toward the final results.

In practice, it is not uncommon for program developers and researchers to find that programs accomplish one or a few proximate outcomes rather than the hoped-for ultimate outcomes. Proximate outcomes are intermediate outcomes.

Answers:

Underlined text should be replaced with the answer.

A measure has <u>internal consistency</u> (**Answer:** test-retest) reliability if the correlation or reliability coefficient between scores recorded at different times is high.

the 28-item revised **Children's Manifest Anxiety Scale**. These measures, according to the researchers, have *adequate test-retest and internal consistency reliability and construct and predictive validity*.

Items from the **Monitoring the Future Scale** were used at the six-year follow-up. The researcher states that *this scale has adequate reliability and construct validity*. To *maximize validity of responses*, adolescents responded on **a self-administered questionnaire. Alcohol and marijuana use** were measured by a 7-point scale of times used (1 = 0 to 7 = 40) in the past year. **Other drug use** was computed as the sum of ratings on this scale for 13 other drugs (e.g., heroin). **Polydrug use** was assessed by counting the number of different drugs, including alcohol, used in the past year.

Adolescents responded to a **self-administered question on the number of different sexual partners** they had had since completion of the New Beginnings Program.

5. Read these articles and compare each in terms of the adequacy of its data collection flow chart and discussion of how the researchers handled missing data.

MacMillan, H. L., Wathen, C. N., Jamieson, E., Boyle, M., McNutt, L.-A., Worster, A., et al. (2006). Approaches to screening for intimate partner violence in health care settings: A randomized trial. *Journal of the American Medical Association, 296*, 530–536.

Riggs, N. R., Elfenbaum, P., & Pentz, M. A. (2006). Parent program component analysis in a drug abuse prevention trial. *Journal of Adolescent Health, 39*, 66–72.

Answer:

The first article by MacMillan and colleagues describes in detail how they defined missing data and tells how they handled these data statistically. The researchers found that, although proportions of missing data differed by instrument, statistical analysis revealed the differences were not significant. MacMillan and colleagues also provide a detailed flow chart that shows how many participants were assessed for inclusion into the study and how many remained for the analysis—even if they had missing data (intention to treat analysis).

In the second article, Riggs and colleagues do not provide a flow diagram. They do discuss in the text that they started with 1,267 parents, 584 completed a Time 1 survey and 351 completed a survey at Time 2. No information (e.g., demographics) is provided on parents who did not complete either of the surveys or on those who completed only one. No information is provided on whether the 351 participants completed all survey questions or just a proportion.

Riggs et al. found no differences between experimental and control group parents who completed the second survey, so they concluded that "although the current sample is 28% of all parents reached at baseline, the lack of group differences at baseline coupled with a lack of program group differences in survey completion rates at follow-up allows us to reasonably expect that the current sample is representative of the overall study sample."

REFERENCES

Ajzen, I., & Fishbein, M. (1980). *Understanding attitudes and predicting social behavior*. Englewood Cliffs, NJ: Prentice Hall.

Bandura, A. (2001). Social cognitive theory: An agentic perspective. *Annual Review of Psychology*, *52*, 1–26.

Barch, C. A. (1996, December). *Seeking health care following stroke: Public education*. Paper presented at the National Symposium on Rapid Identification and Treatment of Acute Stroke, Bethesda, MD. Retrieved from http://www.ninds.nih.gov/news_and_events/proceedings/stroke_proceedings/Barch.htm

Becker, M. H. (Ed.). (1974). The health belief model and personal health behavior. *Health Education Monographs*, *2*, 324–473.

Bifulco, A., Bernazzani, O., Moran, P. M., & Jacobs, C. (2005). The childhood experience of care and abuse questionnaire (CECA.Q): Validation in a community series. *British Journal of Clinical Psychology*, *44*, 563–581.

Booth, B. M., Kirchner, J. E., Fortney, S. M., Han, X., Thrush, C. R., & French, M. T. (2006). Measuring use of health services for at-risk drinkers: How brief can you get? *Journal of Behavioral Health Services and Research*, *33*, 254–264.

Brockington, I. F., Fraser, C., & Wilson, D. (2006). The Postpartum Bonding uestionnaire: A validation. *Archives of Women's Mental Health, 9*, 233–242.

Centers for Disease Control and Prevention. (2009). *The socio-ecological model: A framework for prevention*. Retrieved from http://www.cdc.gov/violenceprevention/overview/social-ecologicalmodel.html

Chen, P.-H., Rovi, S., Vega, M., Jacobs, A., & Johnson, M. S. (2005). Screening for domestic violence in a predominantly Hispanic clinical setting. *Family Practice*, *22*, 617–623.

Cohen, J. A., Mannarino, A. P., & Iyengar, S. (2011). Community treatment of posttraumatic stress disorder for children exposed to intimate partner violence: A randomized controlled trial. *Archives of Pediatrics and Adolescent Medicine*, *165*, 16–21.

Feuerstein, M., & Nicholas, R. A. (2006). Development of a short form of the Workstyle measure. *Occupational Medicine*, *56*, 94–99.

Fix, G. A., & Schaefer, C. (2005). Note on psychometric properties of playfulness scales with adolescents. *Psychological Reports*, *96*, 993–994.

Foa, E. B., Johnson, K. M., Feeny, N. C., & Treadwell, K. R. H. (2001). The Child PTSD Symptom Scale: A preliminary examination of its psychometric properties. *Journal of Clinical Child Psychology*, *30*, 376–384.

Gache, P., Michaud, P., Landry, U., Accietto, C., Arfaoui, S., Wenger, O., et al. (2005). The Alcohol Use Disorders Identification Test (AUDIT) as a screening tool for excessive drinking in primary care: Reliability and validity of a French version. *Alcoholism, Clinical and Experimental Research*, *11*, 2001–2007.

Garrow, D., & Egede, L. E. (2006). Association between complementary and alternative medicine use, preventive care practices, and use of conventional medical services among adults with diabetes. *Diabetes Care, 29*, 15–19.

Godin, G., Belanger-Gravel, A., Amireault, S., Vohl, M. C., & Perusse, L. (2011). The effect of mere-measurement of cognitions on physical activity behavior: A randomized controlled trial among overweight and obese individuals. *Internaitonal Journal of Behavioral Nutrition and Physical Activity*, *8*, 2.

Hartman, C., Luteijn, E., Serra, M., & Minderaa, R. (2006). Refinement of the Children's Social Behavior Questionnaire (CSBQ): An instrument that describes the diverse problems seen in milder forms of PDD. *Journal of Autism and Developmental Disorders*, *36*, 325–342.

Herbert, R. J., Gagnon, A. J., O'Loughlin, J. L., & Rennick, J. E. (2011). Testing an empowerment intervention to help parents make homes smoke-free: A randomized controlled trial. *Journal of Community Health*, *36*, 650–657.

Kärnä, A., Voeten, M., Little, T. D., Poskiparta, E., Kaljonen, A., & Salmivalli, C. (2011). A large-scale evaluation of the KiVa antibullying program: Grades 4–6. *Child Development, 82*, 311–330.

King, C. A., Kramer, A., Preuss, L., Kerr, D. C. R., Weisse, L., & Venkataraman, S. (2006). Youth-nominated support team for suicidal adolescents (version 1): A randomized controlled trial. *Journal of Consulting and Clinical Psychology*, *74*, 199–206.

Klesges, R. C., Obarzanek, E., Kumanyika, S., Murray, D. M., Klesges, L. M., Relyea, G. E., et al. (2010). The Memphis Girls' health Enrichment Multi-site Studies (GEMS): An evaluation of the efficacy of a 2-year obesity prevention program in African American girls. *Archives of Pediatrics and Adolescent Medicine*, *164*, 1007–1014.

Landis, J. R., & Koch, G. G. (1977). The measurement of observer agreement for categorical data. *Biometrics*, *33*, 159–174.

Lieberman P., Morey, A., Hochstadt, J., Larson, M., Mather, S. (2005). Mount Everest: A space analogue for speech monitoring of cognitive deficits and stress. *Aviation, Space, and Environmental Medicine*, *76*, 1093–1101.

Lindqvist, J. K., Daderman, A. M., & Hellstrom, A. (2005). Internal reliability and construct validity of the Novaco Anger Scale-1998-S in a sample of violent prison inmates in Sweden. *Psychology Crime & Law*, *11*, 223–237.

MacMillan, H. L., Wathen, C. N., Jamieson, E., Boyle, M., McNutt, L.-A., Worster, A., et al. (2006). Approaches to screening for intimate partner violence in health care settings: A randomized trial. *Journal of the American Medical Association*, *296*, 530–536.

McFarlane, J. M., Groff, J. Y., O'Brien, J. A., & Watson, K. (2006). Secondary prevention of intimate partner violence: A randomized controlled trial. *Nursing Research*, *55*, 52–61.

McLeroy, K. R., Bibeau, D., Steckler, A., & Glanz, K. (1988). An ecological perspective on health promotion programs. *Health Education Quarterly*, *15*, 351–377.

McQuay, H. J., & Moore, R. A. (1997). Using numerical results from systematic reviews in clinical practice. *Annals of Internal Medicine*, *126*, 712–720.

Montaño, D. E., Kasprzyk, D., & Taplin, S. H. (1997). The theory of reasoned action and theory of planned behavior. In K. Glanz, F. M. Lewis, & B. K. Rimer (Eds.), *Health behavior and health education: Theory, research, and practice* (pp. 85–112). San Francisco, CA: Jossey-Bass.

Nemet, D., Barkan, S., Epstein, Y., Friedland, O., Kowen, G., & Eliakim, A. (2005). Short- and long-term beneficial effects of a combined dietary-behavioral-physical activity intervention for the treatment of childhood obesity. *Pediatrics*, *115*, e443–449.

Prochaska, J. O., Redding, C. A., & Evers, K. E. (2002). The transtheoretical model and stages of change. In K. Glanz, B. K. Rimer, & F. M. Lewis (Eds.), *Health behavior and health education: Theory, research, and practice* (3rd ed., pp. 99–120). San Francisco, CA: Jossey-Bass.

Riggs, N. R., Elfenbaum, P., & Pentz, M. A. (2006). Parent program component analysis in a drug abuse prevention trial. *Journal of Adolescent Health*, *39*, 66–72.

Rosenstock, I. M. (1996). Why people use health services. *Milbank Memorial Fund Quarterly*, *44*, 94–124.

Santa Mina, E. E., Gallop, R., Links, P., Heslegrave, R., Pringle, D., Wekerle, C., et al. (2006). The Self-Injury Questionnaire: Evaluation of the psychometric properties in a clinical population. *Journal of Psychiatric and Mental Health Nursing*, *13*, 221–227.

Sapp, S. G. (n.d.). *The theory of reasoned action.* Retrieved from http://www.soc.iastate.edu/sapp/soc-401FAM.html

Shah, R., & Ogden, J. (2006). "What's in a face?" The role of doctor ethnicity, age and gender in the formation of patients' judgements: An experimental study. *Patient Education and Counseling*, *60*, 136–141.

Stein, B. D., Jaycox, L. H., Kataoka, S. H., Wong, M., Tu, W., Elliott, M. N., et al. (2003). A mental health intervention for schoolchildren exposed to violence: A randomized controlled trial. *Journal of the American Medical Association*, *290*, 603–611.

Stutts, J., Feaganes, J., Reinfurt, D., Rodgman, E., Hamlett, C., Gish, K., et al. (2005). Driver's exposure to distractions in their natural driving environment. *Accident Analysis & Prevention*, *37*, 1093–1101.

U.S. Department of Health and Human Services. (2011). *Adolescent health.* Retrieved from http://healthypeople.gov/2020/topicsobjectives2020/objectiveslist.aspx?topicId=2

Wei, M., Russell, D., & Zakalik, R. (2005). Adult attachment, social self-efficacy, self-disclosure, loneliness, and subsequent depression for freshman college students: A longitudinal study. *Journal of Counseling Psychology*, *52*, 602–614.

Wolchik, S. A., Sandler, I. N., Millsap, R. E., Plummer, B. A., Greene, S. M., Anderson, E. R., et al. (2002). Six-year follow-up of preventive interventions for children of divorce: A randomized controlled trial. *Journal of the American Medical Association*, *288*, 1874–1881.

CHAPTER 6

THE BEST AVAILABLE EVIDENCE

Quality, Strength, Implementation, and Evaluation

This chapter discusses how to evaluate the research literature's quality and assess the strength of its evidence on programs and practices. Many health and medical journals require authors to use standardized reporting checklists as a condition of publication. The checklists provide an inventory of the domains that should be covered in a transparent study report. The domains include the research question, inclusion of participants and settings, comparability of participants and programs, outcomes, measures, statistical analysis, results, discussion, and funding or sponsorship. Reporting checklists are valuable aids in reviewing study quality and strength, and this chapter explains how to use six of them: CONSORT (randomized controlled trials), TREND (nonrandomized trials), STROBE (observational studies), PRISMA (systematic reviews and meta-analysis), MOOS (meta-analysis of observational studies), and SQUIRE (quality improvement).

The chapter also discusses specific scoring and grading systems (the U.S. Preventive Services Task Force, GRADE) to evaluate the strength of the evidence, and concludes with a discussion of criteria for selecting, implementing, and evaluating evidence-based programs in public health practice.

❖ CHAPTER OBJECTIVES

After reading this chapter, you will be able to

- Explain the characteristics of high-quality research as they apply to each of the following domains: derivation and clarity of the research questions; criteria for including participants and settings; methods for ensuring comparability of participants; and justification for and description of the program, its outcomes, data collection measures, statistical analysis, results, discussion, and funding or sponsorship
- Describe and use standardized reporting checklists as a basis for evaluating study quality and evidence strength; among the checklists are CONSORT (randomized controlled trials), TREND (nonrandomized trials), and STROBE (observational studies)
- Describe the features and uses of formal reporting checklists for systematic literature reviews and meta-analyses, such as PRISMA (systematic reviews and meta-analysis), MOOS (meta-analysis of observational studies), and the Institute of Medicine's standards
- Discuss the advantages and limitations of systems for grading study quality and the strength of the evidence; the systems include those developed by the U.S. Preventive Services Task Force and GRADE
- Prepare an abstraction form or questionnaire to extract data from the research literature on programs to improve health
- Describe the main features of charts and tables to display the results of research literature reviews
- Identify the important characteristics to look for in high-quality systematic research literature reviews and meta-analyses
- Discuss criteria to consider when selecting and implementing evidence-based public health programs
- Distinguish effectiveness from improvement evaluations
- Identify the important characteristics to look for in quality improvement studies using guidelines such as those encompassed by the SQUIRE checklist
- Discuss criteria for selecting and implementing programs
- Describe the main characteristics of the logic model for planning and evaluating public health programs

❖ SYNTHESIZING AND REPORTING RESULTS OF RESEARCH REVIEWS

Research literature reviews are used to help make informed decisions about potential programs and policies to meet public health needs. Doing a literature review means (a) applying highly systematic, explicit, and reproducible methods to identify relevant articles and reports and (b) selecting criteria for evaluating their quality and the strength of the evidence.

High-quality research meets certain methodological standards at certain levels. What are the standards and which levels assure quality? Here is a discussion between two literature reviewers about methods.

Reviewer 1:   I think we should focus on whether the study's sample is any good and whether its research design is internally and externally valid.

Reviewer 2:   OK. What would you look for?

Reviewer 1:   Well, I would read each study and ask questions: Was the sample randomly selected? Is the design internally valid? Externally valid?

Reviewer 2:   Is that it?

Reviewer 1:   What more do you want?

Reviewer 2:   Well, I can think of a whole bunch of things. For instance, I wouldn't just be concerned with random sampling, because sample size counts too. Also, I don't know how you would decide if a design was internally valid on the whole. Don't you need to ask specific questions? Is this design subject to maturation, selection, history, instrumentation, statistical regression, or history? If more than one group is included in the research, are the participants randomly assigned to each? Are participants blinded to which intervention they are in? Are participants measured over time? If so, is the number of observations explained? Justified? Shall I go on?

Reviewer 1:   There is no need to go on. I can see you know about research design and data collection, but I am not sure that all of the questions you raise are relevant to this particular literature review. For example, I doubt that we will find any blinded studies. We are relying primarily on nonrandomized research. Also, I am not certain we have the resources to answer all of your questions. We have at least 55 studies to review, and each review takes an hour under usual circumstances. Moreover, we plan on having two people review each article, and if they disagree on any aspect of the review, a third person will be called in to adjudicate. So you can see that we need at least 2 full weeks of personnel time to do the review, and we have already spent 3 weeks going through the process of identifying and obtaining access to the 55 studies. That comes to a total of 5 personnel weeks.

Reviewer 2:   Literature reviews are really time-consuming and very expensive. Let us examine each criterion to see how important it is to our review.

Reviewer 1 is correct in calling attention to the time and expense of doing reviews. But, increasingly, researchers are being asked to follow a set of reporting guidelines, and these almost always makes the reviewers' job a little easier by focusing it on accepted quality criteria.

In 1999, the U.S. Congress directed the Agency for Healthcare Research and Quality (AHRQ) to analyze systems to rate the strength of the scientific evidence underlying health care practices, research recommendations, and technology assessment. AHRQ commissioned the Evidence-Based Practice Center at Research Triangle Institute International–University of North Carolina to produce a report that would describe systems that rate the quality of evidence in individual studies or grade the strength of entire bodies of evidence and provide guidance on the best practices in the field of grading evidence (West et al., 2002). The researchers reviewed the literature and relied on experts to help them uncover and compare systems. They specified desirable domains, and, of those, they chose domains considered absolutely critical for a grading scheme. Table 6.1 lists the domains (e.g., study population) that compose the criteria for evaluating quality of individual randomized controlled trials (RCTs) and observational or nonrandomized studies. The critical domains are italicized.

As you can see from Table 6.1, for RCTs, an adequate statement of the study question is a *desirable* domain that a grading scheme should cover, but adequate descriptions of the study population, randomization, and blinding are *critical* domains that a grading scheme must cover. For observational and nonrandomized trials, the critical domains are the comparability of the participants, the program, statistical analysis, and funding or sponsorship.

In response to a growing demand for precise information about study purpose, design, methods, and findings, health and medical researchers as well as journal editors have endorsed checklists of items that should be addressed in transparent, high-quality research.

Table 6.1 Domains for Evaluating the Quality of RCTs and Observational/
Nonrandomized Studies

Randomized Controlled Trials	Observational/Nonrandomized Studies
Study question	Study question
Study population	Study population
Randomization	Comparability of participants
Blinding	Exposure or program/intervention
Interventions	Outcome measures
Outcomes	Statistical analysis
Statistical analysis	Results
Results	Discussion
Discussion	Funding or sponsorship
Funding or sponsorship	

SOURCE: Adapted from West et al., 2002.

CONSORTing With the Best

Perhaps the most famous reporting checklist is the **Consolidated Standards of Reporting Trials** (**CONSORT**). The CONSORT Statement consists of standards for reporting on randomized controlled trials (www.consort-statement.org). The statement is available in several languages and has been endorsed by prominent medical, clinical, and psychological journals.

CONSORT consists of a checklist and flow diagram. The checklist includes items that need to be addressed in the report; the flow diagram provides readers with a clear picture of the progress of all participants in the research, from the time they are randomized until the end of their involvement. The intent is to make the experimental process more clear so that consumers of RCTs can more appropriately evaluate their validity.

The original CONSORT Statement was based on the standard two-group parallel research design. However, there are several different types of randomized trials, some of which have different research designs (e.g., cluster), interventions (e.g., herbal medicinal), and data (e.g., harms-related data), and the CONSOSRT Statement has been continually revised to reflect these changes in methodology and focus. Example 6.1 is an excerpt from the CONSORT statement.

Example 6.1   Excerpts From the CONSORT 2010 Checklist of Information to Include When Reporting a Randomized Trial

Section/Topic	Item No.	Checklist item
Title and abstract		
	1a	Identification as a randomized trial in the title
	1b	Structured summary of trial design, methods, results, and conclusions (for specific guidance see CONSORT for abstracts)
Introduction		
Background and objectives	2a	Scientific background and explanation of rationale
	2b	Specific objectives or hypotheses
Methods		
Trial design	3a	Description of trial design (such as parallel, factorial), including allocation ratio
	3b	Important changes to methods after trial commencement (such as eligibility criteria), with reasons
Participants	4a	Eligibility criteria for participants
	4b	Settings and locations where the data were collected
Interventions	5	The interventions for each group, with sufficient details to allow replication, including how and when they were actually administered
Outcomes	6a	Completely defined prespecified primary and secondary outcome measures, including how and when they were assessed
	6b	Any changes to trial outcomes after the trial commenced, with reasons
Sample size	7a	How sample size was determined
	7b	When applicable, explanation of any interim analyses and stopping guidelines
Randomization:		
Sequence generation	8a	Method used to generate the random allocation sequence
	8b	Type of randomization; details of any restriction (such as blocking and block size)
Allocation concealment mechanism	9	Mechanism used to implement the random allocation sequence (such as sequentially numbered containers), describing any steps taken to conceal the sequence until interventions were assigned
Other information		
Registration	23	Registration number and name of trial registry
Protocol	24	Where the full trial protocol can be accessed, if available
Funding	25	Sources of funding and other support (such as supply of drugs), role of funders

SOURCE: http://www.consort-statement.org/index.aspx?o=3489

The CONSORT website provides an explanation of each of the items on the checklist. For instance, to better understand how to report on participants, it offers the information presented in Example 6.2.

Example 6.2   CONSORT Statement: Explanation and Illustration of How to Report on Participants' Eligibility

---

Item 4a—Eligibility criteria for participants

Example

"Eligible participants were all adults aged 18 or over with HIV who met the eligibility criteria for antiretroviral therapy according to the Malawian national HIV treatment guidelines (WHO clinical stage III or IV or any WHO stage with a CD4 count < 250/mm3) and who were starting treatment with a BMI < 18.5. Exclusion criteria were pregnancy and lactation or participation in another supplementary feeding programme."(93)

Explanation

A comprehensive description of the eligibility criteria used to select the trial participants is needed to help readers interpret the study. In particular, a clear understanding of these criteria is one of several elements required to judge to whom the results of a trial apply—that is, the trial's generalisability (applicability) and relevance to clinical or public health practice (see item 21).(94) A description of the method of recruitment, such as by referral or self selection (for example, through advertisements), is also important in this context. Because they are applied before randomisation, eligibility criteria do not affect the internal validity of a trial, but they are central to its external validity.

Typical and widely accepted selection criteria relate to the nature and stage of the disease being studied, the exclusion of persons thought to be particularly vulnerable to harm from the study intervention, and to issues required to ensure that the study satisfies legal and ethical norms. Informed consent by study participants, for example, is typically required in intervention studies. The common distinction between inclusion and exclusion criteria is unnecessary; the same criterion can be phrased to include or exclude participants.(95)

Despite their importance, eligibility criteria are often not reported adequately. For example, eight published trials leading to clinical alerts by the National Institutes of Health specified an average of 31 eligibility criteria in their protocols, but only 63% of the criteria were mentioned in the journal articles, and only 19% were mentioned in the clinical alerts.(96) Similar deficiencies were found for HIV clinical trials.(97) Among 364 reports of RCTs in surgery, 25% did not specify any eligibility criteria.

Note: The numbers in parentheses correspond to the authors' references and can be found by clicking on them in the website. Item 21, discussed under Explanation, refers to another item on the CONSORT checklist.

SOURCE: http://www.bmj.com/cgi/content/full/340/mar23_1/c869

The CONSORT statement is not just about methods. It requires researchers to also include information on the scientific rationale for the study, the source of funding, the funders' roles, and other factors that may affect the study's quality. Adherence to the CONSORT Statement results in transparent reporting, and transparency is essential for assessing the quality of research.

Nonrandomized and Observational Studies: TREND and STROBE

Many public health interventions are nonrandomized controlled trials or observational studies. The AHRQ critical domains for reporting nonrandomized trials (Table 6.1) include comparability of participants, exposure or program/intervention, outcome measures, and statistical analysis. These domains are addressed in the **TREND** (Transparent Reporting of Evaluations with Nonrandomized Designs) Statement of the American Public Health Association (Des Jarlais, Lyles, Crepaz, & the TREND Group, 2004) and Centers for Disease Control and Prevention (CDC; 2009). Example 6.3 is representative of a questionnaire based on the TREND Statement and shows how it is linked to AHRQ's quality domains. Like CONSORT, the TREND website gives examples of how its terms should be used.

Example 6.3 Questionnaire to Obtain Information on a Report of a Nonrandomized Trial's Adherence to Critical Quality Domains

Domain Specified by AHRQ	Quality Questions Based on the TREND Statement
Comparability of participants	1. Do the researchers provide data on study group equivalence at baseline?
	2. If baseline differences exist, is information given on the statistical methods used to take those differences ("control for") into account?
Program/intervention	3. Do the researchers thoroughly describe the experimental programs?
	4. Do the researchers provide an adequate explanation of the choice of comparison or control programs?
	5. Do the researchers thoroughly describe the comparison programs?

Domain Specified by AHRQ	Quality Questions Based on the TREND Statement
Outcome measures	6. Are all important outcomes considered?
	7. Do the researchers provide information on the size and precision of effects for main outcomes and intermediary or proximal outcomes?
	8. Do the researchers summarize all important adverse events or unintended effects?
Statistical analysis	9. Do the researchers discuss the statistical methods used to compare study groups for the primary outcomes?
	10. Do the researchers describe statistical methods for additional analyses such as subgroup analyses and adjusted analyses?
	11. Do the researchers describe methods for imputing missing data?

The STROBE (STrengthening the Reporting of OBservational studies in Epidemiology) Statement (von Elm et al., 2007), like CONSORT and TREND, provides guidance on how to report research, in this case, observational studies. The STROBE Statement, according to its authors, provides guidance to researchers on how to improve the reporting of observational studies and facilitates critical appraisal and interpretation of studies by reviewers, journal editors, and readers.

The STROBE Statement consists of a checklist of 22 items, which relate to the title, abstract, introduction, methods, results, and discussion sections of articles. Eighteen items are common to cohort studies, case-control studies, and cross-sectional studies, and 4 are specific to each of the three study designs. An Explanation and Elaboration article (Vandenbroucke et al., 2007) discusses each checklist item and gives methodological background and published examples of transparent reporting.

Example 6.4 contains a brief excerpt from a questionnaire using STROBE's standards for reporting methods in cohort studies. AHRQ's critical criteria of comparability of participants and outcomes are included. (For more on TREND, CONSORT, and STROBE, and to find additional reporting guidelines, see *Introduction to Reporting Guidelines,* n.d.)

Example 6.4   A Brief Portion of a Questionnaire Using STROBE

Domain Specified by AHRQ	Quality Questions Based on the STROBE Statement
Comparability of participants	1. Do the researchers describe the study's inclusion criteria?
	2. Do the researchers describe the study's exclusion criteria?
	3. Is there a description of the source of potential participants (e.g., all persons who visit the clinic in a certain month)
	4. Do the researchers describe how participants were selected from the pool of potential participants?
	5. If the study uses matching, do the researchers justify the choice of matching criteria?
Outcome Measures	6. Did the researcher define each of these:
	Outcomes
	Predictors
	Potential confounders

Scoring and Grading: Distinguishing Good From Poor-Quality Research Articles

Reviewers sometimes score each article and then, based on the score, assign a grade to represent the article's quality. Here are three commonly used grading and scoring methods:

1. **Assign a point for each quality criterion that is met, sum the points, and set a cutoff score for high quality.** For instance, the questionnaire in Example 6.3 consists of 11 questions. A scoring system can be set up in which an article must achieve a score of, say, 9 yeses or more in response to the questionnaire if it is to receive a high-quality grade. Example 6.5 shows how one study used the original AHRQ criteria to score study quality.

Example 6.5   Scoring Study Quality (Ciampa et al., 2010)

We assessed the quality of all articles included based on criteria by West et al. (AHRQ criteria). Every study was rated by 2 of us (P.J.C. and D.K.) in each of the following categories: (1) adequacy of the study population, (2) description of the study intervention, (3) comparability of study subjects, (4) maintenance of comparison groups, (5) measurement of outcomes, (6) appropriateness of the statistical analysis, and (7) control of confounding. Ratings were assigned numerical scores (2 is good; 1, fair; and 0, poor). A composite score was generated for each article by summing the category scores and dividing by the number of categories reviewed. These summary scores were then used to give an overall qualitative rating for the article. Articles with quality scores of 0.00 to 0.99 were considered of poor quality, 1.00 to 1.49 of fair quality, and 1.50 to 2.00 of good quality.

The Cochrane Collaboration (www.cochrane.org) provides its reviewing handbook and glossary online for free. The handbook contains the most comprehensive scoring system available.

Reviewers should use grading systems cautiously. Almost all systems assume that research consists of discrete activities and that poor performance of one or two activities may have little or no bearing on the quality of the remainder. Scientific research is, however, an amalgamated set of activities, and failure to meet high standards in one domain is likely to diminish the validity of all. The grading approach is easy to implement and understand, but it must be used with care.

2. **Weigh one or more criteria more heavily than others.** A reviewer can assume that each article absolutely must attain satisfactory performance on one or several specific criteria to be assigned a high-quality score. For instance, reviewers may decide that to receive a high-quality grade, a study must (without exception) meet two criteria: (1) describe the procedures for randomization and (2) describe, in both the experimental and comparison groups, the number of participants who withdrew and the reasons they withdrew. If a study meets only one of these two criteria, regardless of which one, the study is downgraded.

3. **Assign all criteria equal weight**, and assume that all high-quality studies must achieve all criteria, that is, get a perfect score. This is a very stringent approach to grading, and it may be difficult to enforce, especially if good (but not perfect) studies are downgraded or eliminated from consideration.

The following is a checklist of activities that should occur in applying any system.

Checklist for Scoring and Grading a Study's Methodological Quality

✓ Decide on all the factors that are important standards of high quality, such as randomization, thorough program descriptions, and appropriate and effectively reported statistical analysis.

✓ Select a scoring system (e.g., all study participants must be random-ized, all participants must be included in the analysis regardless of whether they completed all data collection activities).

✓ Define all key terms (e.g., reliable data collection) in advance of the review.

✓ Create a questionnaire or other template for recording the informa-tion abstracted from the literature review.

✓ Review 5 to 10 articles to test the reviewing process. If necessary, revise the process. Be sure to anticipate the need for revisions, which can take time and use up resources.

✓ Decide if the reviewers should be blinded to the authors' names or institutions. Some experts believe that removing names removes the temptation to favor one's friends or reject one's enemies. The evidence on the value of blinding in reducing such bias is ambiguous.

✓ All reviewers should jointly review 5 to 10 articles. The articles can be the same as those used in the first round. Each article should be dis-cussed among reviewers after it is reviewed. Reviewers must agree on the meaning and answer to each item on the questionnaire. In cases of disagreement, another person not directly involved in the review should adjudicate. This person should understand the objectives of the review and be trained to do literature reviews.

✓ Begin the review in earnest when the reviewers are confident that they are likely to agree on the meaning of all concepts (e.g., what constitutes an "adequate" program description, the definition of *validity*).

✓ Monitor the quality of the review. Ask reviewers to jointly re-review every 5th or 10th article to ensure that each has been consistent in his or her responses and that the reviewers agree on the responses. Alternatively, ask an uninvolved person—the "gold standard"—to do a review of every 5th or 10th article. If only one reviewer is doing the review, that person should randomly select 3 articles from the first 10 he or she reviewed and review them again 1 week after the first review. If inconsistencies are found in the joint or individual review, check the definitions of all terms and, if necessary, retrain the reviewers.

Quality, Quantity, and Consistency = Strength of Evidence

AHRQ defines the strength of the evidence as a combined index of its *quality, quantity,* and *consistency.* The quality of evidence is a sum of the grading of the individual articles. The quantity of evidence is the magnitude of effects. The consistency of results reflects the extent to which the research findings consist of effects of similar magnitude and direction.

The **U.S. Preventive Services Task Force (USPSTF)** is an independent panel of experts in primary care and prevention that systematically reviews the evidence of effectiveness and develops recommendations for clinical preventive services. The USPSTF is now under the auspices of AHRQ. In making its recommendations, the USPSTF grades by combining assessments of quality, quantity, and consistency of evidence.

The USPSTF's quality grading system is similar to that used by health authorities in Canada and the United Kingdom. Level I, the highest quality, consists of evidence obtained from at least one properly randomized controlled trial. Level II is divided into three parts. Level II–1 is evidence that is obtained from well-designed controlled trials without randomization. Level II–2 consists of evidence obtained from well-designed cohort or case-control analytic studies—preferably from more than one center or research group. And Level II–3 is evidence obtained from multiple time-series studies with or without the intervention. Dramatic results in uncontrolled experiments (e.g., the results of the introduction of penicillin treatment in the 1940s) can also be regarded as Level II evidence. The weakest evidence is Level III, which consists of opinions of respected authorities, based on their clinical experience; descriptive studies and case reports; and reports of expert committees.

The USPSTF grades its recommendations according to one of five classifications (A, B, C, D, and I) reflecting the strength of evidence and magnitude of net benefit (benefits minus harms). Table 6.2 describes the grading system.

Table 6.2 U.S. Preventive Services Task Force (USPSTF) Recommendations and the Strength of the Evidence

A.—The USPSTF strongly recommends that clinicians provide [the service] to eligible patients. The USPSTF found good evidence that [the service] improves important health outcomes and concludes that benefits substantially outweigh harms. **Good:** Evidence includes consistent results from well-designed, well-conducted studies in representative populations that directly assess effects on health outcomes.

(Continued)

Table 6.2 (Continued)

B.—The USPSTF recommends that clinicians provide [this service] to eligible patients. The USPSTF found at least fair evidence that [the service] improves important health outcomes and concludes that benefits outweigh harms. **Fair:** Evidence is sufficient to determine effects on health outcomes, but the strength of the evidence is limited by the number, quality, or consistency of the individual studies, [their] generalizability to routine practice, or [the] indirect nature of the evidence on health outcomes.

C.—The USPSTF makes no recommendation for or against routine provision of [the service]. The USPSTF found at least fair evidence that [the service] can improve health outcomes but concludes that the balance of benefits and harms is too close to justify a general recommendation.

D.—The USPSTF recommends against routinely providing [the service] to asymptomatic patients. The USPSTF found at least fair evidence that [the service] is ineffective or that harms outweigh benefits.

I.—The USPSTF concludes that the evidence is insufficient to recommend for or against routinely providing [the service]. Evidence that the [service] is effective is lacking, of poor quality, or conflicting, and the balance of benefits and harms cannot be determined. **Poor:** Evidence is insufficient to assess the effects on health outcomes because of [the] limited number or power of studies, important flaws in their design or conduct, gaps in the chain of evidence, or lack of information on important health outcomes.

SOURCE: The Guide to Clinical Preventive Services 2006: Recommendations of the U.S. Preventive Services Task Force. Agency for Healthcare Research and Quality. http://www.ahrq.gov/clinic/pocketgd.pdf

The **Grades of Recommendation, Assessment, Development, and Evaluation** (**GRADE**; Guyatt, Oxman, Schünemann, Tugwell, & Knotterus, 2011) offers a system for rating the quality of evidence in systematic reviews and provides guidelines and for grading the strength of recommendations guiding practice. The system is designed for reviews and guidelines that examine alternative interventions, which may include no intervention or current best management (usual care).

GRADE is designed to provide a systematic framework for clarifying questions, determining the outcomes of interest, summarizing the evidence that addresses a question, and moving from the evidence to a recommendation or decision (see Figure 6.1).

In the GRADE approach, RCTs start as high-quality evidence and observational studies as low-quality evidence supporting estimates of program effects. Five factors may lead to rating down the quality of evidence, and three factors may lead to rating up (see Figure 6.2).

Figure 6.1 GRADE's Process for Developing Recommendations

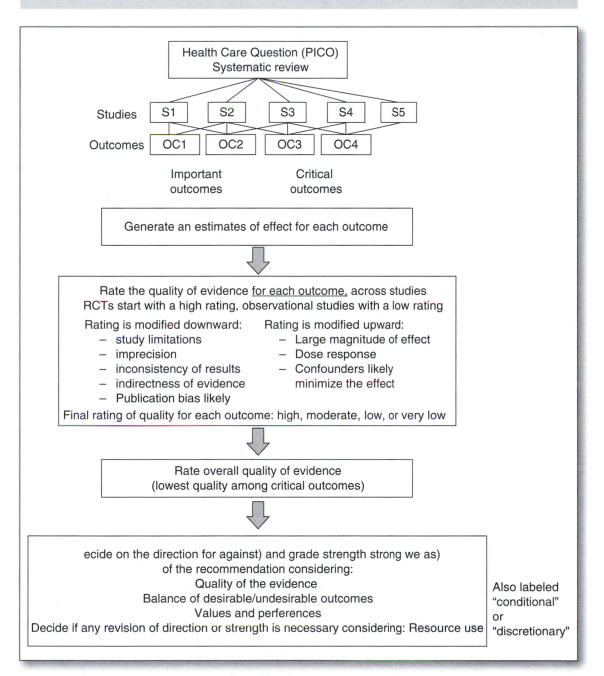

Figure 6.2 Quality Criteria

Study Design	Quality of Evidence	Lower if	Higher if
Randomized trial ➡	High	Risk of bias −1 Serious −1 Very serious	Large effect +1 Large +2 Very large
	Moderate	Inconsistency −1 Serious −2 Very serious	Dose response +1 Evidence of a gradient
Observational Study ➡	Low	Indirectness −1 Serious −2 Very serious	All plausible confounding +1 Would reduce a demonstrated effort
	Very low	Imprecision −1 Serious −2 Very serious	+1 Would suggest a spurious effect when results show no effect
		Publication bias −1 Likely −2 Very likely	

GRADE specifies four categories (high, moderate, low, very low) that are applied to a body of evidence, not to individual studies. In the context of a systematic review, quality in the GRADE system reflects confidence that the estimates of the effect are correct. *Quality* as used in GRADE is defined as more than risk of bias because quality may also be compromised by imprecision, inconsistency, indirectness of study results, and publication bias.

Does The Evidence Make the Grade?

Most reviewers rely on a form that tells them what to look for (e.g., "Describe the program's objectives") and provides them with a place to record the data. The process of reading and recording is called *abstracting the literature*. An abstraction form may be a printed questionnaire, an Microsoft Access data table or spreadsheet, or any other systematic method of recording information. The results are placed in evidence tables (see Example 6.7). Evidence tables are often so large that rather than being published in their entirety, they are made available online.

Example 6.7 **A Part of an Evidence Table From a Review of the Literature on Health Literacy (Berkman et al., 2011)**

Author, Date of Publication, Quality	Study Design	Control Group	Intervention	Sample Size	% Population with Limited Literacy	Outcome	Difference
DeWalt et al., 2006[202] Fair	RCT	Usual Care + low literacy pamphlet Management program on CHF	CHF Self-	127	41% S-TOFHLA inadequate	CHF related Quality of Life by MLHF (range of scores 0-105)	Heart failure-related quality of life (adjusted): 2 (95% CI, 9 to -5) Adequate Health Literacy Subgroup (adjusted) -4.2 (95% CI -14 to S) Inadequate Health Literacy Subgroup (adjusted): -1.6, 95% CI -15 to 12 within intervention Group
Murray et al., 2007[182] Good	RCT	Usual Care	CHF Adherence Intervention	314	29% "not literate" on S-TOFHLA (NOS)	Mean score on Chronic Heart Failure Questionnaire (range from 1 to 7; better functioning = higher)	(unadjusted): +0.39

(Continued)

Example 6.7 (Continued)

Author, Date of Publication, Quality	Study Design	Control Group	Intervention	Sample Size	% Population with Limited Literacy	Outcome	Difference
Rudd et al., 2009[209] Fair	RCT	Arthritis Management Intervention (arthritis pamphlet medicine calendar, hospital map)	Arthritis Management Intervention + Individual Counseling	127	19% REALM ≤ high school	HAQ scores (range of scores 0–3,0 best)	Mean percent change in HAQ scores at 12 months: 6 months: −3.60%a*, p 0.45 12 months: −2.12%a″, p 0.64
Schillinger et al., 2008[187] Schillinger et al., 2009[210]	RCT	Usual Care	(1) Diabetes Self Management Program (automated telephone delivery) (2) Diabetes Self-Management Program (group medical visit delivery)	339	59% S-TOFHLA ≤ 22 (inadequate or marginal)	SF12-Mental health scale (score range 0 – 100) SF-12 Physical health scale (score range 0–100) Mean # days in bed in last month due to health	SF-12 mental health: ATSM-Usual Care (adjusted): 3.7 (−2 to 9.4) GMV-Usual Care (adjusted): −2.9 (−2.6 to 2.9) ATSM-GMV (adjusted): −6.5 (0.7 to 12.4)

Data tables are visual guides. They assist the reviewer in reporting findings and conclusions, and they enable readers to evaluate the reviewer's logic.

RELIABLE AND VALID REVIEWS ❖

A reliable review is one that consistently provides the same information about methods and content for every study reviewed, whether the review is conducted by one person (reliable "within") or by several reviewers (reliable "across"). A valid review is an accurate one.

Large literature reviews nearly always have more than one reviewer, and small ones should aim for at least two. The idea is that each reviewer examines each evaluation, and the results of the examinations are compared. Perfect agreement between (or among) reviewers means perfect inter-rater reliability.

Sometimes, to promote objectivity, one or more of the reviewers are not told the names of the authors of the study, the name of the publication, or when or where the study took place; they are blinded. In relatively smaller reviews (those with scant resources and just one reviewer), objectivity can be improved by having the single reviewer re-review a randomly selected sample of studies. Perfect agreement from the first to the second review is considered perfect intra-rater reliability.

Measuring Review Reliability: The Kappa Statistic

Suppose two reviewers are asked to evaluate independently the quality of 100 studies on the effectiveness of prenatal care programs in preventing low-weight births. Each reviewer is asked, "Do the study's authors include low-risk as well as high-risk women in their analysis?" Here are the reviewers' answers to this question.

		Reviewer 2		
		No	**Yes**	**Total**
Reviewer 1	No	20[C]	15	35[B]
	Yes	10	55[D]	65
	Total	30[A]	70	

Reviewer 2 says that 30 ([A]) of the studies fail to collect prospective data, while Reviewer 1 says that 35 ([B]) fail to do so. The two reviewers agree that 20 ([C]) studies (out of the 30 and 35 each picked) do not collect prospective data.

What is the best way to describe the extent of agreement between the reviewers? A 20% (^{C}) agreement is probably too low; the reviewers also agree that 55% (^{P}) of studies include low-risk women. The total agreement arrived at through this calculation—55% + 20%—is an overestimate because, with only two categories (yes and no), some agreement may occur by chance.

The measuring of agreement between two reviewers is called *kappa*, defined as the agreement beyond chance divided by the amount of agreement possible beyond chance. This is shown in the following formula, in which O is the observed agreement and C is the chance agreement.

$$K = \frac{O - C}{1 - C} \quad \begin{array}{l} \text{(Agreement beyond chance)} \\ \text{(Agreement possible beyond chance)} \end{array}$$

Here is how the formula works with the above example:

1. Calculate how many studies the reviewers may agree by chance *do not* collect prospective data. This is done by multiplying the number of no answers and dividing by 100 because there are 100 studies: $30 \times 35/100 = 10.5$.

2. Calculate how many studies they may agree by chance *do* collect prospective data by multiplying the number of studies each found collected prospective data. This is done by multiplying the number of yes answers and dividing by 100: $70 \times 65/100 = 40.5$.

3. Add the two numbers obtained in Question 1 and 2 and divide by 100 to get a proportion for chance agreement: $(10.5 + 45.5)/100 = 0.56$.

The observed agreement is 20% + 55% = 75% or 0.75. Therefore, the agreement beyond chance is $0.75 - 0.56 = 0.19$: the numerator.

The agreement possible beyond chance is 100% minus the chance agreement of 56%, or $1 - 0.56 = 0.44$: the denominator.

$$K = \frac{0.19}{0.44}$$

$$K = 0.43$$

As with other measurements of reliability, a kappa of 0.0–0.2 = slight; 0.2–0.4 = fair; 0.4–0.6 = moderate; 0.6–0.8 = substantial, and 0.8–1.0 = almost perfect. In a literature review, you should aim for a kappa of 0.6 to 1.0.

How do you achieve substantial or almost perfect agreement—reliability—among reviewers? You do this by making certain that all reviewers collect and record data on exactly the same topics and that they agree in advance on what each important variable means. The "fair" kappa of 0.43 obtained by the reviewers above can be due to differences between the reviewers' definitions of high- and low-risk women or between the reviewers' and researchers' definitions.

Reviewing Other Reviews: Narrative Reviews and Systematic Reviews

Until now, we have been discussing how to find relevant *single* articles and evaluate their quality. In your search, you may find that others have already produced a literature review on the topic of interest. These good people appear to have done all the work by searching the literature, identifying several pertinent articles, and summarizing the results. However, if you find an existing review, you still need to evaluate its quality and timelines. To evaluate the quality means first determining the type of review you are dealing with.

Reviews of the literature are either systematic or narrative. A systematic review follows a detailed set of procedures, or a **protocol**, that includes a focused study question (e.g., PICO); a specific search strategy (that defines the search terms and databases that are used as well as the criteria for including and excluding studies); and specific instructions on the types of data to be abstracted on study objectives, methods, findings, and quality.

Narrative reviews often do not have a specific protocol. For example, they rarely describe their search strategy or inclusion and exclusion criteria. Such reviews may be subject to selection bias because the reviewer may include or exclude studies at will. Narrative reviews do not apply quality standards, so they may contain studies of unknown or varying reliability and validity. The credibility of a narrative review is almost entirely dependent upon the reviewer's credibility.

Systematic literature reviews take two forms. The first produces **qualitative** (or descriptive) **summaries** of the literature based on trends the review finds across the initially reviewed studies. In some fields (e.g., nursing) this review is called *meta-synthesis*. The second form of literature review uses statistical methods to produce a quantitative summary of the program effects that were presented in the initial reviews. It is called **meta-analysis**.

Example 6.8 contains descriptions of systematic literature reviews whose methods and results are qualitative: No attempt is made to combine the studies statistically. Note that in the Methods section of both studies in the example, the investigators record that they searched more than one database and reviewed multiple articles. The review of research on exposure to interpersonal violence in childhood and risk for obesity and central adiposity used two databases and evaluated 36 articles. The review of research on mothers who murder used four databases and summarized 39 articles.

Example 6.8   Qualitative (Descriptive) Systematic Literature Reviews

1. **Interpersonal Violence in Childhood as a Risk Factor for Obesity: A Systematic Review of the Literature and Proposed Pathways (Midei & Matthews, 2011)**

We examined the associations between exposure to interpersonal violence in childhood and risk for obesity and central adiposity. Interpersonal violence is defined as behavior that threatens, attempts or causes physical harm. In addition, we evaluated the evidence for three mechanisms that may connect interpersonal violence to obesity: negative affect, disordered eating and physical inactivity. Based on a literature search of Medline and PsycInfo databases, 36 separate studies were evaluated and ranked based on quality. Approximately 81% of the studies reported a significant positive association between some type of childhood interpersonal violence and obesity, although 83% of the studies were cross-sectional. Associations were consistent for caregiver physical and sexual abuse and peer bullying, and there was mixed evidence for community violence. Although few studies explored mechanisms, early evidence suggests that negative affect and disordered eating may be involved. More prospective studies are needed, as well as studies that examine the mechanisms connecting early childhood victimization to obesity and central adiposity.

2. **Child Murder by Mothers: A Critical Analysis of the Current State of Knowledge and a Research Agenda (Friedman, Horwitz, & Resnick, 2005)**

Background. Maternal filicide, or child murder by mothers, occurs more frequently in the United States than in other developed nations. However, little is known about factors that confer risk to children. The authors review the literature to identify predictors of maternal filicide and identify gaps in knowledge about maternal filicide.

Method. Databases [PubMed (Medline), PsychINFO, the Psychology and Behavioral Sciences Collection, and Sociological Abstracts] were systematically searched for studies of maternal filicide and neonaticide (murder in the first day of life) that were conducted in industrialized countries and were published in peer-reviewed, English-language publications after 1980. Search terms included "filicide," "infanticide," "neonaticide," and "fatal child maltreatment." The database search yielded more than 250 references in the extant literature. The majority consisted of case reports, reports on a series of filicide cases, and conceptual theoretical papers, and these publications were excluded. Eighty-three studies of child homicide were identified. Forty-two of these 83 studies reported on child homicide but did not distinguish maternal filicide from paternal filicide or murder by a stepparent or a nonparent. Those studies were not included in our analysis because they did not yield specific information about maternal perpetrators. Two studies of maternal filicide were excluded because they presented data that were primarily historical (dating to 1850 or the early 1900s) and did not separately consider more recent data. After exclusions, there remained 39 studies that were appropriate for use in our analysis.

Results. Women who committed filicide varied greatly by the type of sample studied. Neonaticide was often committed by young, poor, unmarried women with little or no prenatal care.

Conclusions. The results of the review suggest that little is known about the predictors of maternal filicide and that a systematic, focused program of research on reliable markers for maternal filicide is needed to better prevent these events.

Systematic Reviews: Meta-Analysis

A meta-analysis (Example 6.9) is a systematic review of the literature that uses formal statistical techniques to sum up the results of separate studies on the same topic. The idea is that the larger numbers obtained by combining study findings provide greater statistical power than any of the individual studies do.

Example 6.9   Abstract of a Meta-analysis: Effectiveness of Brief Alcohol Interventions in Primary Care Populations (Kaner et al., 2007)

Background. Many trials reported that brief interventions are effective in reducing excessive drinking. However, some trials have been criticised for being clinically unrepresentative and unable to inform clinical practice.

Objectives. To assess the effectiveness of brief intervention, delivered in general practice or based primary care, to reduce alcohol consumption. To assess whether outcomes differ between trials in research settings and those in routine clinical settings.

Search Strategy. We searched the Cochrane Drug and Alcohol Group specialised register (February 2006), MEDLINE (1966 to February 2006), EMBASE (1980 to February 2006), CINAHL (1982 to February 2006), PsycINFO (1840 to February 2006), Science Citation Index (1970 to February 2006), Social Science Citation Index (1970 to February 2006), Alcohol and Alcohol Problems Science Database (1972 to 2003), reference lists of articles.

Selection Criteria. Randomised controlled trials [RCTs], patients presenting to primary care not specifically for alcohol treatment, brief intervention of up to four sessions.

Data Collection and Analysis. Two authors independently abstracted data and assessed trial quality. Random effects meta-analyses, sub-group, sensitivity analyses, and meta-regression were conducted.

Main Results. Meta-analysis of 22 RCTs (enrolling 7,619 participants) showed that participants receiving brief intervention had lower alcohol consumption than the control group after follow-up of one year or longer (mean difference: –38 grams/week, 95% CI: –54 to –23), although there was substantial heterogeneity between trials (I2 = 57%). Sub-group analysis (8 studies, 2,307 participants) confirmed the benefit of brief intervention in men (mean difference: –57 grams/week, 95% CI: –89 to –25, I2 = 56%), but not in women (mean difference: –10 grams/week, 95% CI: –48 to 29, I2 = 45%). Meta-regression showed little evidence of a greater reduction in alcohol consumption with longer treatment exposure or among trials which were less clinically representative. Extended intervention was associated with a non-significantly greater reduction in alcohol consumption than brief intervention (mean difference = –28, 95%CI: –62 to 6 grams/week, I2 = 0%).

Conclusions. Overall, brief interventions lowered alcohol consumption. When data were available by gender, the effect was clear in men at one year of follow up, but not in women. Longer duration of counselling probably has little additional effect. The lack of evidence of any difference in outcomes between efficacy and effectiveness trials suggests that the current literature is relevant to routine primary care. Future trials should focus on women and on delineating the most effective components of interventions.

The concept of effect size is central to meta-analysis. An effect is the extent to which an outcome is present in the population, and it is a crucial component of sample size selection. The likelihood that an evaluation will be able to uncover an association between program participation and a good outcome—an **effect**—depends on the actual magnitude of that association in the target population.

How Many People and What Effect?

Target populations are the people who are supposed to benefit from a program, even though only a sample of them actually participates in it. For example, suppose a program aims to prevent child neglect (the outcome or the desired effect) on the part of young parents who have a history of neglect (the target) by providing them with parental coping skills (the program). Suppose also that the researchers cannot enlist all young parents with histories of neglect in their study because the study's resources are not able to handle all, and besides, some live far from the research site. Moreover, good statistical practice says that not every member of a population needs to participate anyway if a representative subgroup is carefully selected. The research team decides to select a sample of parents and not worry about including all.

The researchers set specific eligibility criteria for participation: parents must (a) be 21 years of age or younger, (b) have a previous history of child neglect, and (c) attend any one of the city's prenatal care clinics.

Ideally, the researchers would like to see an effect (prevention of child neglect) that is clearly linked to participation in the program (which aims to provide parental coping skills). Previous research shows that, if the effect in the target population is large, you can detect it more easily if the sample is small, but that small effects may go unnoticed unless the sample is large. In fact, the smaller the effect, the larger the sample needs to be in order to detect it. Unfortunately, the researchers have no way of knowing the size of the association in the target population. In fact, one of the jobs of the study is to find that out. Without that advance knowledge, the researchers are forced to figure out how large an association they would *like* to find or that *is meaningful* (or both). That quantity—the size of the association—is known as the **effect size**.

Expert researchers do not just come up with uninformed effect sizes. They find data from prior studies in related areas to make estimates. Sometimes, these are confirmed with experts who can help decide the clinical relevance of hoped-for effect sizes. When programs are designed to influence large numbers of people, small differences (e.g., 5 points on a standardized test of reading) might be important, especially if they are relatively easy to achieve. The choice of effect size is always somewhat arbitrary, however, with feasibility always uppermost in the researcher's mind. Sometimes, when the number of available participants is limited, researchers will work backward and ask this question: If I have this many participants, what is the effect size I can hope to see?

The researchers use statistical techniques to determine how large a sample is needed to uncover the hoped-for effect. If the sample for the evaluation is too small, a true difference in effect may be missed. This can be a serious error. You will find many studies in which neither the sample nor effect size is justified.

The determination of sample size is also referred to as **power analysis** because the number of persons in the study determines (to some degree) the power the researcher has to detect an effect or a true difference in experimental and control groups.

Experts in research design and sampling encourage researchers to choose one primary outcome on which to base sample size calculations. Sample size calculators can be found on the Internet.

Odds, Risks, and Effects

Risks and **odds** are alternative methods for describing the likelihood that a particular effect will or will not take place, but they do so in different ways. For example, suppose that, for every 100 persons who have headaches, 20 people have headaches that can be described as severe. The risk of a severe headache is 20/100 or 0.20. The odds of having severe headaches are calculated by comparing the number of persons with severe headaches (20) against the number without (100 − 20 or 80) or 20/80 = 0.25. The difference between risks and odds is shown in the table below.

Number of Persons With Outcome	Risk	Odds
20 of 100	20/100 = 0.20	20/80 = 0.25
40 of 100	40/100 = 0.40	40/60 = 0.66
50 of 100	50/100 = 0.50	50/50 = 1.00
90 of 100	90/100 = 0.90	90/10 = 9.00

Because risks and odds are really just different ways of talking about the same relationship, one can be derived from the other. Risk converts to odds by dividing risk by 1 minus the risk, and odds can be converted to risk by dividing odds by odds plus 1.

$$ODDS = (RISK)/(1 - RISK)$$

$$RISK = (ODDS)/(1 + ODDS)$$

When an outcome is infrequent, little difference exists in numerical values between odds and risks. When the outcome is frequent, however, differences emerge. If, for instance, 20 of 100 persons have headaches, the risks and odds are similar: 0.20 and 0.25, respectively. If 90 of 100 persons have headaches, then the risks are 0.90 and the odds are 9.00.

Both risks and odds are used to describe the likelihood that a particular outcome will occur within a group (e.g., the group with or the group without headaches). But risks and odds can also be used in comparing groups (e.g., experimental and control groups). When they are, you are comparing the *relative* likelihood that an outcome will take place. The **relative risk** expresses the risk of a particular outcome in the experimental group relative to the risk of the outcome in the control group. The **odds ratio** is a description of the comparison of the odds of the outcome in the experimental group with the odds in the control group.

The relative risk and the odds ratio will be less than 1 when an outcome occurs less frequently in the experimental than in the control group. Similarly, both will be greater than 1 if the outcome occurs more frequently in the experimental than in the control group. The direction of the relative risk and odds ratio (less than or greater than 1) is always the same. The extent to which the odds ratio and relative risk deviate from one another can be quite different.

But what significance do measurements of risk or odds have for meta-analysis? These measurements are crucial in any systematic, quantitative review because it is the effect sizes that are combined statistically in meta-analysis, and these are sometimes expressed as relative risk or an odds ratio. Suppose you do a literature review to find out the effect of a low-fat diet on your blood pressure. Typically, an effect size that expresses the magnitude and direction of the results would be calculated for each study in the review. For example, a positive effect of fish oil might be expressed as the difference in mean blood pressure levels between a group given a low-fat diet and a group not on a low-fat diet (possibly divided by a within-group standard deviation). A positive sign can be given if the low-fat diet group has lower postintervention blood pressure and a negative sign given when the opposite is true. As a second example, think of a group of studies examining whether attitude toward reading is associated with age. The effect size can be the correlation between age and satisfaction (as a component of the concept of *attitude*), with positive correlations indicating that older students are more satisfied than are younger students. In this example, the effect size is an expression of the degree of relationship between two variables.

There are many ways to define the average or typical effect size. Among the most commonly reported is the weighted mean, where weighting is by the size of the study. The idea is that effect sizes based on larger studies have more stability and should be weighted more heavily than the more variable effect sizes based on smaller studies. But this may be misleading. Suppose, for example, interventions in larger studies were intrinsically weaker and had less of an impact than the more intensive interventions that might be possible in smaller studies; the average effect size weighted by study size would be systematically biased toward the weaker interventions and could lead to a pessimistic conclusion. Because of this, many statisticians and epidemiologists urge the reporting of both weighted and unweighted average effect sizes.

A Checklist of Questions to Guide in Evaluating the Quality of a Meta-Analysis

A meta-analysis is an observational study in which the participants are research articles and not people. You need to be able to evaluate the quality of a synthesis of research just as you must when you review a single study. The following are seven questions to use in the evaluation.

✓ 1. Are the objectives of the meta-analysis unambiguous?

The objectives are the purposes for doing the analysis. Meta-analyses have been done about subjects as diverse as school-based smoking prevention programs, adolescent gambling disorders, consumer choice and subliminal advertising, cesarean childbirth and psychosocial outcomes, and the effectiveness of intravenous streptokinase during acute myocardial infarction and of the use of electroshock in the treatment of depression. But just listing a topic is not the same as describing how the literature will be used to learn more about the topic (see Example 6.10).

Example 6.10   Unambiguous Meta-Analysis Objectives or Questions

Objective 1: To examine the association between birth spacing and relative risk of adverse perinatal outcomes, we performed a systematic review, including meta-analysis, of the relationship between birth spacing and the risk of adverse perinatal outcomes that provided an overall summary of the effect measure and determined both the riskiest and the optimal interpregnancy intervals. In addition, we determined whether estimates of the effect size depend on dimensions of study quality of the primary studies.

Comment: This statement is unambiguous because it describes exactly what to expect from the analysis. For instance, the reviewer can expect to obtain information on

Birth spacing and relative risk of adverse perinatal outcomes

An overall summary of the effect

The riskiest and optimal intervals between pregnancies

Estimates of whether the effect size depends on study quality

Objective 2: A key prevention strategy is improved screening of depressed patients by primary care physicians and better treatment of major depression. This review considers what is known about this and other prevention strategies to permit integration into a comprehensive prevention strategy.

Comment: This analysis will provide information on what is known about improved screening for depression and other prevention strategies.

Objective 3: The purpose of this article is to conduct a meta-analysis on the facilitative effects of offering young children the opportunity to draw as part of an interview process and to determine if sufficient evidence exists to include drawings in research and clinical protocols and practice as a method of facilitating communication with children.

Comment: This analysis will provide information on what is known about offering children the opportunity to draw when interviewing them and if the strength of the evidence is sufficient to include drawing as part of clinical protocol and practice.

✓ 2. Are the inclusion and exclusion criteria explicit?

Very conservative statisticians and epidemiologists assert that only true experiments or randomized trials are eligible to be included in a systematic review. More liberal statisticians and epidemiologists will accept all high-quality studies. They often group them by study design characteristics, such as random or nonrandom assignment, to estimate if differences exist between the findings of higher and lower quality studies. The technique used to conduct separate analyses of studies of different quality is **sensitivity analysis**. When doing the review, check that the meta-analyst specifies and justifies quality criteria and that high-quality studies are not analyzed together with studies of lower quality.

✓ 3. Are the search strategies described in detail?

Electronic and manual literature searches that are supplemented by consultation with experts in the field are the order of the day for all literature reviews. In meta-analyses, it may be important to make certain that data are included from ongoing studies that have not yet been published. If they are not, the analysis may fall victim to **publication bias**, a term used to mean that a review unfairly favors the results of published studies. Published studies may differ from unpublished ones in that they tend to have positive findings; negative findings or findings of no difference between groups do not get published as frequently (in the English-language literature). The general rule in estimating the extent of the bias is to consider that, if the available data uncovered by the review are from high-quality studies and are reasonably consistent in direction, then the number of opposite findings will have to be extremely large to overturn the results.

A number of statistical techniques are available to help deal with publication bias. Formulas are available that you can use to estimate the number of published studies showing no differences between programs that are needed to convert a statistically significant pooled difference into an insignificant difference. If the number of unpublished studies needed to overturn your findings is small relative to the number of published studies pooled in the meta-analysis, then you should be concerned about potential publication bias.

Other methods include estimating the size of the population from which each study group is drawn. Using this information and the study's sample size, potential publication bias can be calculated for individual studies. Software is available for investigating publication bias by graphically displaying sample size plotted against effect size. Some researchers suggest that this graphic display (which is called a *funnel plot*) should always be examined as part of a meta-analysis if a sufficient number of studies are available.

✓ 4. Is a standardized protocol used to screen the literature?

Usually, two or more reviewers determine the quality of each study in the total number of potential studies to be included in the review. To ensure a consistent review, researchers should prepare a screening protocol. This means that each study is reviewed in a uniform manner.

✓ 5. Is a standardized protocol or abstraction form used to collect data?

Once studies are selected, they are reviewed and information is abstracted. The best meta-analyses describe the coding of information.

Information may, for example, be coded by type of intervention, sample size, setting, age of participants, or any number of factors.

As with the screening process, valid data collection often requires at least two reviewers using a standard protocol.

Check to see who conducted the review, if they were trained, and how disputes were handled.

✓ 6. Do the authors fully explain their method of combining, or pooling, results?

An underlying assumption of one of the most commonly used meta-analytic approaches is that the reason you can **pool** (merge) individual study results to produce a summary measure is that all study results are homogeneous in that they reflect the same "true" effect. Differences, if you find any, are due to chance alone (sampling error). If the assumption is correct, then when the results are combined, any random errors will be canceled out and one meta-study will be produced. A meta-study—a merging of many studies—is presumed to be better than just one.

In large meta-analyses, you can expect disagreement in results among studies. Sometimes the differences may be due just to chance. But not always. Other factors, such as variations in study settings or the age or socio-economic status of the participants, may be the culprits. Rather than being **homogenous** (with any observed variations due to chance) studies may be **heterogeneous** (with observed variations due to initial differences in design, setting, or sample).

In reviewing the results of a meta-analysis that assumes that study results are homogeneous, check to see if the authors systematically examine their assumption of homogeneity or compatibility of the study results. Investigations of homogeneity may be done graphically, statistically, or both. It is generally considered good practice for a meta-analysis to examine sources of variation based on theoretical or other empirical considerations regardless of the outcomes of the homogeneity tests. These tests alert the investigator to the likelihood that differences in effect size may be due to influences on the intervention that vary from study to study. Thus, a significant test result for homogeneity obligates the meta-analyst to search for variations in study settings or participants' characteristics; a nonsignificant test does not preclude the search.

One method of describing the results of a meta-analysis is by plotting the results on a graph. The objective of the meta-analysis shown in Figure 6.3 was to estimate the effects of international adoption on behavioral problems and mental health referrals. The investigators used a statistical technique called Cohen's criteria, represented by d, to describe the difference between international adoptees and nonadopted controls.

Figure 6.3 Meta-Analysis of Mental Health Referals in International Adoptees

Source	Effect Size, *d* (95% CI)	Favors Cases	Favors Controls
Cederbiad,[99] 1991	0.25 (0.04 to 0.47)		
Déry-Alfrecisson and Katz,[100] 1986	0.18 (0.03 to 0.33)		
Hoksbergen and Bakker-Van Zel,[107] 1983	0.37 (0.23 to 0.51)		
Hoksbergen et al.,[108] 1988	0.71 (0.60 to 0.82)		
Howard et al.,[74] 2004 (International)	0.21 (−0.09 to 0.51)		
Treffers et al.,[127] 1998	0.46 (0.17 to 0.76)		
Vertrulst and Versluis-den-Bieman,[128] 1989	0.29 (−1.09 to 1.68)		
Combined	**0.37 (0.17 to 0.57)**		

Effect Size, *d*: −1.00 −0.50 0 0.50 1.00

SOURCE: Juffer, F., & van IJzendoorn, M. H. (2005). Behavior Problems and Mental Health Referrals of International Adoptees: A Meta-analysis. *Journal of the American Medical Association, 293,* 2501–2515. Reprinted by permission of the American Medical Association.

International adoptees were overrepresented in mental health referrals (*d*, 0.37; Figure 6.3), and this effect size was medium. According to Cohen's criteria, *d*s of <0.20 are considered small effects; *d*s of about 0.50, moderate effects; and *d*s of about 0.80, large effects.

Fixed Versus Random Effects. In reviewing meta-analyses, critics often focus on the reviewers' choice of one or two models: **fixed effects** versus **random effects**. The fixed effects model assumes that all experiments are similar in that they share the same underlying treatment effect. Thus, the observed differences in their results are considered to be due to chance alone (sampling error within each study).

The random effects model incorporates the potential heterogeneity of the treatment effect among different studies by assuming that each study estimates a unique treatment effect that, even given a large amount of data, might still differ from the effect in another study. Compared with the fixed effects model, the random effects model weights smaller studies more heavily in its pooled estimate of treatment effect. Fixed effects and random effects models are equivalent when there is no heterogeneity of the treatment effect among different studies.

Cumulative Meta-Analysis. A **cumulative meta-analysis** is a technique that permits the identification of the year when the combined results of many studies (almost always randomized controlled trials or true experiments) first achieve a given level of statistical significance. The technique also reveals whether the temporal trend seems to be toward superiority of one intervention or another or whether little difference in treatment effect can be expected, which allows investigators to assess the impact of each new study on the pooled estimate of the treatment effect.

✓ 7. Does the report summarize the flow of studies, provide descriptive data for each study, and summarize key findings?

A report of a meta-analysis should describe how the reviewers arrived at the final number of articles that were included. For instance, the reviewers should report on how many potentially relevant studies were identified for retrieval, screened (with the practical screen), and excluded. The reasons should be stated (e.g., "Closer review revealed that the setting was inappropriate"). The reviewers should then discuss how many articles were excluded from the final number because they did not meet methodological or nonmethodological criteria.

The meta-analysis report should also present descriptive data for each study, including the study's objectives, outcomes, sample size, intervention, settings, data collection methods and the reliability and validity of data collection, effect sizes, results, and conclusions. Key findings should also be summarized, and clinical and policy implications should be given. The meta-analysis' limitations should also be discussed. These may include concerns about the comprehensiveness of the review (e.g., only articles and reports in English) and its quality (e.g., only a few high-quality randomized controlled trials).

Many health and medical journals (e.g., *Journal of Clinical Epidemiology, British Medical Journal, Annals of Internal Medicine*) now require that reports of systematic reviews and meta-analyses follow standardized guidelines.

PRISMA Guidelines for Systematic Reviews and Meta-Analysis

PRISMA stands for Preferred Reporting Items for Systematic Reviews and Meta-Analyses (Moher, Liberati, Tetzlaf, Altman, & PRISMA Group, 2009). It is a minimum set of items whose primary aim is to help authors improve the reporting of systematic reviews and meta-analyses. Although PRISMA focuses on reports of randomized trials, it can also be used as a basis for reporting systematic reviews of other types of research, particularly evaluations of interventions.

PRISMA is useful for the critical appraisal of published systematic reviews because it focuses on an established set of times that a review should include. The PRISMA Statement consists of a 27-item checklist, a flow diagram, and an explanation of its items with examples. Example 6.11 contains two items from the Statement, an explanation of potentially ambiguous terms, and examples of how to apply it. The two items focus on what to look for in a meta-analysis or systematic review's statement of objectives and information sources.

Example 6.11   Sample of Explanation of Two Items in the PRISMA Statement (Liberati et al., 2009)

Item 4: Objectives

Provide an explicit statement of questions being addressed with reference to participants, interventions, comparisons, outcomes, and study design (PICOS).

Example. "To examine whether topical or intraluminal antibiotics reduce catheter-related bloodstream infection, we reviewed randomized, controlled trials that assessed the efficacy of these antibiotics for primary prophylaxis against catheter-related bloodstream infection and mortality compared with no antibiotic therapy in adults undergoing hemodialysis."

Explanation. The questions being addressed, and the rationale for them, are one of the most critical parts of a systematic review. They should be stated precisely and explicitly so that readers can understand quickly the review's scope and the potential applicability of the review to their interests. Framing questions so that they include the following five "PICOS" components may improve the explicitness of review questions: 1) the patient population or disease being addressed (P), 2) the interventions or exposure of interest (I), 3) the comparators (C), 4) the main outcome or endpoint of interest (O), and 5) the study designs chosen (S). Good review questions may be narrowly focused or broad, depending on the overall objectives of the review. Sometimes broad questions might increase the applicability of the results and facilitate detection of bias, exploratory analyses, and sensitivity analyses. Whether narrowly focused or broad, precisely stated review objectives are critical as they help define other components of the review process such as the eligibility criteria (Item 6) and the search for relevant literature (Items 7 and 8).

Item 7: Information sources

Describe all information sources in the search (such as databases with dates of coverage, contact with study authors to identify additional studies) and date last searched.

Example. "Studies were identified by searching electronic databases, scanning reference lists of articles and consultation with experts in the field and drug companies. . . . No limits were applied for language and foreign papers were translated. This search was applied to Medline (1966–Present), CancerLit (1975–Present), and adapted for Embase (1980–Present), Science Citation Index Expanded (1981–Present) and Pre-Medline electronic databases. Cochrane and DARE (Database of Abstracts of Reviews of Effectiveness) databases were reviewed. . . . The last search was run on 19 June 2001. In addition, we handsearched contents pages of Journal of Clinical Oncology 2001, European Journal of Cancer 2001 and Bone 2001, together with abstracts printed in these journals 1999–2001. A limited update literature search was performed from 19 June 2001 to 31 December 2003."

Explanation. The National Library of Medicine's Medline database is one of the most comprehensive sources of healthcare information in the world. Like any database, however, its coverage is not complete and varies according to the field. Retrieval from any single database, even by an experienced searcher, may be imperfect, which is why detailed reporting is important within the systematic review.

(Continued)

Example 6.11 (Continued)

At a minimum, for each database searched, authors should report the database, platform, or provider (such as Ovid, Dialog, PubMed) and the start and end dates for the search of each database. This information lets readers assess the currency of the review, which is important because the publication time-lag outdates the results of some reviews. This information should also make updating more efficient. Authors should also report who developed and conducted the search.

In addition to searching databases, authors should report the use of supplementary approaches to identify studies, such as handsearching of journals, checking reference lists, searching trials registries or regulatory agency websites, contacting manufacturers, or contacting authors. Authors should also report if they attempted to acquire any missing information (such as on study methods or results) from investigators or sponsors; it is useful to describe briefly who was contacted and what unpublished information was obtained.

Additional guides for undertaking and evaluating systematic reviews and meta-analyses include the **Meta-analysis of Observational Studies in Epidemiology (MOOS)** statement (Stroup et al., 2000) and the Center for Review and Dissemination's (2009) guidelines for doing reviews.

The most comprehensive standards for systematic reviews of comparative effectiveness research of therapeutic medical or surgical interventions have been issued by the Institute of Medicine (IOM; 2011). Many, if not all, of the standards can be used in evidence-based public health practice. Example 6.12 contains an excerpt from the IOM's standards.

Example 6.12   Excerpt From the Institute of Medicine's Standards for Systematic Reviews

Standard 3.1: Conduct a comprehensive systematic search for evidence

3.1.1   Work with a librarian or other information specialist trained in performing systematic reviews to plan the search strategy

3.1.2   Design the search strategy to address each key research question

3.1.3   Use an independent librarian or other information specialist to peer review the search strategy

3.1.4   Search bibliographic databases

3.1.5   Search citation indexes

3.1.6   Search literature cited by eligible studies

3.1.7   Update the search at intervals appropriate to the pace of generation of new information for the research question being addressed

3.1.8   Search subject-specific databases if other databases are unlikely to provide all relevant evidence

3.1.9   Search regional bibliographic databases if other databases are unlikely to provide all relevant evidence

Standard 3.2: Take action to address potentially biased reporting of research results

3.2.1 Search grey literature databases, clinical trial registries, and other sources of unpublished information about studies

3.2.2 Invite researchers to clarify information about study eligibility, study characteristics, and risk of bias

3.2.3 Invite all study sponsors and researchers to submit unpublished data, including unreported outcomes, for possible inclusion in the systematic review

3.2.4 Handsearch selected journals and conference abstracts

3.2.5 Conduct a web search

3.2.6 Search for studies reported in languages other than English if appropriate

SELECTING AND IMPLEMENTING PROGRAMS ❖

Program selection and implementation involves matching evidence-based programs to communities and populations and then evaluating the effectiveness of the match. The following is list of criteria to use in selecting and implementing programs.

1. *Theoretical Basis of the Program.* Health behavior change theories, such as the Health Belief Model or Social Cognitive Theory, are often used to guide the development of programs. Make certain that the activities and measures (e.g., self-efficacy, certain behaviors or cultural norms) are consistent with the health-related values and preferences of the community and are acceptable to the staff.

2. *Program Content.* If the program is to consist of an educational campaign, who will design or obtain the educational materials? If it is an online program, who will maintain the website? Is the content comprehensive?

3. *Participant Eligibility.* Make certain that the eligibility criteria are clearly described by the program developers and that you can easily implement them in practice. For instance, if certain members of the community are not eligible, can you provide alternative services?

4. *Program Organization.* Who will be responsible for some or all activities? Is there an organization chart? Who will be responsible for hiring and supervising staff?

5. *Program Delivery.* Is space adequate? Who is responsible for overseeing that sufficient space is available for staff and participants?

6. *Program Services.* Who is responsible for ordering medical and other supplies? Is child care available? Translation service? Is a referral network set up to handle additional services?

7. *Location.* Where will the program be delivered? Is transportation available?

8. *Implementation.* To facilitate implementation, it is useful to create a time line of events and to keep track of progress. At the same time, be sure to monitor the use of financial and other resources.

For more information on program planning and implementation, see Peoples-Sheps, Foshee, and Bender (2001) and CDC (n.d.).

❖ PLANNING AND EVALUATING PROGRAMS

Logic Models

Logic models are sometimes used in planning and evaluating programs. The most basic model consists of a depiction (often in graphic form) and an explanation of the resources that go into a program, the activities it undertakes, and the changes or benefits that result. The relationships are logical. In most cases, the relationships have not been tested empirically. Figure 6.4 shows the components of a basic logic model developed by the CDC (2010).

According to advocates (e.g., Taylor-Powell, Jones, & Henert, 2003), a logic model describes the sequence of events thought to bring about benefits or change over time. It portrays the chain of reasoning that links investments to results. Additionally, a logic model is termed a *systems model* because it shows the connection of interdependent parts that together make up the whole.

There is no one correct way to create a logic model (CDC, 2010). The stage of development of the program (i.e., planning, implementation, or maintenance) leads to one of two approaches to creating the model: right to left or left to right.

Figure 6.4 A Basic Logic Model (CDC, 2010)

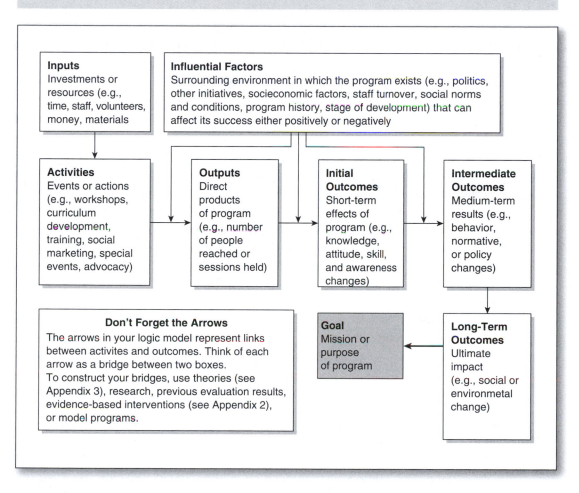

Right-to-Left Logic Model

This approach, also called *reverse logic*, starts with desired outcomes and requires working backward to develop activities and inputs. Usually used in the planning stage, this approach ensures that program activities will logically lead to the specified outcomes if the arrow bridges are well founded (see Figure 6.5). Ask "How?" as you move to the left in the logic model. This

Figure 6.5   Right-to-Left Logic Model (CDC, 2010)

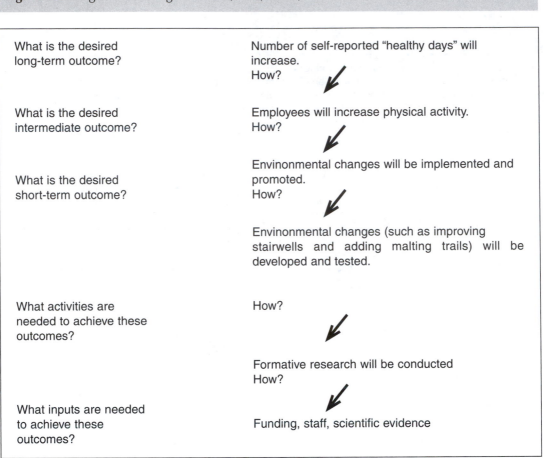

What is the desired long-term outcome?	Number of self-reported "healthy days" will increase. How?
What is the desired intermediate outcome?	Employees will increase physical activity. How?
	Envinonmental changes will be implemented and promoted.
What is the desired short-term outcome?	How?
	Envinonmental changes (such as improving stairwells and adding malting trails) will be developed and tested.
What activities are needed to achieve these outcomes?	How?
	Formative research will be conducted How?
What inputs are needed to achieve these outcomes?	Funding, staff, scientific evidence

approach is also helpful for a program in the implementation stage that still has some flexibility in its program activities.

Left-to-Right Logic Model

This approach, also called *forward logic,* may be used to evaluate a program in the implementation or maintenance stage that does not already have a logic model. You start by articulating the program inputs and activities (see Figure 6.6). To move to the right in your model, ask "Why?" You can also think of this approach as an "If . . ., then . . ." progression.

Logic models are complex and experience in their use is recommended.

Figure 6.6   Left-to-Right Logic Model (CDC, 2010)

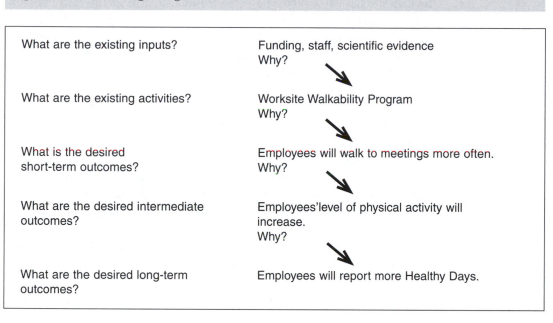

What are the existing inputs?

Funding, staff, scientific evidence
Why?

What are the existing activities?

Worksite Walkability Program
Why?

What is the desired
short-term outcomes?

Employees will walk to meetings more often.
Why?

What are the desired intermediate
outcomes?

Employees'level of physical activity will
increase.
Why?

What are the desired long-term
outcomes?

Employees will report more Healthy Days.

IMPROVEMENT EVALUATIONS: DID THE PROGRAM ❖ CHANGE BEHAVIOR? DO WE NEED TO IMPROVE?

Evaluation has a long history as a mechanism for improvement. The American Evaluation Association states that purposes of evaluation include bettering practices, personnel, programs, organizations, governments, consumers, and the public interest; contributing to informed decision making and more enlightened change; precipitating needed change; and empowering all stakeholders by collecting data from them and engaging them in the evaluation process.

A defining characteristic of evidence-based public health practice is its focus on evaluating the impact on quality and outcomes of care of the selected programs and practices. Did quality of care improve? Improving quality of care usually means changing clinician behavior. Did behavior change, and did it lead to improvements in community health? Did all participants benefit equally? Participants include patients, providers, and people who administer the system. Was the entire process worth the effort and costs? The type of evaluation that is used to answer questions like these is an **improvement evaluation**, or a **quality improvement (QI) evaluation**.

QI evaluations aim to change patient, provider, and system behavior through the use of evidence-based and established programs and interventions. The expectation is that if the programs are appropriate for the community and properly put into place, improvements in clinician practice and subsequent public health outcomes are likely. When high-quality evidence of intervention effectiveness is available, rigorous evaluation using RCTs—the type needed to demonstrate effectiveness—may not always be necessary.

Alternative designs (e.g., before-and-after studies that include concurrent control groups and time-series designs involving multiple pre- and post-test measurements) may provide robust results. But anecdotal reports and simple before-and-after studies, although sometimes adequate to justify local quality-improvement efforts, are probably not sufficient to support widespread initiatives. Anecdotal reports come with the risks of expending tremendous resources without obtaining a true benefit and, possibly, introducing new problems. Anecdotal QI reports can generate new hypotheses, fuel innovative changes, and motivate clinicians to change. If no dissemination of a local QI intervention to other settings is planned, lower quality evidence may be acceptable. However, given the potential for widespread implementation of QI interventions, there is a need for robust study methods in QI research (Fan, Laupacis, Pronovost, Guyatt, & Needham, 2010).

The value of randomized study designs lies in the random assignment of participants with unknown characteristics that affect outcomes to intervention and control groups. With random assignment, these unknown characteristics are assumed to be equally distributed between the two groups, so their potential effects on outcomes are neutralized. In clinical medicine, important confounders are often well known and easily planned for so that observational studies can adjust for these factors, thereby producing results that often agree with the results of randomized trials. However, outcomes of quality-improvement interventions in communities and large populations depend on many factors related to patients, providers, and organizations. According to current thinking, the complexity of health care and the dearth of evidence with respect to how these multiple components interact to influence outcomes provides a strong rationale for conducting randomized trials to evaluate the quality and safety of interventions whenever feasible (Auerbach, Landefeld, & Shojania, 2007).

The growing interest in the importance of QI evaluations has generated guidelines for reporting QI studies, among them the **Standards for QUality Improvement Reporting Excellence** (**SQUIRE**; www.squire-statement .org). The SQUIRE Guidelines describe and explain the recommended contents of each quality improvement article, including what should be included in the title, abstract, introduction, methods, analyses, results, and discussion (Ogrinc et al., 2008). Example 6.13 is an excerpt from the SQUIRES Methods guidelines.

Example 6.13   A Portion of the SQUIRE Guidelines for Reporting Quality Improvement Evaluations

10. Planning the study of the intervention

1. Outlines plans for assessing how well the intervention was implemented (dose or intensity of exposure)

2. Describes mechanisms by which intervention components were expected to cause changes, and plans for testing whether those mechanisms were effective

3. Identifies the study design (for example, observational, quasi-experimental, experimental) chosen for measuring impact of the intervention on primary and secondary outcomes, if applicable

4. Explains plans for implementing essential aspects of the chosen study design, as described in publication guidelines for specific designs, if applicable (see, for example, http://www.equator-network.org)

5. Describes aspects of the study design that specifically concerned internal validity (integrity of the data) and external validity (generalizability)

11. Methods of evaluation

1. Describes instruments and procedures (qualitative, quantitative, or mixed) used to assess a) the effectiveness of implementation, b) the contributions of intervention components and context factors to effectiveness of the intervention, and c) primary and secondary outcomes

2. Reports efforts to validate and test reliability of assessment instruments

3. Explains methods used to assure data quality and adequacy (for example, blinding; repeating measurements and data extraction, training in data collection; collection of sufficient baseline measurements)

SOURCE: Reproduced from Qual Saf Health Care. Davidoff, F., Batalden, P., Stevens, D., Ogrinc, G., and Mooney, S., 17, i3–i9, 2008 with permission from BMJ Publishing Group Ltd.

SUMMARY OF CHAPTER 6: THE BEST AVAILABLE EVIDENCE

Words to Remember

abstraction, CONSORT, cumulative meta-analysis, effect, effect size, evidence table, fixed effects, GRADE, Healthy People 2020, heterogeneous studies, homogenous studies, improvement evaluation, Institute of Medicine reporting standards, logic model, meta-analysis, methodological quality, MOOS, narrative reviews, nonmethodological quality, odds, pool, power analysis, PRISMA, protocol, publication bias, qualitative summaries, quality improvement evaluation, random effects, risks, sensitivity analysis, SQUIRE, STROBE, systematic literature review, TREND, U.S. Preventive Services Task Force, usual care

Literature reviews for evidence-based public health result in information about effective programs and practices. Doing a review means using highly systematic, explicit, and reproducible methods to identify, evaluate, and report on one or more studies, articles, or reports.

Literature reviews are either systematic or narrative. A systematic review follows a detailed set of procedures or a protocol that defines a focused study question, poses a specific search strategy, explains the types of data on study quality and findings to be abstracted, and details how the data will be synthesized (either qualitatively, as text, or in a quantitative summary accompanied by text).

Systematic literature reviews take two forms. The first produces qualitative summaries of the literature based on trends the reviewer finds across studies. The second uses statistical methods to produce a quantitative summary of program effects, and it is called a meta-analysis. Materials produced by the Cochrane Collaboration are excellent sources of information.

Guidelines and checklists, such as CONSORT, TREND, and STROBE, can be used to study the transparency and adequacy of reporting. The USPSTF and GRADE have systems for grading the quality and strength of the evidence. Reviewers themselves can be guided in their studies by using PRISMA, a checklist and guideline for reporting systematic reviews and meta-analyses.

A key characteristic of evidence-based public health practice is an evaluation of whether the program or intervention that was selected for a particular community or population was effective. Did it achieve the hoped-for outcomes in the community? Did all participants benefit equally? Was the entire process worth the effort and costs? The type of evaluation that is used to answer questions like these is called an *improvement evaluation* or a *quality improvement evaluation.* Guidelines for reporting include SQUIRE. Logic models can be used to guide program planning and evaluation. Another approach to evaluating the effectiveness of public health programs can be found through HealthyPeople.gov.

EXERCISES

1. Find these three articles. Are they systematic or narrative reviews? Explain why.

   a. Bair-Merritt, M. H., Blackstone, M., & Feudtner, C. (2006). Physical health outcomes of childhood exposure to intimate partner violence: A systematic review. *Pediatrics, 117,* 278–290.

   b. Crook, J., Milner, R., Schultz, I. Z., & Stringer, B. (2002). Determinants of occupational disability following a low back injury: A critical review of the literature. *Journal of Occupational Rehabilitation, 12,* 277–295.

   c. Weyandt, L. L., & Dupaul, G. (2006). ADHD in college students. *Journal of Attention Disorders, 10,* 9–19.

2. You are interested in programs to enhance the health and development of children under 4 years of age and of their families, who live in poor communities. Your search of the literature has led you to the article below. You have been asked to create an abstraction form that can be used to evaluate the article's methodological quality.

    Belsky, J., Melhuish, E., Barnes, J., Leyland, A. H., Romaniuk, H., & National Evaluation of Sure Start Research Team. (2006). Effects of Sure Start local programmes on children and families: Early findings from a quasi-experimental, cross sectional study. *British Medical Journal, 332*, 1476.

    a. Which methodological domains should you include in the abstraction form?

    b. Write at least three questions for abstracting nonmethodological information.

3. Read the following two meta-analyses. Compare and contrast each with respect to whether they adhered to the following recommendations for reporting meta-analytic results.

    a. Mitchell, T. L., Haw, R. M., Pfeifer, J. E., & Meissner, C. A. (2005). Racial bias in mock juror decision-making: A meta-analytic review of defendant treatment. *Law and Human Behavior, 29*, 621–637.

    b. Horowitz, J. L., & Garber, J. (2006). The prevention of depressive symptoms in children and adolescents: A meta-analytic review. *Journal of Consulting Clinical Psychology, 74*, 401–415.

Recommendations	Mitchell et al.		Horowitz & Garber	
1. Describes eligibility for inclusion and exclusion	Yes	No	Yes	No
2. Discusses databases that were searched	Yes	No	Yes	No
3. Gives specific search terms	Yes	No	Yes	No
4. Discusses effect size and why chosen	Yes	No	Yes	No
5. Provides results of tests of study homogeneity	Yes	No	Yes	No
6. Discusses effects of publication bias	Yes	No	Yes	No
7. Depicts the flow of literature from potentially useful through those that passed through all screens (e.g., practical, methodological)	Yes	No	Yes	No

4. Two reviewers evaluate 110 studies on the impact of home-safety education in preventing accidents. The reviewers are asked to state whether the study investigators adequately describe the education intervention by defining its objectives, activities, participants, and settings. Reviewer 1 says that, in total, 30 of the studies do not adequately describe the intervention, but Reviewer

2 says that 45 do not give an adequate description. The two reviewers agree that 20 specific studies do not adequately describe the intervention. Use the kappa statistic to describe the extent of agreement between the reviewers. Is the kappa slight, fair, moderate, or nearly perfect?

5. Locate the following article. List the study's limitations as described by the researchers.

Hovell, M. F., Seid, A. G., & Liles, S. (2006). Evaluation of a police and social services domestic violence program: Empirical evidence needed to inform public health policies. *Violence Against Women, 12*, 137–159.

6. Locate the following studies, and evaluate the quality of their reporting using CONSORT, TREND, STROBE, or SQUIRE as appropriate. You may also use the guidelines suggested by Fan et al. (2010).

   a. Belansky, E. S., Cutforth, N., Delong, E., Litt, J., Gilbert, L., Scarbro, S., et al. (2010). Early effects of the federally mandated local wellness policy on school nutrition environments appear modest in Colorado's rural, low-income elementary schools. *Journal of the American Dietetic Association, 110*, 1712–1717.

   b. Ciaranello, A. L., Molitor, F., Leamon, M., Kuenneth, C., Tancredi, D., Diamant, A. L., et al. (2006). Providing health care services to the formerly homeless: A quasi-experimental evaluation. *Journal of Health Care for the Poor and Underserved, 17*, 441–461

   c. Klesges, R. C., Obarzanek, E., Kumanyika, S., Murray, D. M., Klesges, L. M., Relyea, G. E., et al. (2010). The Memphis Girls' health Enrichment Multi-site Studies (GEMS): An evaluation of the efficacy of a 2-year obesity prevention program in African American girls. *Archives of Pediatrics and Adolescent Medicine, 164*, 1007–1014.

   d. Samoutis, G. A., Soteriades, E. S., Stoffers, H. E., Philalithis, A., Delicha, E. M., & Lionis, C. (2010). A pilot quality improvement intervention in patients with diabetes and hypertension in primary care settings of Cyprus. *Family Practice, 27*, 263–270.

7. Describe the basic outlines of the logic model.

Answer:

The most basic model consists of a depiction (often in graphic form) and an explanation of the resources that go into a program, the activities it undertakes, and the changes or benefits that result.

REFERENCES

Auerbach, A. D., Landefeld, C. S., & Shojania, K. G. (2007). The tension between needing to improve care and knowing how to do it. *New England Journal of Medicine, 357*, 608–613.

Bair-Merritt, M. H., Blackstone, M., & Feudtner, C. (2006). Physical health outcomes of childhood exposure to intimate partner violence: A systematic review. *Pediatrics, 117*, 278–290.

Belansky, E. S., Cutforth, N., Delong, E., Litt, J., Gilbert, L., Scarbro, S., et al. (2010). Early effects of the federally mandated local wellness policy on school nutrition environments appear modest in Colorado's rural, low-income elementary schools. *Journal of the American Dietetic Association*, *110*, 1712–1717.

Belsky, J., Melhuish, E., Barnes, J., Leyland, A. H., Romaniuk, H., & National Evaluation of Sure Start Research Team. (2006). Effects of Sure Start local programmes on children and families: Early findings from a quasi-experimental, cross sectional study. *British Medical Journal*, *332*, 1476.

Berkman, N., Sheridan, S., Donahue, K., Halpern, D., Viera, A., Crotty, K., et al. (2011). *Health literacy interventions and outcomes: An updated systematic review.* Rockville, MD: Agency for Healthcare Research and Quality.

Center for Review and Dissemination. (2009). *Systematic reviews: CRD's guidelines for undertaking reviews in healthcare.* York, UK: Author. Retrieved from http://www.york.ac.uk/inst/crd/SysRev/!SSL!/WebHelp/SysRev3.htm

Centers for Disease Control and Prevention. (2009). *Transparent Reporting of Evaluations with Nonrandomized Designs.* Retrieved from http://www.cdc.gov/trendstatement/

Centers for Disease Control and Prevention. (2010). *Logic model.* Retrieved from http://www.cdc.gov/nccd php/dnpao/hwi/programdesign/logic_model.htm

Centers for Disease Control and Prevention. (n.d.). Building our understanding: Key concepts of evaluation. Retrieved from http://www.cdc.gov/healthycommunitiesprogram/tools/pdf/eval_planning.pdf

Ciampa, P. J., Kumar, D., Barkin, S. L., Sanders, L. M., Yin, H. S., Perrin, E. M., et al. (2010). Interventions aimed at decreasing obesity in children younger than 2 years: A systematic review. *Archives of Pediatrics and Adolescent Medicine*, *164*, 1098–1104.

Ciaranello, A. L., Molitor, F., Leamon, M., Kuenneth, C., Tancredi, D., Diamant, A. L., et al. (2006). Providing health care services to the formerly homeless: A quasi-experimental evaluation. *Journal of Health Care for the Poor and Underserved*, *17*, 441–461.

Crook, J., Milner, R., Schultz, I. Z., & Stringer, B. (2002). Determinants of occupational disability following a low back injury: A critical review of the literature. *Journal of Occupational Rehabilitation*, *12*, 277–295.

Des Jarlais, D. C., Lyles, C., Crepaz, N., & the TREND Group. (2004). Improving the reporting quality of nonrandomized evaluations of behavioral and public health interventions: The TREND statement. *American Journal of Public Health*, *94*, 361–366.

Fan, E., Laupacis, A., Pronovost, P. J., Guyatt, G. H., & Needham, D. M. (2010). How to use an article about quality improvement. *Journal of the American Medical Association*, *304*, 2279–2287.

Friedman, S. H., Horwitz, S. M., & Resnick, P. J. (2005). Child murder by mothers: A critical analysis of the current state of knowledge and a research agenda. *American Journal of Psychiatry*, *162*, 1578–1587.

Guyatt, G. H., Oxman, A. D., Schünemann, H. J., Tugwell, P., & Knotterus, A. (2011). GRADE guidelines: A new series of articles in the *Journal of Clinical Epidemiology. Journal of Clinical Epidemiology*, *64*, 380–382.

Horowitz, J. L., & Garber, J. (2006). The prevention of depressive symptoms in children and adolescents: A meta-analytic review. *Journal of Consulting and Clinical Psychology*, *74*, 401–415.

Hovell, M. F., Seid, A. G., & Liles, S. (2006). Evaluation of a police and social services domestic violence program: Empirical evidence needed to inform public health policies. *Violence Against Women*, *12*, 137–159.

Institute of Medicine. (2011). *Standards for systematic reviews.* Retrieved from http://www.iom.edu/Reports/2011/Finding-What-Works-in-Health-Care-Standards-for-Systematic-Reviews/Standards.aspx

Introduction to reporting guidelines. (n.d.). Retrieved from http://www.equator-network.org/resource-centre/library-of-health-research-reporting/reporting-guidelines/

Juffer, F., & van IJzendoorn, M. H. (2005). Behavior problems and mental health referrals of international adoptees: A meta-analysis. *Journal of the American Medical Association*, *293*, 2501–2515.

Kaner, E. F., Beyer, F., Dickinson, H. O., Pienaar, E., Campbell, F., Schlesinger, C., et al. (2007). Effectiveness of brief alcohol interventions in primary care populations. *Cochrane Database of Systematic Reviews*, *2*, CD004148.

Klesges, R. C., Obarzanek, E., Kumanyika, S., Murray, D. M., Klesges, L. M., Relyea, G. E., et al. (2010). The Memphis Girls' health Enrichment Multi-site Studies (GEMS): An evaluation of the efficacy of a 2-year obesity prevention program in African American girls. *Archives of Pediatrics and Adolescent Medicine*, *164*, 1007–1014.

Liberati, A., Altman, D. G., Tetzlaff, J., Mulrow, C., Gøtzsche, P. C., Ioannidis, J. P. A., et al. (2009). The PRISMA statement for reporting systematic reviews and meta-analyses of studies that evaluate healthcare interventions: Exlanation and elaboration. *British Medical Journal*, *339*, b2700.

Midei, A. J., & Matthews, K. A. (2011). Interpersonal violence in childhood as a risk factor for obesity: A systematic review of the literature and proposed pathways. *Obesity Reviews*, *12*, e159–e172.

Mitchell, T. L., Haw, R. M., Pfeifer, J. E., & Meissner, C. A. (2005). Racial bias in mock juror decision-making: A meta-analytic review of defendant treatment. *Law and Human Behavior*, *29*, 621–637.

Moher, D., Liberati, A., Tetzlaf, J., Altman, D. G., & the PRISMA Group. (2009). Preferred Reporting Items for Systematic Reviews and Meta-Analyses: The PRISMA Statement. *PLoS Medicine*, *6*, e1000097. Retrieved from http://www.plosmedicine.org

Ogrinc, G., Mooney, S. E., Estrada, C., Foster, T., Goldmann, D., Hall, L. W., et al. (2008). The SQUIRE (Standards for QUality Improvement Reporting Excellence) guidelines for quality improvement reporting: Explanation and elaboration. *Quality and Safety in Health Care*, *17*(Suppl 1), i13–i32.

Peoples-Sheps, M. D., Foshee, V., & Bender, D. (2001). *Program and implementation.* Chapel Hill: University of North Carolina at Chapel Hill, School of Public Health. Retrieved from http://www .shepscenter.unc.edu/data/peoples/programming.pdf

Samoutis, G. A., Soteriades, E. S., Stoffers, H. E., Philalithis, A., Delicha, E. M., & Lionis, C. (2010). A pilot quality improvement intervention in patients with diabetes and hypertension in primary care settings of Cyprus. *Family Practice*, *27,* 263–270.

Scales, D. C., Dainty, K., Hales, B., Pinto, R., Fowler, R. A., Adhikari, N. K. J., et al. (2011). A multifaceted intervention for quality improvement in a network of intensive care units. *Journal of the American Medical Association*, *305,* 363–372.

Stroup, D. F., Berlin, J. A., Morton, S. C., Olkin, I., Williamson, G. D., Rennie, D., et al. (2000). Meta-analysis of observational studies in epidemiology. *Journal of the American Medical Association*, *283*, 2008–2012.

Taylor-Powell, E., Jones, L., & Henert, E. (2003). *Enhancing program performance with logic models.* Retrieved from http://www.uwex.edu/ces/pdande/evaluation/pdf/lmcourseall.pdf

Vandenbroucke, J. P., von Elm, E., Altman, D. G., Gøtzsche, P. C., Mulrow, C. D., Pocock, S. J., et al. (2007). Strengthening the Reporting of Observational Studies in Epidemiology: Explanation and elaboration. *Epidemiology*, *18*, 805–835.

von Elm, E., Altman, D. G., Egger, M., Pocock, S. J., Gøtzsche, P. C., Vandenbroucke, J. P., et al. (2008). The Strengthening the Reporting of Observational Studies in Epidemiology (STROBE) statement: Guidelines for reporting observational studies. *Journal of Clinical Epidemiology*, *61*, 344–349.

West, S., King, V., Carey, T. S., Lohr, K. N., McKoy, N., Sutton, S. F., et al. (2002). Systems to rate the strength of scientific evidence. *Evidence Reports/Technology Assessments*, *47*, 1–11.

Weyandt, L. L., & Dupaul, G. (2006). ADHD in college students. *Journal of Attention Disorders*, *10*, 9–19.

GLOSSARY

An **abstract** is an abbreviated version of the objectives, methods, findings, and conclusions of a much larger report.

Abstracting the literature is the process of reading and recording data from research articles and reports.

Administrative needs refer to policies and resources that exist in the organizations and institutions (e.g., schools, hospitals, businesses, nongovernmental organizations) that might facilitate or hinder the adoption of a new program.

Alternate-form reliability refers to the extent to which two instruments measure the same concepts at the same level of difficulty.

Analysis of covariance (ANCOVA) is a statistical procedure that results in estimates of intervention or program effects adjusted for participants' background and for potentially confounding characteristics or covariates (e.g., age, gender, educational background, severity of illness, type of illness, motivation).

Article databases consist of citations and abstracts of articles that have been published either in print or online pertaining to a particular subject, such as psychology (e.g., PsycINFO) or medicine (e.g., MEDLINE). Article databases can be found online.

Asset mapping aims to create an in-depth understanding of a community by identifying local resources, networks, places of importance, prevalent issues, how these are already connected, and where potential connections exist. Asset mapping identifies needs by comparing a community's assets or resources with its current services.

Attrition is the loss of participants during the course of an evaluation (also called **loss to follow-up**). Participants who are lost during the study are often called *dropouts*. Attrition can be a threat to an evaluation's internal validity if participants drop out from one or more study groups on a nonrandom basis.

Baseline information refers to information collected about study participants and staff before the program begins (sometimes referred to as **pretest** data).

Behavioral needs refer to individual and communal lifestyles and beliefs that affect a community's well-being.

Beneficence is an ethical principle. It requires that the research design be scientifically sound and that the risks of the research be acceptable in relation to the likely benefits. The principle of beneficence also means that persons are treated in an ethical manner. Researchers must not only respect people's decisions and protect research participants from harm but also make efforts to secure their well-being.

Best available evidence comes from an objective and reproducible study of the quality of existing research results.

Bibliographic databases: see **article databases**.

Blinding is the process of preventing those in an experiment from knowing to which comparison group a particular participant belongs. The risk of bias is minimized when as few people as possible know who is receiving the experimental program and who the control program. All participants, including members of the research team, are candidates for being blinded.

Blocked randomization is a method of randomization ensuring that, at any point in an evaluation study, roughly equal numbers of participants have been allocated to all the comparison groups.

Boolean operators are words such as AND, OR, and NOT. They are used to combine search terms to either broaden or narrow the retrieval results of a research literature search.

Case-control studies or **designs** are generally retrospective. They are used to explain why a phenomenon currently exists by comparing the histories of two different groups, one of which is involved in the phenomenon. For example, a case-control design might be used to help understand the social, demographic, and attitudinal variables that distinguish people who, at the present time, have been identified with frequent headaches from those who do not, at the present time, have frequent headaches.

Clinical expertise, according to evidence-based medical practitioners, means the ability to use clinical skills and past experience to identify rapidly each patient's unique health state and diagnosis, his or her individual risks and benefits of potential interventions, and his or her personal values and expectations.

Clinical trials are evaluations of medical and surgical treatments, drugs, and other interventions that are conducted in health care settings such as clinics and hospitals. The outcomes investigated in clinical trials may be medical (e.g., reductions in blood pressure), psychosocial (e.g., improvements in health-related quality of life), and economic (e.g., which of two equally effective programs costs less).

Clusters are naturally occurring groups (e.g., classrooms, hospitals, social work agencies) that are used as single sampling units.

A **cohort** is a group of people who have something in common and who remain part of a study group over an extended period of time. In public health research, cohort studies are used to describe and predict the risk factors for a disease and the disease's cause, incidence, natural history, and prognosis.

Communal or **epidemiological needs** refer to problems that can be documented to affect a large number of people in the community.

Community-based participatory research includes stakeholders as partners in setting the evaluation agenda and doing all phases of the research, including analyzing and reporting on the results.

A **community forum,** also called a **public forum,** consists of a group of people who meet to discuss a common problem. The meeting is open to all members of the community.

The **Community Guide** is a maintained by the Centers for Disease Control and Prevention and contains evidence-based preventive services. It also has glossaries and detailed explanations of methods for identifying best evidence. Its full name is the Guide to Community Preventive Services (www.the communityguide.org).

Community needs are gaps in available programs and policies to prevent disease and promote well-being.

Concurrent controls are those in which two or more groups are randomly constituted, and they are studied at the same time (concurrently). Concurrent controls are sometimes called **parallel controls**.

Concurrent validity is demonstrated when two measures agree with one another or when a new measure compares favorably with one that is already considered valid.

A **confidence interval (CI)** is a measure of the uncertainty around the main finding of a statistical analysis.

A **conflict of interest** is a situation in which someone in a position of trust (e.g., researcher, practitioner, policy maker) has competing professional or personal interests.

A **confounding variable** is an extraneous variable that affects the dependent variables but either has not been considered or has not been controlled for. The confounding variable can lead to a false conclusion that the dependent variables are in a causal relationship with the independent variable. Such a relation between two observed variables is termed a *spurious relationship*. An experiment that fails to take a confounding variable into account is said to have poor internal validity.

Consensus development conferences aim to produce "state-of-the-science" reports using best evidence and expertise (http://consensus.nih.gov).

CONSORT (the Consolidated Standards of Reporting Trials) consists of standards for reporting on randomized controlled trials in public health and medicine.

Construct validity is established experimentally to demonstrate that a measure distinguishes between people who do and do not have certain characteristics.

Content analysis is the process of systematically reviewing, analyzing, and interpreting data from open-ended questions, observations, and records—from all types of human communication. A content analysis relies on trained personnel to search the data for themes that consistently occur.

Content validity refers to the extent to which a measure thoroughly and appropriately assesses the skills or characteristics it is intended to measure. A depression scale may lack content validity if it only assesses the affective dimension of depression but fails to take into account the behavioral dimension.

Continuous measures use response options that result in numerical data. They can have an infinite number of values (e.g., weight) or be discrete (e.g., number of drinks per day).

A **control group** is a group assigned to an experiment, but not for the purpose of being exposed to the program under investigation. The performance of the control group usually serves as a standard against which to measure the effect of the program on the experimental group. The control program may be typical practice (usual care), an alternative practice, or a placebo (a treatment or program believed to be inert or innocuous).

A **controlled experiment** generally compares the outcomes obtained from an experimental group against a control group, which is practically identical to the experimental group except for the one aspect (the experimental program) whose effect is being tested.

Convergent validity means that performance on the new measure correlates with one or more measures of a similar characteristic.

A **correlation** is a numerical index that reflects the linear relationship (described by a straight line) between two numerical measurements made on the same group of people. A **correlation coefficient** (r) ranges from −1 to +1, with 0 indicating no relationship. The absolute value of the coefficient reflects the strength of the correlation so that a correlation of −.60 is stronger than a correlation of +.50.

Cost is the value of money that has been used to produce something, so it is not available for use anymore. In deciding on the costs of programs, the evaluator might consider the amount of money expended to train personnel, to administer the program, and to design the intervention.

Having a **cost benefit** means that a program has value because its benefits (expressed in monetary terms) are equal to or exceed its costs. To determine whether this is the case, a researcher might perform a cost-benefit analysis.

Cost-effective programs save costs and offer equal or better outcomes than the alternative. A program is also cost-effective when no other program is as effective at lower cost.

Cost minimization refers to attempts to determine which of two equally effective programs has lower costs.

Cost utility means that the outcomes of hypothetical Programs A and B are weighted by their value or quality and measured by a common metric such as "quality of life" years.

In statistics, a **covariate** is a variable that is possibly predictive of the outcome under study. A covariate may be of direct interest or be a confounding (mediator) variable.

Criterion validity is a general term for predictive and concurrent validity because both involve comparing a measure to something else (the criterion).

Cronbach's alpha is a measure of internal consistency that reflects the extent to which a set of test items can be treated as measuring a single latent variable. Latent variables, as opposed to observable variables, are those that cannot be directly observed but rather are inferred from other variables that can be observed and directly measured. Cronbach's alpha can range between 0 and 1. A measure with an alpha .61 and above is usually considered to be internally consistent.

A **cross-sectional study** is a one that measures the distribution of some characteristics in a population at a particular point in time. (It is also called a *survey study*.)

Cumulative meta-analysis is a technique that permits the identification of the year when the combined results of many studies (almost always randomized controlled trials or true experiments) first achieve a given level of statistical significance.

A **data set** consists of a subset of information that was extracted from a database for a specific analytic purpose. A researcher who extracts the information on all persons 85 years of age and older from a database consisting of statistics on all people in the nation who are 65 years of age and older has created a data set.

A **database** contains all the information collected on a population of people.

The **Delphi technique** is a structured method of determining the degree of agreement on a topic, of selecting alternatives, or of setting priorities. Delphi techniques use questionnaires that are completed by participants on their own, in groups, or both. The questionnaires are structured to ask people to rate or rank the importance or validity of certain ideas.

A **dependent variable** is a variable (e.g., improved health) that may be predicted by or caused by one or more other variables called *independent variables* (e.g., a health education intervention). In evaluation research, outcomes are dependent variables.

Descriptors are terms used by some article databases to describe the articles listed (e.g., their content, subject, or language); they are similar to key words except that, like identifiers, they are taken from a controlled language prepared and monitored by the librarians or indexers who categorize, sort, and store information in the database.

Discriminant validity means that performance on the new measure does not correlate with measures of dissimilar characteristics.

Educational needs refer to individual and community knowledge, attitudes, skills, self-efficacy, and beliefs.

An **effect** is an association between program participation and an outcome.

Effect size is a generic term for an estimate of the effect of being in a study. It is viewed as a dimensionless measure of effect that is typically used for continuous data and is usually defined as the difference in means (average scores) between the intervention and control groups (on the primary outcome of interest) divided by the standard deviation (a measure of variation from the average scores) of the control or both groups.

An **effectiveness evaluation** is a form of research whose purpose is to find out if a program works in real-life situations. A program is effective if its outcomes compare favorably to comparable alternative or currently available programs.

Effectiveness studies examine the outcomes and impact of programs that evaluators observe in real-life settings.

Efficacy studies consider the outcomes and impact of programs that evaluators observe in laboratory-like or ideal settings.

Epidemiological needs refer to problems (e.g., asthma, obesity) that can be documented to affect a large number of people in the community.

Epidemiology is the study of patterns of health and illness in the population.

Equipoise means that current evidence does not favor the superiority of the experimental over the control program. Equipoise is associated with randomized controlled trials.

Ethics, also called *moral philosophy,* involves systematizing, defending, and recommending concepts of right and wrong behavior.

An **ethics committee**, sometimes called an **institutional review board (IRB)**, is an administrative body whose purpose is to protect the rights and welfare of human research subjects who are recruited to participate in research activities.

Evaluation researchers use scientific methods to assess the process, outcomes, impact, or costs of programs and to provide new knowledge about social behavior.

Evidence-based medicine (**EBM**) is the conscientious, explicit, and judicious use of current best evidence in making decisions about the care of individual patients.

Evidence-based public health practice is characterized by use of the best available evidence to make informed public health practice decisions. It means identifying community needs, tracking down information from evaluation research to find potentially effective programs, assessing the quality of the research or evidence supporting the programs, and evaluating the impact of introducing the programs into practice.

Evidence tables contain the results of a literature abstraction or review.

Expectancy is a threat to an evaluation's internal validity that is caused by the expectations of the evaluator, the participants, or both.

The **experimental group** is the group in an experiment that receives the program that is being studied.

Experimental research designs involve the collection of information to compare two or more groups, one of which participates in a new program while the other does not. An example of an experimental design is the randomized controlled trial in which the groups are constituted at random, which means that chance dictates which participants receive the experimental program.

Experimental studies are tests that are conducted under controlled conditions to examine the validity of a hypothesis or determine the effectiveness or efficacy of something (e.g., program, intervention) previously untried.

External validity refers to the extent to which the design produces results that are applicable to other programs, populations, and settings. Another term for external validity is **generalizability**.

Face validity refers to how a measure appears on the surface: Does it seem to cover all the important domains? Ask all the needed questions?

Factorial designs enable researchers to evaluate the effects of varying the features of an intervention or practice to see which combination works best. In a two-by-two, or 2×2, factorial design, there are four study groups: a and b, a and c, d and b, d and c.

Factors are independent variables in factorial designs.

False negatives occur as a result of measures with poor specificity. They incorrectly classify people as not having a disease (e.g., alcohol-related risk) when in fact they actually do.

False positives occur when people without a disease get a positive test anyway, one that says they do have the disease. Insensitive, invalid measures lead to false positives.

A **feasibility test,** also known as a **pilot test**, is a scaled-down version of a study in which the primary aim is to find out if the program can be implemented in the community.

Fidelity of program implementation, also called **integrity of implementation**, refers to the extent to which a program's protocol was followed.

The **fixed effects model** assumes that all experiments are similar in that they share the same underlying treatment effect. (Compare with **random effects model**.)

A **focus group** is designed to collect information from "insiders" or "people in the know." The group usually consists of about 10 carefully selected participants and a trained moderator.

Forced-choice questions, also called *closed questions,* are those in which respondents provide answers from a list of response options.

Formative evaluations focus on the program's activities and organization rather than on the outcomes of participation. These evaluations are sometimes called **implementation** or **process evaluations**.

Generalizability refers to the extent to which the design produces results that are applicable to other programs, populations, and settings. Another term for generalizability is **external validity**.

Genetic needs predict the risk of disease and possibly the outcomes of interventions. Heart disease, cancer, and diabetes are estimated to account for 7 of every 10 deaths in the United States. Like rare genetic disorders, these common diseases run in families and may be considered genetic diseases. Members of these families may have risks for these genetic diseases.

GRADE (Grades of Recommendation, Assessment, Development, and Evaluation) offers a system for rating the quality of evidence in systematic reviews and provides guidelines and for grading the strength of recommendations guiding practice.

The **Hawthorne effect** is a threat to an evaluation's external validity that occurs when participants know that they are participating in an experiment. These sorts of threats are also described as the **reactive effects of experimental arrangements**.

Health behavior change models provide a framework for understanding the variables that need to be influenced in order to get people to modify their health habits.

According to the **Health Belief Model**, the likelihood that people will take action to prevent illness depends on their perception that they are personally vulnerable to a particular condition, that the consequences of the condition can be serious, that if they take precautions the condition will be prevented, and that the benefits of reducing the threat of the condition exceed the costs.

Health services researchers examine how people get access to health care, how much care costs, and what happens to patients as a result of this care.

Healthy People, a program maintained by the U.S. Department of Health and Human Services, describes public health goals for the United States. It is updated every decade (e.g., Healthy People 2010, Healthy People 2020).

Heterogeneous studies are those with observed variations due to initial differences in their design, setting, or sample. (Compare with **homogenous studies**.)

Using **historical controls** means comparing the outcomes for participants who receive a new program with the outcomes for a previous group of participants who received the standard intervention. Selection bias often arises because subjects who receive the new intervention are typically not comparable to subjects who received the standard intervention.

History is a threat to internal validity that is caused by unanticipated events that occur while the evaluation is in progress.

Homogenous studies are those in which any observed variations are due to chance. (Compare with **heterogeneous studies**.)

A **human research subject** is a living individual about whom an investigator (whether professional or student) conducting research obtains (a) data through intervention or interaction with the individual (e.g., in a counseling session, in a classroom) or (b) identifiable private information (e.g., birth date, school record number).

A **hypothesis** is an unproven theory that can be tested through research. To properly test a hypothesis, it should be prespecified and clearly articulated, and the study to test it should be designed appropriately.

Identifiers: see **descriptors**.

Impact refers to the magnitude and duration of program effects.

researchers important or expert information. The purpose of the key informant method is to collect information about a community's needs by interviewing community leaders who are likely to be in a position to know what the needs are.

Key words are informative words chosen to indicate the content of a document; these words can be used to search indexes and databases.

Kuder-Richardson refers to a statistical technique for estimating internal consistency in measures with dichotomous response choice (e.g., yes or no, true or false).

The **last observation carried forward** uses the last value observed before the participant left, regardless of when the dropout occurred.

Levels of measurement refers to measures (e.g., online or paper-and-pencil surveys, achievement tests, interviews, record reviews) that result in either categorical, ordinal, or numerical data.

The **Likert scale** is a type of response format that shows responses on a continuum and has response categories such as *strongly agree, agree, disagree,* and *strongly disagree.*

A **linear relationship** between two numerical measurements is described by a straight line.

Logic models are used in planning and evaluating programs. The most basic model consists of a depiction (often in graphic form) and an explanation of the resources that go into a program, the activities it undertakes, and the changes or benefits that result.

Longitudinal studies provide information on changes over time (from one time to the next). See **time-series designs.**

Loss to follow-up: see **attrition**.

Matching is the process of ensuring that participants in a study's experimental and control groups are as alike as possible in age, gender, problem severity, motivation, and so on at baseline.

Maturation is a threat to internal validity that is the result of processes occurring inevitably within participants as a function of time (e.g., physical and emotional growth).

Measurement error is a term used to describe the discrepancy between responses to a measure and the true value of the concept.

Measures refer to data collection devices or instruments such as self-administered surveys or achievement tests.

A **mediator variable**, also known as a **confounding variable**, can adversely affect the relation between the independent variable and dependent variable.

A **meta-analysis** is the use of statistical techniques in a systematic literature review to integrate the results of included studies.

Methodological quality is the extent to which all aspects of a study's design and implementation combine to protect its findings against biases. A focus on methodological quality means intensively examining factors such as the scientific soundness of the research design and sampling strategy, measurement, and data analysis.

MOOS (Meta-analysis of Observational Studies in Epidemiology) is a statement for evaluating systematic reviews and meta-analyses.

The **Morbidity and Mortality Weekly Report (MMWR)**, is a resource through which the Centers for Disease Control and Prevention provides public health data.

Multiple program interference is a threat to an evaluation's external validity that results when participants are in other complementary activities or programs that interact with the one being tested.

Narrative literature reviews are interpretations of the research literature that do not describe their research question or search strategy. (Compare with **systematic literature review**.)

A **needs assessment** is a systematic effort to identify user needs.

The **negative predictive value** is the probability that the patient will not have the disease when restricted to all patients who test negative.

In the **nominal group technique**, participants are brought together for a discussion session led by a moderator. After the topic of concern has been presented to session participants and they have had an opportunity to ask questions or briefly discuss the scope of the topic, they are asked to take a few minutes to think about and write down their responses.

Nominal response choice: see **categorical response choices**.

Nonmethodological quality means analyzing the clarity and relevance of the program's objectives, theoretical basis, and content; the trustworthiness of the research's funding source; and the adequacy of the resources, setting, and ethical considerations.

Nonrandomized controlled design is the same as **quasi-experimental design**.

The **null hypothesis** is the statistical hypothesis that one variable (e.g., the program a study participant was allocated to receive) has no association with another variable or set of variables (e.g., whether or not a study participant acquired a skill), or that two or more population distributions do not differ from one another. In simplest terms, the null hypothesis states that the factor of interest (e.g., the program) has no impact on outcome (e.g., acquiring a skill).

The **number needed to treat (NNT)** is an estimate of how many people need to receive the program before one person would experience a beneficial outcome. For example, if you need to give violence prevention therapy to 20 people before one violent act is prevented, then the number needed to treat to benefit for that violence prevention program is 20.

Numerical is a type of response choice. It may be continuous (e.g., weight) or discrete (number of witnesses).

Observational research designs are those in which the evaluators do not seek to intervene; they simply observe the course of events. Changes or differences in one characteristic (e.g., whether or not people received the program of interest) are studied in relation to changes or differences in other characteristics (e.g., whether or not they reduced their harmful drinking), without action by the evaluator.

The **odds** are a way of expressing the chance of an event, calculated by dividing the number of individuals in a sample who experienced the event by the number for whom it did not occur. For example, if, in a sample of 100, 20 people did not improve and 80 people improved, the odds of improving are $20/80 = 1/4$, 0.25 or 1:4.

An **odds ratio** (**OR**) is the ratio of the odds of an event in one group to the odds of this event in another group. In studies of treatment effect, the odds in the treatment group are usually divided by the odds in the control group. An odds ratio of one (OR = 1.0) indicates no difference between comparison groups. For undesirable outcomes, an OR that is less than one (OR < 1) indicates that the intervention was effective in reducing the risk of that outcome. When the risk is small, odds ratios are very similar to risk ratios.

Online bibliographic or article databases contain bibliographic citations, abstracts, and sometimes the full text of documents and articles; these databases can be searched online.

Online or electronic journals can be found directly online or through online databases.

An **open-ended question** is one in which respondents provide answers in their own words. (Compare with **forced-choice questions**.)

Ordinal response choices have a built-in order to them (e.g., highest level of education attained). The order may be imposed (e.g., poor, fair, good, very good, excellent).

Outcomes are the results of program participation. Beneficial outcomes include improvements in health, education, social well-being, and economic prospects.

P-value is the probability (ranging from zero to one) that the results observed in a study (or results more extreme) could have occurred by chance if, in reality, the null hypothesis was true.

Parallel controls are those in which two (or more) groups are randomly constituted, and they are studied at the same time (parallel). Parallel controls are sometimes called **concurrent controls.**

Participant observation requires the researcher actually to live within or somehow join in the community being observed.

Participatory evaluations include stakeholders as partners in setting the evaluation agenda and in doing all phases of the research, including analyzing or reporting on the results.

Patient values, according to evidence-based medical practitioners, are the unique preferences, concerns, and expectations that each patient brings to a clinical encounter and that must be integrated into clinical decisions if they are to serve the patient.

The **Pearson product-moment correlation coefficient** is a statistical technique for estimating test-retest reliability.

With **per protocol analysis**, participants' data are included even if they have not completed all study activities (e.g., they dropped out of the program).

Physical needs refer to social or physical factors that are external to an individual or a community.

PICO is a framework for asking research questions. It consists of four components: the **p**opulation or problem of concern; the **i**ntervention, practice, or program; a **c**omparison program; and the hoped-for **o**utcomes.

A **pilot test,** also known as a **feasibility test,** is a scaled-down version of a study in which the primary aim is to find out if the program can be implemented in the community.

Pool is a term associated with meta-analysis and means merging the results of several studies. An underlying assumption of one of the most commonly used meta-analytic approaches is that the reason you can pool individual study results to produce a summary measure is that all study results are homogenous in that they reflect the same "true" effect.

The **positive predictive value** of a test is the probability that a person has the disease when restricted to those patients who test positive.

Posttest data are collected about the program outcomes or effectiveness after all activities are completed. Posttest data can be collected just once (e.g., immediately after program participation) or more than once over a period of time (e.g., 1 and 2 years after program completion).

Power, also called *statistical power,* is the probability of rejecting the null hypothesis when a specific alternative hypothesis is true. The power of a hypothesis test is one minus the probability of Type II error. In clinical trials, power is the probability that a trial will detect, as statistically significant, an intervention effect of a specified size. If an evaluation study had a power of 0.80 (or 80%), and assuming that the prespecified treatment effect truly existed, then, if the trial was repeated 100 times, it would find a statistically significant treatment effect in 80 of those repetitions. Ideally, we want a test to have high power, close to the maximum, which is one (or 100%). For a given size of effect, studies with more participants have greater power. Studies with a given number of participants have more power to detect large effects than a small effect.

The determination of sample size is also referred to as **power analysis** because the number of persons in the study determines (to some degree) the power the evaluator has to detect an effect or a true difference in experimental and control groups.

Practical clinical trials, also called **pragmatic clinical trials**, are studies in which the hypothesis and study design are developed specifically to answer questions faced by patients, healthcare providers, and policy makers as compared to researchers. These trials compare two or more interventions and assess effectiveness in real-world practice. They use broad eligibility criteria and recruit participants from a variety of settings to ensure inclusion of people whose health will actually be influenced by the study's results. Internal validity may be compromised in favor of external validity or generalizability.

The **practical screen** consists of criteria that an article or report absolutely must achieve if it is to be included in the literature review. The criteria include attention to the language of the article or report, study design, the nature of the program and its participants, date of publication, and the study's funding source.

Practical significance is an outcome or result (e.g., program effect) that is large enough to be of practical importance to participants and all others (e.g., teachers, prison officials) concerned with program outcomes. This is not the same thing as statistical significance. Assessing practical significance takes into account factors such as the size of the program's effect, the severity of the need being addressed, and the cost.

Pragmatic clinical trial: see **practical clinical trial**.

Predictive validity refers to the extent to which a measure forecasts future performance.

Predictor variable: see **independent variable**.

Pretest information refers to information collected about study participants and staff before the program begins. This information is sometimes referred to as **baseline data**.

Pretest-posttest designs, also called **self-controlled research designs**, are those in which each participant is measured on some important program variable and serves as his or her own control. Participants are usually measured twice (at baseline and after program participation), but they may be measured multiple times afterward as well.

Primary data collection means selecting and validating measures specifically to answer a study's unique research questions. It is often contrasted with secondary data collection.

PRISMA (Preferred Reporting Items for Systematic Reviews and Meta-Analyses) is a minimum set of items for reporting on systematic reviews and meta-analyses.

Process evaluations focus on program activities and organization. (They are sometimes called **formative** or **implementation evaluations**.)

A **program** consists of activities and resources that have been specifically selected to achieve beneficial outcomes.

Program processes refer to the staff, activities, materials, and methods that are used to accomplish the outcomes.

Propensity score analysis is a technique for dealing with confounding variables; it is used in analyzing data from quasi-experiments. The goal is to create subgroups of study participants who are similar across a broad range of confounding variables or covariates and then to test the program effect within those groups. That is, within homogenous subgroups (e.g., all older participants, all participants at risk for dropping out), the evaluator compares the outcomes of those who did and did not receive the program.

With a **prospective design**, the direction of inquiry is forward in time. (Compare with **retrospective design**.)

A **protocol** is a planned set of procedures to follow in a research study or systematic literature review. In literature reviews, the protocol includes a focused study question; a specific search strategy (that defines the search terms and databases that are used as well as the criteria for including and excluding studies); detailed instructions on which data are to be abstracted on study objectives, methods, findings, and quality; and a plan for how the data will be synthesized (either qualitatively, as text, or in a quantitative summary accompanied by text).

Proximate outcomes are intermediate outcomes. They are chosen because they are meaningful in themselves and because previous research and clinical insight suggest that they are associated with the hoped-for outcome.

Psychometrics is a discipline concerned with the theory and technique of psychological measurement, which includes the measurement of knowledge, abilities, attitudes, and personality traits.

Public forum: see **community forum**.

Public health identifies risks, regardless of disease, and devises strategies to enable people and populations to avoid the risks. This role is often described as health promotion, that is, changing exposure to risks in the environment or modifying unhealthy behaviors (www.hsph .harvard.edu/foph/foph_web.html).

Publication bias means unfairly favoring the results of published studies.

Qualitative methods involve investigating participants' opinions, behaviors, and experiences from their point of view and using logical deduction.

Qualitative summaries of the literature describe and analyze trends across studies. In some fields (e.g., nursing) doing this is called *metasynthesis*.

Quality improvement (QI) evaluations aim to change patient, provider, and system behavior through the use of evidence-based and established programs and interventions.

Quality of evidence depends on factors such as the characteristics of a study's research design, the adequacy of the sample size, the composition of the participants, and the validity of the outcomes.

Quantitative evaluation methods rely on mathematical and statistical models.

A **quasi-experimental design** is one in which the control group is predetermined (without random assignment) to be comparable to the program group in critical ways, such as being in the same school or eligible for the same services.

The **RAND/UCLA Appropriateness Method (RUAM)** is a method for determining the extent of agreement on controversial topics and on those for which the research base is poor or ambiguous (a mixture of positive and negative findings).

Random allocation, also called **random assignment**, is a method that uses the play of chance to assign participants to comparison groups in a trial (e.g., by using a random numbers table, by using a computer-generated random sequence). Random allocation implies that each individual or unit being entered into a study has the same chance of receiving each of the possible interventions.

Random assignment: see **random allocation**.

The **random effects model** incorporates the potential heterogeneity of the treatment effect among different studies by assuming that each study estimates a unique treatment effect that, even given a large amount of data, might still differ from the effect in another study. (Compare with **fixed effects model**.)

Random error occurs when the concept underlying a measure is subject to debate and, thus, imprecise (e.g., quality of life, economic well-being). Random error comes from three sources: variability in the measure itself, variability in the respondents, and variability in the observer.

Randomization is the process of randomly allocating participants into one of the groups that make up a controlled trial. There are two components to randomization: the generation of a random sequence and its implementation, ideally in a way so that those entering participants into a study are not aware of the sequence

A **randomized controlled trial (RCT)** is an experimental study in which eligible individuals or groups of individuals (e.g., schools, communities) are assigned at random to receive one of several programs or interventions. The group in an experiment that receives the specified program is the experimental group. The control is another group assigned to the experiment, but not for the purpose of being exposed to the program. The performance of the control group usually serves as a standard against which to measure the effect of the program on the experimental group. The control program may be typical practice (usual care), an alternative practice, or a placebo (a treatment or a program believed to be inert or innocuous).

Reactive effects of experimental arrangements, or the **Hawthorne effect,** is a threat to an evaluation's external validity that occurs when participants know that they are participating in an experiment.

Reactive effects of testing pose a threat to an evaluation's external validity that occurs when a baseline measure interacts with the program, resulting in an effect that will not generalize.

Record reviews are analyses of an evaluation participant's documented behavior (e.g., school records, medical records). The documentation may be in print, online, or on audio or video.

The **relative risk** expresses the risk of a particular outcome in the experimental group relative to the risk of the outcome in the control group.

Reliability coefficient: see **correlation**.

Reliable means consistency over time and within an instrument.

Research is a diligent and systematic process of inquiry aimed at discovering, interpreting, and revising information about programs and interventions. *Research* is also a term that is used to describe a collection of information about a particular subject and is associated with the scientific method.

Research-based is often used as a synonym for **evidence-based**.

Research consumers use research as the basis for making decisions about programs, practices, and policy. Consumers practice research and are concerned with the practical applications of research findings.

Research design is the structure of research. At its most stingy, the structure consists of the intervention or program that is to be compared to an alternative, participants who are assigned to be part of the new program *or* of the alternative, and a schedule of measurements (e.g., before program participation and immediately after).

Research ethics concern the rights and wrongs associated with research. Evaluations always include human subjects, so research ethics are of great concern. The evaluator must demonstrate that the study design respects participants' privacy, ensure that the benefits of participation are maximized, and provide all participants with equal access to the benefits. Research that is not sound is unethical in itself because it results in misleading or false conclusions, which when applied may result in harm.

The best **research evidence**, according to evidence-based medical practitioners, is clinically relevant research, often from the basic sciences of medicine but especially from patient-centered clinical research. Patient-centered clinical research is analogous to evaluation research, particularly in its advocacy and use of experimental methods to test effectiveness, impact, and cost.

A **research literature review** is a highly systematic, explicit, and reproducible method for identifying, evaluating and synthesizing one or more studies or reports that comprise the existing body of completed and recorded work produced by researchers, scholars, and practitioners about programs.

Research misconduct includes such offenses as fabrication, falsification, and plagiarism. Fabrication means making up results and recording or reporting them. Falsification includes changing or omitting data or results. Plagiarism means taking another person's ideas, results, or work without giving due credit.

A **research question** is the objective of the evaluation, the uncertainty that the evaluator wants to diminish.

Respect for persons is an ethical principle that requires investigators to obtain informed consent from research participants, to protect participants who have impaired decision-making capabilities, and to maintain confidentiality.

A **respondent** is the person who completes a survey.

Response choices are also known as rating or measurement scales and **levels of measurement**. There are three basic measurement types: categorical, ordinal, and numerical.

With a **retrospective design**, the direction of the inquiry is backward in time. (Compare with **prospective design**.)

Risks and odds are alternative methods for describing the likelihood that a particular effect will or will not take place.

The **scientific method** is a set of techniques for investigating phenomena and acquiring new knowledge of the natural and social worlds; this scientific knowledge is based on observable, measurable evidence.

Secondary data analysis refers to statistical analysis of data collected by others for their own research purposes.

Selection of participants is a threat to internal validity that results from the selection or creation of groups that are not equivalent. Selection can interact with history, maturation, and instrumentation.

Self-administered survey questionnaires ask participants to answer questions in writing (paper-and-pencil surveys) or online. Some paper-and-pencil surveys are mailed to participants, and others are completed on site (e.g., at a clinic, at a school).

Self-controlled research designs, also called **pretest-posttest designs**, are designs in which each participant is measured on some important program variable and serves as his or her own control. Participants are usually measured twice (at baseline and after program participation), but they may be measured multiple times afterward as well.

Sensitivity refers to the proportion of people with disease who have a positive test result. Said another way, a sensitive measure will correctly detect disease (e.g., alcohol-related risk) among people who have the disease. A sensitive measure is a valid measure.

Sensitivity analysis is a technique that is used to conduct separate analyses of different quality studies.

The **single time-series design**, also called **interrupted time-series design**, is a research design without a control group (hence, the "single"). It involves repeated measurement of a variable (e.g., reported crime) over time, encompassing periods both before and after implementation of a program. The goal is to evaluate whether the program has interrupted or changed a pattern established before the program's implementation.

According to **Social Learning/ Social Cognitive Theory**, behavior change is affected by environmental influences, personal factors, and attributes of the behavior itself. Each may affect or be affected by either of the other two. A central tenet of this theory is the concept of self-efficacy.

Social needs usually refer to the community's perceptions of its problems.

The **Socio-Ecological Model** incorporates individual, peer and family group, community, and societal factors into a framework for changing behavior.

The **Spearman-Brown prediction formula** is a statistical technique for estimating split-half reliability.

Specificity refers to the proportion of people without disease who have a negative test result. Measures without good specificity lead to false negatives. They invalidly classify people as not having a disease (e.g., alcohol-related risk) when in fact they actually do.

Split-half reliability requires the researcher to divide a measure into two equal halves (e.g., by choosing all odd-numbered questions to be in the first half and all even-numbered questions to be in the second half). Then, using, the Spearman-Brown prediction formula, the researcher calculates the correlation between the two halves.

SQUIRE (Standards for QUality Improvement Reporting Excellence) guidelines describe and explain the recommended contents for quality improvement reports, including what should be included in the title, abstract, introduction, methods, analyses, results, and discussion.

Statistical regression is a threat to an evaluation's internal validity when participants are selected on the basis of extreme scores and regress or go back toward the mean (e.g., average score) of that variable.

A **statistically significant** result is unlikely to have occurred by chance. The amount of evidence required to accept that an event is unlikely to have arisen by chance is known as the *significance level* or *critical P-value.*

Stratified blocked randomization is a method used to ensure that equal numbers of participants with a characteristic thought to affect response to the intervention will be allocated to each comparison group. Stratification variables include age, gender, marital status, and socioeconomic status.

Strength of evidence refers to the number of high-quality studies that consistently support the effectiveness of a program or intervention.

The **STROBE (**STrengthening the Reporting of OBservational studies in Epidemiology) Statement provides guidance on how to report observational studies.

Study quality refers to the validity of the research design, the adequacy of the sample size, the composition of the participants, and the pertinence of the outcomes.

Summative evaluations use historical methods to examine outcomes and impact after most (if not all) of a program's activities are completed. (Compare with **formative** and **process evaluations**.)

A **systematic literature review** is the same as a **research literature review.** It follows a protocol that includes a focused study question; a specific search strategy (that defines the search terms and databases that are used as well as the criteria for including and excluding studies); and specific instructions on the types of data to be abstracted on study objective, methods, findings, and quality. (Compare with **narrative literature reviews**.)

Test-retest reliability refers to the extent to which a measure produces consistent results over time.

Testing is a threat to internal validity; it refers to the effect of previous testing on the scores of subsequent tests.

Themes are fundamental and common ideas, perceptions, values, and attitudes expressed by respondents or participants in a study.

The **Theory of Reasoned Action** and **Theory of Planned Behavior** assume that individual performance of a given behavior is primarily determined by a person's intention to perform that behavior. This intention is affected by the person's attitude toward the behavior (beliefs about the outcomes of the behavior and the value of these outcomes) and the influence of the person's social environment or subjective norms (beliefs about what other people think the person should do, as well as the person's motivation to comply with the opinions of others).

Threats to an evaluation's validity arise because of factors such as imperfect randomization and attrition. Both internal and external validity may be affected.

Time-series designs are longitudinal studies that enable the evaluator to monitor change from one time to the next.

In the **Transtheoretical Model**, behavior change has been conceptualized as a five-stage process or continuum related to a person's readiness to change: precontemplation, contemplation, preparation, action, and maintenance. People are thought to progress through these stages at varying rates, often moving back and forth along the continuum a number of times before attaining the goal of maintenance.

The **TREND (Transparent Reporting of Evaluations with Nonrandomized Designs)** Statement is a checklist developed to guide reporting on studies having a nonrandomized controlled design or a quasi-experimental design.

Triangulation is the use of multiple measures to collect data on a single outcome, with the expectation that, if the findings converge, then confidence in the results is enhanced.

A **true experiment** is the same as a **randomized controlled trial (RCT)**.

A **Type I error**, also called a **false positive**, is a conclusion that a program works when it actually does not work. The risk of a Type I error is often called *alpha*. In a statistical test, the term describes the chance of rejecting the null hypothesis when it is in fact true.

A **Type II error**, also called a **false negative**, is a conclusion that there is no evidence that a program works when it actually does work. The risk of a Type II error is often called *beta*. In a statistical test, the term describes the chance of not rejecting the null hypothesis when it is in fact false. The risk of a Type II error decreases as the number of participants in a study increases.

Unobtrusive measures obtain data about evaluation participants by relying on existing documentation (e.g., medical records, school records).

The **U.S. Preventive Services Task Force (USPSTF)** is an independent panel of experts in primary care and prevention that systematically reviews the evidence of effectiveness and develops recommendations for clinical preventive services. The USPSTF is now under the auspices of the Agency for Healthcare Quality and Research.

Usual care means current best treatment.

Valid refers to the accuracy of a measure, or the extent to which the measure represents the concept of interest.

Validity refers to the degree to which a measure assesses what it is supposed to. For example, a test that asks students to *recall* information is an invalid measure of their ability to *apply* information.

Variables are quantities or factors that may assume any one of a set of values such as age (e.g., 13 through 19 years), educational level (e.g., elementary or high school), reading ability (e.g., reads at the third-grade level or reads below it).

A **vignette** is a short scenario that is used in collecting data in "what if" situations.

A **wait-list control** refers to a research study design in which one group receives the program first and others are put on a waiting list. If the program appears to be effective, participants on the waiting list receive it. Participants are randomly assigned to the experimental and wait-list groups.

AUTHOR INDEX

SUBJECT INDEX

Figures, tables, and examples are indicated by f, t, and e respectively.

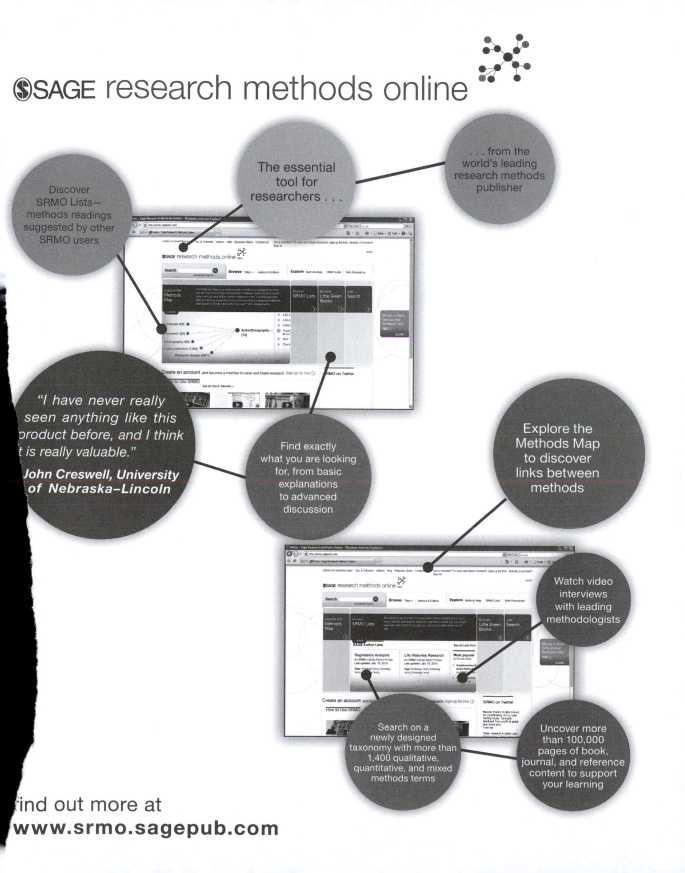